D0586263

THAILAND
A Complete Guide

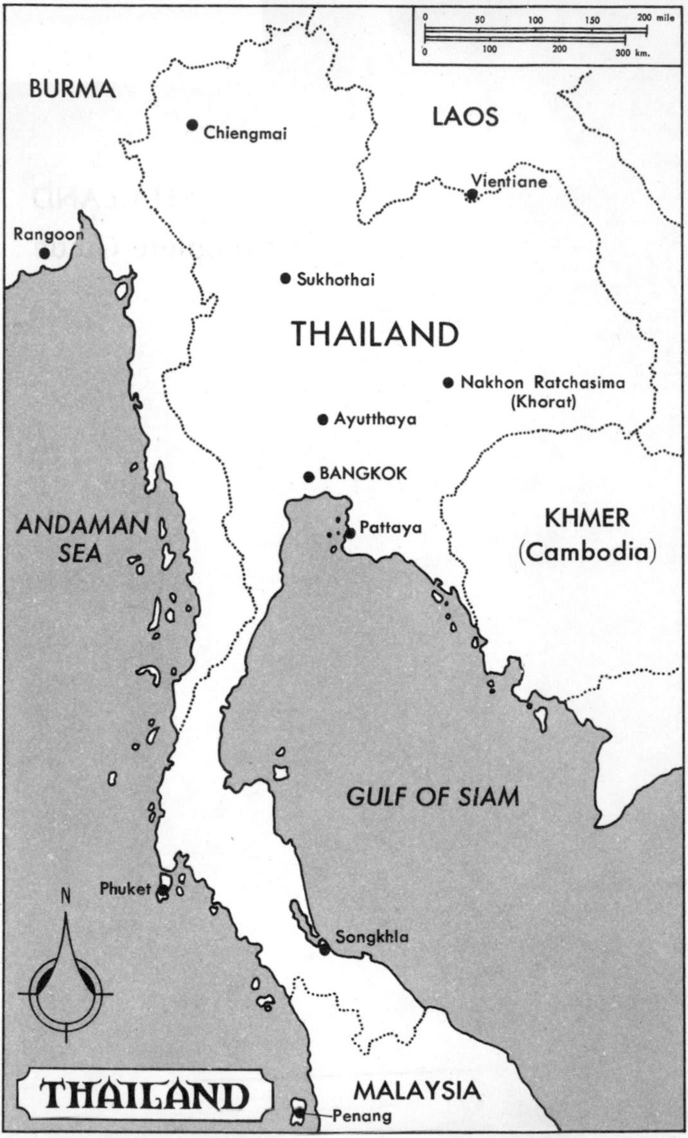

0 50 100 150 200 mile
0 100 200 300 km.
BURMA
LAOS
Chiengmai
Vientiane
Rangoon
Sukhothai
THAILAND
Nakhon Ratchasima
(Khorat)
Ayutthaya
BANGKOK
Pattaya
ANDAMAN
SEA
KHMER
(Cambodia)
GULF OF SIAM
Phuket
N
Songkhla
THAILAND
MALAYSIA
Penang

WILLIAM DUNCAN

THAILAND

A Complete Guide

Sketches by Ikuko Duncan

CHARLES E. TUTTLE COMPANY
Rutland, Vermont and Tokyo, Japan

BY THE SAME AUTHOR

A Guide to Japan (1970)

Japanese Markets Review 1970/75

Doing Business with Japan (1975)

Representatives

For Continental Europe:
BOXERBOOKS, INC., *Zurich*

For the British Isles:
PRENTICE-HALL INTERNATIONAL, INC., *London*

For Canada:
M. G. HURTIG, LTD., *Edmonton*

For Australasia:
BOOK WISE (AUSTRALIA) PTY. LTD.
104–108 Sussex Street, Sydney

Published by the Charles E. Tuttle Company, Inc.
of Rutland, Vermont & Tokyo, Japan
with editorial offices at
Suido 1-chome, 2-6, Bunkyo-ku, Tokyo

Copyright in Japan, 1976
by Charles E. Tuttle Co., Inc.

All rights reserved

Library of Congress Catalog Card No. 75-28719
International Standard Book No. 0-8048 1158-X

First printing, 1976

PRINTED IN JAPAN

46314

ABINGTON LIBRARY
Abington, Mass.

TABLE OF CONTENTS

List of Illustrations 7

Acknowledgments 11

Introduction 13

Tips for Low-Budget Travellers 15

Part I: PRACTICAL INFORMATION

1. Timing Your Visit 19
2. Before You Depart 24
3. What to Wear 31
4. Arriving in Thailand 35
5. Hotels and Accommodation 38
6. Language 45
7. Transport in Thailand 48
8. Meeting a Thai 64
9. Food and Restaurants 68
10. Entertainment and Sports 91
11. Shopping 108

Part II: VILLAGE AND MONASTIC LIFE

12. Village Life 121
13. Buddhism and Monastic Life 135

Part III: WHERE TO GO AND WHAT TO SEE

14. Bangkok 153
15. More Bangkok Sights and a Walking Tour 192
16. Day Excursions from Bangkok 222
17. The Southeast 264
18. The Northeast 281
19. Chiengmai and the North 295
20. Southern Peninsula 345

Useful Addresses and Information 373

Index 377

LIST OF ILLUSTRATIONS

PLATES

1. Classical dancers 81
2. Motor samlors 82
3. Monument of Democracy, Bangkok 82
4. Street merchants, Bangkok 83
5. Country girl at loom 84
6. Umbrella making 84
7. Sellers of Buddhist images 86
8. *Ranad ek,* classical Thai instrument 86
9. Thai food 86
10. Floating market, Bang Khun Thien 86
11. Hill-tribe woman 87
12. Thai boxing 88
13. Elephant round-up, Surin 88
14. Royal Summer Palace, Bang Pa-In 201
15. Logging elephants 202
16. Rice barge on rural *klong* 202
17. Hua Hin Beach 203
18. Floating houses on Yom River, Phitsanulok 203
19. "Sea gypsies" village, Phuket 204
20. Royal Chapel of the Emerald Buddha 205
21. National Museum, Bangkok 205
22. Buddha image, Ayutthaya 206
23. Wat Yai Chai Mongkol, Ayutthaya 207

24. Buddhist sanctuary (Prang Sam Yod), Lopburi 207
25. Ruins, Ayutthaya 208

SKETCHES

Thai hat 34
Siam Intercontinental Hotel 39
Bangkok Hualampong Station, with plan 52–53
Traffic signal signs 56
Samlor 60
Pedicab 61
A *wai* 65
Fruits 71–77
Musical instrument 93
Thai boxing 101
Princess ring 113
Water pot 130
Temple bell 139
Buddhist monk (*bikkhu*) 149
Wat Arun Rajuararm 163
Carved bow of royal barge 167
Giant swing 179
Golden Mount 183
Alexandrian lamp 193
Bronze Buddha head 193
Massive barges in procession 224
Farmers and water buffaloes 237
Village houses and *taln* trees 247
Phra Pathom *chedi* 249
Elephants at TIMland 262
Stone lantern (*toro*) 268
Sky-skiing 271
Ban Chieng pottery 294
Hammering silver 309
Hill-tribe dress 318
Khan toke dinner 326

MAPS

1 (*Frontispiece*). Thailand
2. Bangkok 152–153
3. Day excursions from Bangkok 223
4. The Southeast 265
5. The Northeast 283
6. Chiengmai and the North 297
7. Chiengmai 300–301
8. Southern Peninsula 347

PLAN

Bangkok (Hualampong) Station 52–53

ACKNOWLEDGMENTS

Grateful thanks for kind assistance in making travel arrangements and collecting information are due to: Viroj Palapong; Charoen Saenglor (alias Johnny Lo); the staff of T.O.T. (especially Phajphong Abhijataphong); Thai International Airways; Siam Restaurant, London; and others too numerous to mention.

Thanks are also due to Thai International Airways for the photograph incorporated into the jacket design and to T.O.T. (Tourist Organization of Thailand) for photographs 1, 2, 5, 7, 9, 10, 13, 22, and 24. (The other photographs in this volume are by the author.)

Most thanks, however, go to Ikuko, my wife, who helped in many ways and also did the sketches.

INTRODUCTION

Blessed by Lord Buddha, Thailand has just about everything to offer as a tropical paradise: deserted palm-fringed beaches, coral islands, and a peaceful rural life where even the "poor" seem to be content.

Bearing a dozen children brings not a visible care in the world. What does it matter if they have no clothes to wear? What does it matter if there is no money? There are always fish in the streams, rice and vegetables in the rich soil, fruit that grows in over-abundance.

Living so close to nature, the rural Thais are delightful, and appear, to the visitor at least, to be completely untroubled. This may be because of their devotion to Buddhism, a religion that knows no guilt, or simply because of the climate and the uncomplicated life in idyllic surroundings. Surely there is something we can learn and enjoy here before our strange economics, problem-wars, and modern-style "civilization" encroach on their blissful peace.

Inexplicably, most tourists stay only in Bangkok, the modern capital, and miss seeing Thailand. The rest of the country offers exciting, exotic, and primitive scenes—dense jungles, ruined cities, undiscovered lost kingdoms for the archeologist/explorer, and the curious Thai art and culture that evolved from a mixture of Khmer (with its Hindu cults), Mon, Burmese, and Mongol influences, supplemented by Sinhalese Buddhism. Yet, somehow, it is an art and culture far removed from any of these.

Thailand has been sadly overlooked. Even the film "The King and I," which put Thailand on the map throughout the Western world, is so full of misconceptions that the offended Thais banned its screening in Bangkok.

Except for Japan, Thailand is the only country in East Asia that has never been a colony or been dominated by a foreign power.* Like Japan, therefore, Thailand has retained its native traditions and a deep national pride that is distinct from that of other countries of Asia.

This book has been prepared to tell you all you should need to know for a successful visit to Thailand. Suggestions and criticisms from readers will be welcomed so that future editions may be more useful. Please address the author, 76 Raffles House, Brampton Grove, London NW4 4BX, England.

WILLIAM R. DUNCAN

* This statement discounts the period of Japanese occupation during the Second World War, which did not affect Thai traditional life. Some readers may also argue that Japan was once dominated—during the Allied occupation following the Second World War.

TIPS FOR LOW-BUDGET TRAVELLERS

1. Go to the Tourist Organization of Thailand for free help in drawing up an itinerary.
2. Travel by bus. (Ask T.O.T. for bus-route maps and timetables.)
3. Stay in a hotel near the railway station for around 40 *baht* ($2) a night. (Atlanta Hotel or Thai Song Greet Hotel are two to try.) Alternatively, go to a restaurant in Chinatown (avoiding those with signs in English) and explain by sign language that you are looking for a place to sleep. State the price. Someone will surely lead you to a hotel that charges just a little more than the price you named, but the room will be very cheap.
4. Avoid air-conditioned restaurants. Eat Thai food in the open-fronted Thai restaurants for just a few *baht*. But don't eat food sold at temporary street stalls, and avoid, especially, the ice used by street vendors to cool bottled drinks.
5. In Bangkok, see the Grand Palace, several *wat*, the Weekend Market, classical dancing at the National Theatre, the National Museum (admission free on Sundays), and then get away into the provinces.
6. Use this book.

Note: Prices quoted here, based on exchange rates of 20 *baht* to one U.S. dollar and 2.50 dollars to one pound sterling, are given for comparison and guidance; the reader should not be surprised to find that there have been increases.

The metric system is used: a metre equals 39.37 inches; a kilometre, 0.62 mile; a litre, 1.057 quarts; a gramme, 0.035 ounce.

1

TIMING YOUR VISIT

Climate

Thailand has three seasons—hot, rainy, and cool. To say which is the best is a matter of conjecture although there can be no doubt which is the worst. The hot season, from March to May, should be avoided if possible.

From June to October the country is visited by the southwest monsoons bringing billowing clouds and cool showers. Far from hindering sightseeing, the sudden torrents of rain that usually come during the late afternoon lower the temperature and are refreshing. However, in Bangkok and in the central plains, occasional floods follow the heavier rainstorms, sometimes disrupting transport services. On the other hand, the rainy season is best for photography. The cloudy sky diffuses the fierce sunlight, and early mornings especially are good.

The cool season, from November to February, would be better named "warm" season. In these months, foreign residents have been known to don jackets during the daytime. Normally, Europeans will still find air-conditioned rooms a welcome relief from the strong sun. Snow is unknown.

If you have to visit Thailand during the hotter months you could escape the oppressive humidity by going to a hill resort such as Khao Yai or by making a trip to Chiengmai, which has a lower humidity and is usually, but not always, cooler. In Chiengmai the temperature drops considerably after sunset.

At any time of the year try to take advantage of the early mornings, which are bright and cool.

AVERAGE TEMPERATURE IN BANGKOK

	Jan	Feb	Mar	Apr	May	Jun	Jul	Aug	Sept	Oct	Nov	Dec
Temp F°	78	82	84	86	85	82	82	82	82	82	79	77
Temp C°	25	28	29	30	29	28	28	28	28	28	26	25
Rain (in.)	0.4	0.8	1.3	2.9	7.1	6.2	6.3	6.6	12.1	8.3	2.6	0.3

Festivals and Annual Events

Dates change from year to year according to the lunar calendar.

JANUARY 1–3, *New Year's*—Monks gather on the Phramane Grounds in Bangkok to receive offerings from devout Buddhists, most of whom give food.

END OF JANUARY/BEGINNING OF FEBRUARY, *Chinese New Year*—The Chinese celebrate for three days, sometimes with firecrackers.

SECOND OR THIRD WEEK OF FEBRUARY, *Phra Buddhabaht Festival*—Pilgrims flock to a temple near Sara Buri, about 108 kilometres (sixty-eight miles) north of Bangkok, where there is a holy footprint of Buddha. A fair is held there.

FEBRUARY, *Magha Puja Day*—Occurs on the full-moon day of the third month in the Thai lunar calendar. This is to commemorate the day when 1,250 disciples of Buddha were supposed to have gathered, without prior summons, before Buddha. Buddha then preached his cardinal doctrines. On Magha Puja Day Buddhist followers make candle processions around the temple halls, reciting prayers.

FEBRUARY, MARCH, AND APRIL, *Kite-fighting season*—See Chapter 10 for details (p. 100).

APRIL 6, *Chakri Day*—The Thais pay homage to King Rama I, whose statue stands at the Memorial Bridge, Bangkok. He founded Bangkok in 1782 and was also the founder of the Chakri Dynasty, to which the present King belongs. The Pantheon, in the grounds of the Grand Palace, is open to the public on this day. It contains life-sized statues of all the Rama kings.

APRIL 13–15, *Songkran or Water Festival Day*—This is still unofficially recognized as the Thai New Year's Day, especially in the provinces. People sprinkle water over Buddha images, monks, and elders as a sign of veneration and respect. Relatives, friends, and even strangers throw water at one another just for fun. The King also takes a ceremonial bath for purification. Chiengmai people love this festival. Tourists on this day are advised to wear either a raincoat or a swimsuit!

MAY 5, *Coronation Anniversary Day*—The King and Queen attend a special ceremony in the Royal Chapel.

MAY, *Ploughing Ceremony Day*—A colourful ceremony takes place on the Phramane Grounds, Bangkok, to mark the beginning of the rice-planting season. Buddhist monks chant and Brahmins predict the rainfall while the King looks on. Traditional costumes are worn.

MAY, *Visakha Piya Day*—This Buddhist holy festival commemorates Buddha's birth, enlightenment, and death or passing into Nirvana. Followers take part in candle processions at the temples, which are specially decorated with lanterns.

MAY/JUNE, *Buddha's Cremation Ceremonies*—These take place in the villages on the eighth day following the full moon of the sixth lunar month.

JUNE/JULY, *Buat Nak Day*—Buddhists who wish to stay in a monastery for their "Lent" are ordained on this day which immediately precedes Khao Pansa Day, actually the first day of the waning moon of the eighth lunar month. *Khao* means "enter" and *pansa* means "rain." Thai youths when they are twenty years old are ordained as monks to spend the following three months of the rainy season studying and practising Buddhism. (The rainy season actually continues for four months but the last month of it is reserved for Tod Kathin. See below.)

AUGUST 12, *Queen Sirikit's Birthday*—She presents offerings to the monks in the morning at Chit Lada Palace.

OCTOBER/NOVEMBER, *Tod Kathin*—This festival is celebrated for a period of one month, the last month of the rainy season. People give new saffron robes and new utensils to the monks. Processions, singing, dancing, and general enjoyment typify this religious occasion. To mark the end of the Buddhist "Lent," the King travels in the ancient Royal Barge in a very grand procession of boats along the Chao Phya River to Wat Arun (the Temple of the Dawn).

OCTOBER 23, *Chulalongkorn Day*—This commemorates the death of King Chulalongkorn (fifth king of the Chakri Dynasty), who died in 1910. People flock to place flowers and incense in front of his equestrian statue, which stands before the National Assembly Hall. This venerable king instituted great reforms during his reign.

LATE OCTOBER/NOVEMBER, *Phra Chedi Klang Nam Festival*—Held at Paknam, a town nineteen miles south of Bangkok, this festival centers around the above named *chedi* or pagoda. Colourful processions, boat races, water games, and a fair make this interesting for visitors.

NOVEMBER, *Loy Krathong (Festival of Lights)*—This festival takes place at the time of the full moon in the twelfth lunar month. *Krathong,* or banana-leaf cups, are made to float down all the rivers and canals in Thailand, loaded with little offerings such as flowers, incense, and lighted candles. Some *Krathong* are very elaborate and quite beautiful. Hundreds of these little candlelit floats make a lovely sight as they bob gently and drift downstream in the moonlight.

Loy Krathong is mentioned in early Thai literature of the Sukhothai period as a way to worship the holy footprint of Buddha on the bank of the Nammada River. Nowadays it is just another way for Buddhists to "make merit" (and have fun at the same time). It seems there may be a connection with the Hindu rite of giving thanks to the goddess of water.

SECOND OR THIRD WEEK OF NOVEMBER, *Elephant Round-up*—A special train is reserved to take sightseers from Bangkok to Surin to watch spectacular demonstrations showing how elephants are caught and trained. The event is organized by T.O.T. See also pages 291–2.

DECEMBER 5, *The King's Birthday*—Buildings in Bankkok are decorated with illuminations, and there is a parade of the Royal Guards.

DECEMBER 10, *Constitution Day*—A government-declared national holiday.

DECEMBER 25, *Christmas Day*—A national holiday.

Because many of the holidays celebrate Buddhist events, the dates will change from year to year in keeping with the lunar calendar. The Thai lunar year ends with the last full moon in November and begins with the new moon in that month.

2

BEFORE YOU DEPART

Visas

The following information is for guidance, and it is advisable to check with your airline or a Thai embassy for any changes. An Alien Occupation Control Bill has recently been enacted into law, imposing more restrictions on foreigners who want to take up employment or who are working in Thailand. If there is no Thai embassy or consulate nearby, write directly to: The Immigration Division, Sathorn Nua Road, Phya Pipat Lane, Bangkok, Thailand. The Division's official letter of permission for entry can be used in lieu of a visa.

Anyone who infringes the immigration laws is placed, with military precision, in jail. Only then, it seems, are matters able to be reconciled. Foreigners are detained until they have obtained guarantees or air tickets to leave the country. Visitors are particularly advised to make sure not to remain in Thailand even for one day after their visas expire. A minor mistake may result in a few days in jail or a fine.

Is a visa necessary?—This depends primarily on your length of stay, nationality, purpose of visit, and a number of other less lucid factors. Except in the straightforward circumstances mentioned below, the issuance of visas seems to be considered "case by case." As a result, a visa refused in a Thai embassy of one country may well be obtained without question in another.

WHEN TRAVELLING BY AIR ONLY—Visas are not required by any foreigner for a stay of less than seventy-two hours, providing an air ticket for the outgoing flight can be shown on arrival.

Citizens of the U.S.A. or the Federal Republic of Germany may stay up to fifteen days, and citizens of ASEAN countries (Indonesia, Malaysia, Philippines, and Singapore) may stay up to seven days without a visa. The Thai government intends to extend this privilege to other nationalities in the near future.

BONA FIDE TOURISTS—You may apply for either a tourist visa, which allows the holder to stay for up to thirty days, or for a transit visa valid for a stay of up to eight days.

VISITORS ON BUSINESS—You should apply for a non-immigrant visa allowing the bearer to stay up to thirty days. For certain nationalities the application may require the approval of the Immigration Division of the Foreign Ministry in Thailand, in which case plenty of time must be allowed.

VISA FEES—For a single entry visa 70 *baht* ($3.50) is charged. Citizens of the following countries, however, are exempt from the fees for the above visas: Federal Republic of Germany, Sweden, Norway, Denmark, Malaysia, Singapore, the Republic of Korea, and the Republic of the Philippines.

VALIDITY OF VISAS—Holders of visas should visit Thailand within ninety days from the date of issue. If necessary, at the time of application for a visa one may ask for the duration of validity to be extended to a maximum period of six months (providing the passport also remains valid for that period, of course).

EXTENDING YOUR STAY—You must apply to the Immigration Department on the corner of Sathorn Nua Road and Phya Pipat Lane in Bangkok.

Applications are considered "case by case." In general it is not easy for the holder of a tourist visa to extend his stay. He will probably be asked to deposit 5,000 *baht* ($250) in a local bank as security until departure. An extension of stay is granted more easily to a holder of a non-immigrant visa. Often, a letter of guarantee on company-headed paper is all that is required but sometimes it is necessary to deposit 2,000 *baht* ($100) in a local bank as security until departure.

In both cases, it is better to apply as early as possible, at least ten days before the existing visa expires. If an extension is granted it can be for a maximum of a further thirty days. With a non-immigrant visa, it may be possible to extend the stay a second time.

If personal efforts fail, it is worth asking a local travel agency. Often, they can find a way to arrange an extension for a small fee. Otherwise one must leave Thailand to apply for another visa.

RE-ENTRY PROCEDURE—If one wishes to make a trip outside Thailand for a short period (for example, to Rangoon or Penang) a re-entry visa can be obtained. A local travel agent or T.O.T. will arrange this.

EMPLOYMENT IN THAILAND—There is a quota for each nationality limiting the number of foreigners who are permitted to live and work in Thailand. Within the quota, visas are granted. The applicant must be able to show adequate means of support and/or letters of guarantee.

It is not practical to think of obtaining employment after arriving in Thailand.

Foreigners employed in Thailand have to obtain a tax certificate from the Revenue Department which must be produced on departure to show that no tax is due to the Thai government.

Medical Requirements

An international smallpox vaccination certificate, showing vaccination within three years, and an international cholera certificate, showing vaccination within six months, are all that are required. However, if you intend travelling to remote districts or will be in Thailand during the rainy season, there is a possibility of the drinking water being contaminated. It is advisable to have a vaccination against typhoid and paratyphoid fevers as a precaution. Some remote areas are still malarial. One should check and take anti-malarial tablets if intending to travel upcountry extensively.

Insurance

Since Thailand is in the tropics it is common sense to insure against illness. A minor infection or sickness may be accelerated by the change of food and climate. Imported drugs are very expensive. Doctors' fees and hospitalization charges are also fairly high.

It is always better to be covered against personal accidents and for loss of luggage. Also, since a journey to Thailand is an expensive affair, it is wise to insure against cancellation or curtailment, which could involve a substantial amount.

Currency

The better-known travellers' cheques are readily accepted, especially in U.S. dollars, Japanese yen, and pounds sterling. The most recognized are American Express, Bank of Tokyo, and Thomas Cook. American Express are more expensive but well known for their on-the-spot, immediate replacement of lost cheques. Some companies take several days or weeks before replacement or a refund is made (see p. 35).

Hotel Reservations

The airline or travel agent will handle the bookings. There is, at present, an abundance of hotels in Bangkok. At certain times obtaining a room has been difficult—for example, during Expo '70 or the Asian Games—but one need hardly worry about arriving without a reservation (see pp. 38–41).

Taking in Your Car

A *Carnet de Passages en Douanes* from the FIA *(Federation Internationale de l'Automobile)* is necessary to make everything go smoothly. The Royal Automobile Association of Thailand will then sign a re-export guarantee with the Customs Department, valid for 180 days. Alternatively, the car owner must sign the re-export guarantee himself, which entails a deposit amounting to fifty-five per cent of the value of the car with the Customs. (A letter of guarantee from a bank is acceptable too.) One must have an international car licence authorized by the Royal Traffic Convention, 1962, as well as an international driving licence. Within fifteen days, these licences must be presented to the Changwa Automobile Registrar, who will then permit the owner to use the car in Thailand for ninety days with a further ninety-day extension on request. A driver without these documents must apply for a local driving licence.

Motor insurance—is not compulsory. Arrangements should be made before arriving in Thailand.

Making and Confirming Appointments

It is always advisable to confirm the place, time, and date of appointments to avoid any misunderstandings. Most Thais do not seem to mind if they are kept waiting. Neither do they appear to feel uncomfortable if they are late themselves.

Name Cards

Useful among businessmen, they are not as essential as in Japan. In Thailand it is quite easy to have cards printed, one side in English and one side in Thai, within a few days. Many printers who specialize in this work are clustered in a row of rather unattractive shops along the Ti Thong Road in the Chinatown area of Bangkok.

Gifts

Exchanging and giving presents is not common practice. Perhaps this is why Thais are so delighted when they receive presents.

It is worthwhile to take in the bottle of spirits allowed by customs—either brandy or whisky, which is very expensive in Thailand. Thais are not quite as abstemious as the Lord Buddha. Men like neckties and tie clips from abroad, and for women, perfume, brooches, and embroidered handkerchiefs are most acceptable. Any toys or sweets are suitable for children.

Of course anything typical of your own country, such as a doll in national costume, will be appreciated as a gift. Dolls, in particular, have a novelty value. In Thailand the first costume dolls were produced less than twenty years ago. Heavy duties are imposed on foreign goods and, as a result, whatever the gift, it will be more highly regarded if it has "Made in Somewhere" written on it. Presents do not need to be wrapped in any special way.

As a last resort one may give money. Especially among the country people this is quite usual and will not cause offence. A "gift" of money is suitable if you have stayed in a Thai home or in return for some other kindness. It is also customary at a wedding for guests and friends to give money to the bridal couple.

3

WHAT TO WEAR

Although Thailand is a tropical country it would be too easy simply to say "wear as little as possible." Here are some extra tips worth considering when preparing for the journey.

For Gentlemen

SUITS—Because of the high humidity and because the temperature drops very little in the evenings, Thais rarely wear a suit or even a jacket and tie. Dress is informal by Western standards.

For formal social occasions, a white dinner jacket is more comfortable than a dark suit. The other need for a jacket and tie is when visiting the Grand Palace. Only one hotel insists on such attire—the Oriental, for dinner in its Normandie Grill Room.

In the rainy season, trousers are bound to get splashed around the ankles and an extra pair or two are useful.

SHIRTS—*Farang* or foreigners seem to be the only people who wear silk shirts in Thailand. Thais wear cottons, the best choice for the heat. Avoid nylon shirts or drip-dry cotton/synthetic mixtures. All-cotton shirts are coolest. Laundry charges are moderate, and the service is quick.

Colourful Thai cotton or silk sportshirts are popular buys among tourists.

TIES—Any style is acceptable. Good selections of Thai cotton or silk ties are on sale.

UNDERWEAR—Cotton underwear is best. Avoid drip-dry materials.

SOCKS—Pale coloured, summer, mesh socks are the most practical. Avoid wool socks.

SHOES—Open-toed sandals are most comfortable, especially when sightseeing. (Shoes are required for a visit to the Grand Palace.)

In the rainy season a spare pair is essential. Made-to-measure shoes at around 625 *baht* ($12.50) a pair are another good buy in Bangkok. They can be made in a couple of days. See page 115.

SHORTS—Among Thais they are worn by school children only. Quite a number of tourists wear them, but they do attract attention. When visiting places of worship one should wear trousers, although this is not compulsory.

HATS—When sightseeing it is essential to have some protection from the sun's rays. Tourists in the holiday mood may like to sport a local straw hat that can easily be bought for very little.

For Ladies

GENERAL HINTS—Wear pastel shades in lightweight cotton, or, better still, linen clothes. Avoid nylon or drip-dry cotton/synthetic materials and heavy linens.

Linen clothes, although the most comfortable, require a little more attention, but laundry and pressing can be left to the hotel with confidence.

In the cool season, in Chiengmai, and for air-conditioned rooms, a stole or lightweight cardigan will be a boon. Silk dresses are also warm in the evenings.

SHORTS AND SLACKS—Shorts are acceptable at beach resorts but not for wearing in the street. Slacks are very practical for sightseeing and commonly worn by tourists. If slacks are not worn, a wide skirt will save awkwardness when climbing in and out of boats and when floor-sitting.

Smart pants suits can be quickly made to measure in Bangkok from lovely Thai cottons or silks.

COCKTAIL AND EVENING DRESS—Have a cocktail dress tailor-made in Bangkok. Thai silk wears very well so it is a good idea to choose a simple style that will not go out of fashion too quickly. A plain dress with several interchangeable sashes or scarves makes a versatile set.

Unless one is notified beforehand, it is certain that an evening dress will not be needed in Thailand.

HANDBAGS—If one has a dress made, a handbag can be made with the same material. A wide range awaits you at very reasonable prices. See page 117.

GLOVES—Not required except for meeting the King.

STOCKINGS—Not needed at all except for special evening wear.

UNDERWEAR—Avoid nylon underwear and drip-dry materials which are rather on the hot side.

FOOTWEAR—Open-toed sandals or light summery walking shoes are ideal for sightseeing. Shoes with narrow heels are not suitable. The uneven pavements with unexpected gaps make walking in "heels" extremely tiring and have led to many an unhappy moment.

In the rainy season ladies' shoes are susceptible to damage from dirty puddles and splashes of rainwater—really difficult to avoid.

JEWELLERY—Gold necklaces and brooches are said to tempt snatch-thieves who operate a special "twenty-four-hour service" in Bangkok. Although this may be unlikely, foreign residents often warn visitors to use caution.

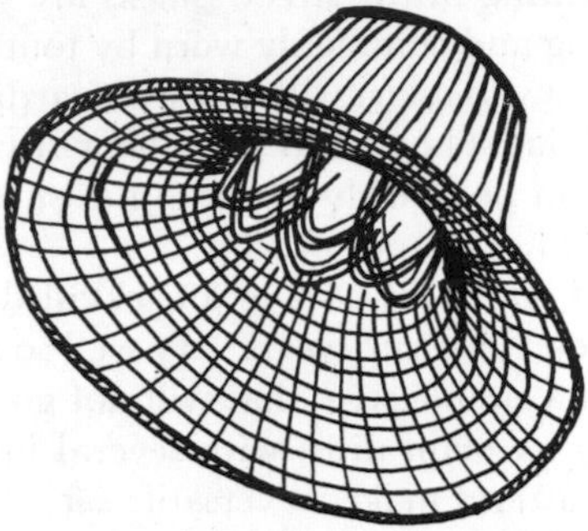

Thai hat.

Surely no woman can resist buying some of the beautiful Thai jewellery. See pages 112–15 before deciding what to pack.

BIKINIS—Nowadays they are normal wear for the beach resorts and hotel pools in sunny Thailand.

In Bangkok it is easy to buy a Thai printed cotton bikini with a matching sun-hat and beach bag of the same material.

HATS—Rather than carry a hat box or a squashed hat to Thailand, buy a floppy, beach-style hat or a locally made straw hat widely available for low prices. Thai-style hats are very becoming.

Miscellaneous

UMBRELLA—An umbrella is more a nuisance than a necessity, even in the rainy season.

HAIR—In a tropical climate hair needs to be washed more often. Shampoo and hair colouring should be packed.

SUNGLASSES—Better take them rather than buy them in Thailand.

4

ARRIVING IN THAILAND

Customs Regulations

Outside the health and immigration sections, customs officers wait to check passengers' luggage. Generally, Thai customs officers are very fair and quite polite. Visitors are allowed to bring into Thailand, free of duty, one bottle of spirits, two hundred cigarettes, one movie camera, one still camera, and a reasonable amount of film. Anything that is not for personal use should be declared. Tourists should have no difficulties.

CURRENCY—Visitors are allowed to take in not more than $500 or £200 in cash. Family passport holders are allowed more—$1,000 or £400. There is no limit on traveller's cheques or drafts. It is forbidden to take in or bring out any more than 500 Thai *baht* (1,600 *baht* for family passport holders).

After customs clearance, one can change money at the bank foreign exchange counter which is almost facing the customs area. The rate is reasonable, usually a little higher than in most hotels.

PROHIBITED ARTICLES—Narcotics and obscene pictures or literature are banned. Firearms can be taken in, in special cases, after an import permit has been obtained from the Police Department.

FURTHER CUSTOMS INFORMATION—Contact Customs Department, Klong Toey, Bangkok, tel: 58011.

Hotel Reservations

At Don Muang Airport (Bangkok) there are always several hotel representatives waiting with cars or mini-buses to meet passengers. They are worth approaching, or one may ask at the desk of the National Travel Service near the airport exit. Beware of touts and taxi drivers who offer to arrange accommodations in "very nice, very cheap hotel." It may not be what you are looking for.

Getting to the Hotel

FROM BANGKOK AIRPORT (Don Muang)—Allow about one hour for the drive to your hotel. The time depends on traffic conditions in the city and the hotel's location. The airport is about sixteen miles from the city.

Just before the airport exit is a "limousine service" counter operated by the National Travel Service. A ticket can be bought there either for 20 *baht* ($1) for the mini-bus service or for 80 *baht* ($4) for a car—new Mercedes—to any of the major hotels in the city. If you would like to have a try at bargaining, negotiate with the taxi drivers. It should not cost more than 50 *baht* per taxi (for a small Japanese car). Porters should be tipped a minimum of 2 *baht* (10 cents) per suitcase.

FROM BANGKOK PORT (Klong Tuey)—Taxis and samlors (see pp. 58–61) will eagerly take newly arrived visitors to the town centre, but one must bargain hard not to be overcharged. Depending on the location of your hotel, the fare should be between 10 and 20 *baht* (50 cents–$1).

The alternative is to catch a public bus. There is a choice—a number 4 to go westwards past Bangkok (Hualampong) Railway Station, through Chinatown and into Thon Buri; a number 27 to go northwards past the Victory Monument and then east away from the town centre; a number 74 to go by the Victory Monument and then east to an industrial and welfare housing area; or a number 79 to go past Bangkok (Hualampong) Railway Station to nearby Wat Trimitr. The fare is 50 *satang* (2½ cents) for any single journey.

5

HOTELS AND ACCOMMODATION

International-Style Hotels

About 65 good hotels, offering more than 8,000 rooms, exist in Bangkok. Their standards, facilities, and comforts are much the same as in other capital cities. The deluxe hotels have such amenities as shopping arcades, choice of restaurants, bars, 24-hour coffee shops, sauna baths, hairdressers, tropical gardens, swimming pools, and round-the-clock room service. Lesser hotels may lack many of these facilities but bedrooms will still be comfortable and clean.

Perhaps the most memorable impression of a stay in a Bangkok hotel is the friendliness of the Thai staff. The service may often be sloppy and unhurried but irritated guests are always soothed by the sincere smiles of the staff, and eventually visitors melt into the same happy-go-lucky attitude.

RATES—Based on the "European plan," prices quoted are for room charge only, with no meals. In general, rates are lower than in most other capital cities. A single room in a good hotel will be easy to find at around $8–10 a night and in a deluxe hotel at about $13–18 a night. In both these price ranges the hotels would have swimming pools.

It causes no surprise to bargain over the room rate before checking in. Sometimes a small reduction or a better room will be offered.

One can also save by paying the bill in *baht*. Hotel cashiers eagerly accept any hard currency in lieu of *baht* but exchange rates are slightly better in the Thai banks.

SERVICE CHARGE—Ten per cent is added to all bills for service.

TIPPING—Not usual among Thais, tipping has become customary in places frequented by foreigners. In the hotels, baggage porters should be tipped a minimum of 2 *baht* (10 cents) per piece. On any occasion, a tip of 1 *baht* will be received as an insult.

Some International-Style Hotels in Bangkok

Each hotel listed here has its own distinctive atmosphere catering to particular tastes. The list is intended to be impartial information. Your travel agent should know which of all the hotels in Bangkok is suitable for you.

SIAM-INTERCONTINENTAL—The centre building has a unique roof with long, overlapping eaves representing an ancient Thai warrior's helmet. Behind it, attractive, two-

Siam Intercontinental Hotel.

story buildings for accommodation face a tropical garden and swimming pool. To one side stands the new wing—a tall, featureless, concrete block. Some guest rooms are quite a walk from the facilities in the centre building.

RAMA—Smart and typical of the Hyatt group; beautiful grill room.

ORIENTAL—This hotel has its own landing pier for river boats. A lovely lawn bordered by rose bushes and a terrace restaurant separate the Oriental from the busy Chao Phya River. It is a delightful place to sit and sip cocktails, watching the evening sun set across this "River of Kings." Established in 1887, the hotel includes a ten-story tower block with split-level rooms and a new wing with simple, first-class rooms. The Oriental still retains, however, the romantic and nostalgic ambiance of the days when Somerset Maugham stayed there. On the top floor is the classical Normandie Grill. Jacket and tie should be worn here.

SHERATON—This is an international-style, air-conditioned hotel with all amenities for comfort and convenience including dining room, grill room, coffee shop, two cocktail lounges, nightclub, swimming pool, steam baths and massage, and more than twenty shops.

NARAI—Second largest hotel in Bangkok, the Narai, in spite of its size, has a cosy atmosphere. The only revolving restaurant in town (French cuisine) is on the rooftop. Another unique feature is a Bavarian-style beer hall in the basement.

ERAWAN—The government, which built this hotel in 1956, uses it for occasional receptions and official guests.

It is luxuriously and graciously furnished, and the staff have the manners of diplomats. The hotel has a very nice tearoom too.

Dusit thani—surely no visitor to Bangkok can miss seeing this striking landmark at Lumpini Park. The building is basically triangular shaped, with a spire at the top. With 525 rooms, it is Thailand's largest hotel, and can also claim to have the best convention facilities in Southeast Asia. The banquet hall can be varied in shape for any group from 50 to 1,600 persons.

Other facilities include a spacious exhibition hall and a 350-seat cinema that shows recently released films. Some of the staff wear attractive ancient-style Thai costumes, but the decor may strike some people as a little garish.

Royal—An old-style hotel with spacious rooms and a swimming pool set in a lovely tropical garden, the Royal has all air-conditioned bedrooms, and most are comfortably large for a standard-grade hotel.

Its main advantage is position, being only a few minutes' walk from the Grand Palace, Emerald Buddha Temple, Wat Po, National Museum, and the National Theatre. The hotel faces the site of the Weekend Market.

Local-Style Hotels

In many of the provincial towns, such as Sukhothai, there may be a great deal to interest a foreign tourist but no alternative to staying in a local-style hotel*—that is, a

* But, as mentioned in a note on p. 336, visitors who wish to study the ruins of the ancient capital may stay at a comfortable guest house recently made available for this purpose in Old Sukhothai. Reservations should be requested well in advance from the Department of Fine Arts of Thailand, Na Phra Lam Road, Bangkok.

hotel built with local capital, managed by Thai nationals (almost always the Chinese/Thai), and not designed to cater to *farang* (foreigners). It would be misleading to call them Thai-style hotels since the accommodation is quite different from that in a traditional Thai home. There are a surprising number of such hotels in any town that has a main road so there is never any need to make a reservation.

Before agreeing to a price at the reception counter, ask to see the room offered. Furnishings are never luxurious. There will be a bed with a thin mattress but only one sheet. Unless you have adopted the Thai attire which is similar to the sarong, you will probably have nothing to lay over you in lieu of the top sheet. Hotel staff are quite puzzled when asked for another sheet but, by persevering with sign language, you can eventually convince them to concede and provide it. Each room has a ceiling fan and electric light, but there will be a switch outside as well as inside the room. Do not expect to have a gentle breeze from the fan all night, or to be able to read if you have insomnia. Many of the hotels turn off the electricity supply every night. Some even turn off the water supply. Every bedroom has its own private bathroom with a washbasin and a shower or tap and bucket. Nowadays the old-style Thai water jar and scoop is rarely found in hotels. There is cold water only (Thais say it's more refreshing), and no soap or towel is provided. The toilet may be the "Asian" type (no pedestal).

In the evening it is advisable to keep the windows closed as the light will attract mosquitoes, moths, and other flying insects. Although the windows may be screened it seems impossible to stop a few mosquitoes' coming in. One solution is to burn a mosquito coil, which can readily be bought in Bangkok. (Kincho, a Japanese brand, smoulders for eight hours.) Anyway, one had better not ask the hotel for an insect spray, as it will smell disgusting. Little *chinchook* (small lizards), scamper across the walls and ceilings, devouring insects, including the mosquitoes. The lizards are absolutely harmless to humans but can be disturbing when they occasionally fall to the floor with a "plop" or onto the bed during the night. The most disturbing insect, however, is the ant. Armies of them can appear from tiny cracks and crevices, attracted by sweet food such as biscuit crumbs or a few grains of sugar. Most horrifying is to wake up in the morning to find thousands in one's suitcase, drawn by the perspiration on underclothes or on a necklace! Wrapping food, clothes, or even the necklace into a polythene bag and sealing it with rubber bands will not necessarily deter the ants. They bite through the bags and feast away just the same. The only answer seems to be to use airtight tins. Also, buy a can of ant killer and spray it around the room and learn to say "*mai pen rai*" (never mind) in the morning.

Service in local-style hotels is limited. Hot Chinese tea in a vacuum flask is automatically brought to one's room. It has an unusual flavour, not quite like the more scented China tea served in Chinese restaurants. This tea has a yellowish, *klong* (canal) colour and sharper taste. It is quite safe to drink but one should be wary of the iced tea or iced water that may be served. Carrying one's own supply of tea and asking for boiling water presents no problems. Sometimes the hotels have a porter. Tipping among Thais is not customary and, because it is not expected, it is much appreciated. Often these hotels have a cheap restaurant on the ground floor.

Prices vary from 30 to 80 *baht* ($1.50–$4) per room, per night, according to the standard of accommodation. By bargaining before checking in, one can usually achieve a ten to thirty per cent reduction, though the manager's apparent incomprehension of English or of your sign language will make bargaining more difficult. The friendly atmosphere and smiling Thai faces more than compensate for the material discomforts of these hotels. A one-night stay is a memorable experience.

Convention Facilities

Bangkok is conveniently placed for international conventions, and facilities are steadily improving. Briefly, the following are suitable sites for major conventions: Thammasart University—accommodates up to 3,000 delegates; Chulalongkorn University—accommodates about 2,000 delegates; ECAFE Headquarters in Rajdamnern Avenue—accommodates 1,200–1,500 delegates; Hua Mark (New Asian Games) Complex—accommodates 880 delegates; hotels, especially the Dusit Thani, Erawan, Narai, Rama, and President hotels. Contact T.O.T. for the latest detailed information.

6
LANGUAGE

The language spoken in Thailand is one of several Thai languages that are spoken in northern Burma, Laos, and by a few clans in Tongking and southern China. In the central part of Thailand more vocabulary is used because new words were taken from Cambodian, Pali, and Sanskrit when the cultures from Cambodia and India were introduced there.

The language has changed little since King Ramkamhaeng of Sukhothai created the first Thai alphabet. There is some relation to the Mon and Khmer scripts, which in turn had derived from India. It is believed that this great warrior king produced the new script to strengthen national unity among his people. In 1292, he made an inscription on stone for posterity which can now be seen in the National Museum. It reads:

> "Sukhothai is good. There is fish in the water, rice in the fields. The King does not levy tax on his subjects. Those who want to trade elephants, trade. Those who want to trade horses, trade. Those who want to trade in silver and gold, trade. The faces of the people shine bright."

With "Sukhothai" changed to "Utopia," this would

have made a fine blurb for Sir Thomas More's account of an ideal state, published in 1516.

Some Difficulties

English is the second language and is taught in schools throughout the country. Except in Bangkok, however, and in hotels frequented by foreigners, there are likely to be language difficulties. On the other hand, many Thais speak a little English, such as "you!" (meaning "I say" or "hey there"), "where you go?" "O.K.," "same-same" (meaning "it's the same"), "no have," and "bye-bye" (sometimes used to express "hello"). Verbs have no past or future tense in Thai so, for example, "I have been to Chiengmai" becomes "I go Chiengmai yesterday" (or last week, last year, etc.).

Generally, you should have no serious language problem, but, to save time, always carry the name and address of your destination or hotel written in Thai script.

Hypothetical questions such as, "Am I going the right way?" or "Is the Erawan Hotel that way?" will invite the polite answer "Yes." If you ask, "Where is the Erawan Hotel?" the informant will have to think before answering, and his answer is more likely to be correct. Remember always to smile and never to raise your voice.

A Few Useful Phrases

Learning the polite phrases will be appreciated, and knowing the numbers will help when haggling over prices and taxi fares. (For additional vocabulary, see p. 109.)

good morning good afternoon good evening goodbye	*sawadee*
please	*dai prod*

thank you	*korb koon*
yes	*krab, kah*
no	*mai chai*
water	*nam*
Where is the toilet?	*Hong nam yu ti nai?*
Never mind That's fate C'est la vie That's the way the cookie crumbles	*Mai pen rai*
one	*nung*
two	*sorng*
three	*sarm*
four	*see*
five	*hah*
six	*hok*
seven	*jet*
eight	*paed*
nine	*kow*
ten	*sib*

7

TRANSPORT IN THAILAND

Using Public Transport

When compared to services in Europe, Thai transportation is not so comfortable and not so fast, but very cheap. In spite of the hardy conditions, travelling around independently can be great fun because the Thais are so friendly. It is an excellent way to observe the life of the local people.

In Bangkok there is less language difficulty than in the provinces, but before setting off anywhere it is wise to have the exact destination written in Thai (hotel receptionists willingly do this for guests). Then, ask a Thai for all alternative routes and services for every step of the journey. When you think you have the information, ask another Thai and see if you get the same answers.

Be prepared for delays and unscheduled stops and beware of relying on a connecting service shown in a timetable. Allow plenty of time between arrival and departure when making connections. Thai travellers are quite accustomed to waiting, sitting, doing nothing contentedly for hours on end. In the rainy season remember that flooding can disrupt some services for days.

The State Railway of Thailand

Perhaps "Sedate Railways" would be a more appropriate term, for even the "express" and "rapid" trains jog along at a leisurely pace.

Unless one is used to the tropical climate and unaffected by "foreign" habits, choose first class and view the country life through the windows of an air-conditioned compartment.

Those who want to "experience" Thailand rather than just observe will prefer sharing a coach with the second-class travellers, a cross-section of the population. Here, one may enjoy not only the views outside—village scenes, farmers' houses, up-country *klong,* plantations, jungle, and distant plains—but also the distraction of fellow passengers inside. Hot foods, cold drinks, and beer are served by a waiter who constantly walks up and down carrying the plates and bottles from the dining car.

At each scheduled stop, tribes of Thais move in with trays and baskets of local foods to sell at incredibly low prices. Curry and rice are served in disposable "bowls" cleverly made entirely from banana leaves. Iced tea is sold in small plastic bags (an increasing menace since these bags never rot when thrown away). Flattened quarter chickens cooked and dipped in a salty curry sauce are available, firmly skewered in a web of split bamboo for easy handling. Nuts, trays of soft coloured sweets (mostly of a coconut basis), and a variety of fruits are also thrust under one's face. One by one, the hawkers, chanting a nasal word or two, try their luck with every passenger until the train begins to chug forward again. Wherever one sits, the smell of food is impossible to avoid.

Second-class coaches have ceiling fans that stir the hot air. Sit on the side facing away from the sun.

Anyone who still has not seen enough of life may like to try the third-class coach. Toothless women chewing betel nut, wearing the *panung* (striped or flower-patterned garments, similar to the Indian *dhobi*), barefooted farmers smoking cheroots, half-naked children, and monks in saffron robes are but a few of the vivid memories that will remain.

THE RAILWAY NETWORK—Thailand's railway system is divided into four regions; each one has a trunk line from Bangkok. Every day there is only one express train each way on each line, except for the international express service which runs only three days a week. Some trains start from Bangkok (Hualampong) Station and some from Thon Buri (Bangkok Noi) Station. (See facing page.)

PASSENGER FARES—Still at the 1955 level, the rates are low in relation to today's costs. First class is 64 *satang* ($3\frac{1}{5}$ cents) per mile; second class is half, or 32 *satang*; third class is half-again. A reduction of ten to twenty per cent is made for round-trip tickets, and rates are forty per cent lower for journeys within a hundred miles from Bangkok. An additional charge of 20 *baht* ($1) is levied for any journey on an "express" train and 10 *baht* (50 cents) for a "rapid" train.

GROUP CONCESSIONS—Parties of ten or more persons can obtain discounts of ten to thirty per cent for trips beyond the hundred-mile cheap zone from Bangkok. A nominal booking charge must be paid.

RESERVATIONS can be made no more than ten days in advance of the journey at the Advance Booking Office of Bangkok (Hualampong) Station or at other major stations. For first- and second-class tickets on "express" and "rapid" trains, there is no seat or berth reservation fee.

EXPRESS TRAIN SERVICES ON THAILAND'S TRUNK LINES

Region	Outgoing from Bangkok	Returning to Bangkok
Northern	Bangkok–Chiengmai 5:05 P.M. 10:10 A.M.	Chiengmai–Bangkok 4.00 P.M. 9:00 A.M.
North-eastern	Bangkok–Nong Khai[1] 6:30 P.M. 6:30 A.M.	Nong Khai–Bangkok 6:40 P.M. 6:30 A.M.
	Bangkok–Ubon Ratchathani 7:30 P.M. 6:35 A.M.	Ubon Ratchathani–Bangkok 7:00 P.M. 6:00 A.M.
Eastern	Bangkok–Aranyaprathet[2] 6:00 A.M. 11:35 A.M.	Aranyaprathet–Bangkok 1:10 P.M. 5:40 P.M.
Southern (International Express Service)	Monday, Wednesday, and Saturday only Bangkok–Hat Yai (for Songkhla)[3] 3:40 P.M. 10:28 A.M.	Singapore to Bangkok[4] (about 48 hours)

[1] Onward travel to Vientiane available (see p. 294).

[2] Formerly connected with the Cambodian railway to Phnom Penh (now closed).

[3] Through coaches or onward services cross the frontier to:
Butterworth (for Penang)—Arr. 4:22 P.M. (Local Malaysia time 30 min. ahead of Thai time.)
Kuala Lumpur—Arr. 7:12 A.M.
Singapore (Sun.)—Arr. 5:00 P.M. (Weekday)—Arr. 3:45 P.M.

[4] *Magic Arrow Express* leaves Singapore every Sun. and Thurs. at 8:10 A.M., arriving at Kuala Lumpur at 3:35 P.M.

Change to the *North Star Night Express* lv. Kuala Lumpur every Sun. and Thurs. at 9:30 P.M. arriving at Butterworth (for Penang) at 6:47 next morning.

Change to the *International Express* lv. Butterworth 7:40 A.M. Mon., Wed., and Fri., arr. Bangkok 24 hours later Tues., Thurs., and Sat.

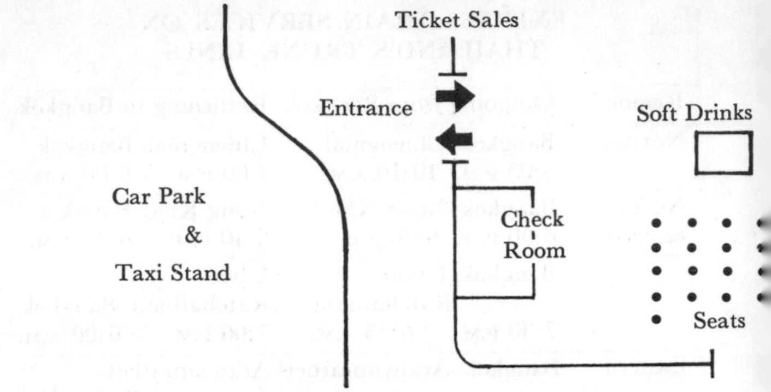

Bangkok (Hualampong) Station.

Ticket conditions—When buying a ticket one must state the time and date on which the journey is to be made. The ticket issued will show this information. Therefore, if one cancels or defers the journey (or misses the train), a refund or endorsement on the ticket must be applied for not later than three hours after the departure time of the train.

It is permitted to stop over en route during any journey of more than 125 miles. Just remember to have the ticket endorsed by the local station master and there will be no extra to pay.

Night train travel—Only "express" trains are fitted with berths. The first-class compartments convert to sleeping compartments with two beds each, while the second-class carriages have two-tier berths that fold down at night on each side of the central corridor. Night trains also have a restaurant car, toilets, shower, and wash basins. Clean sheets are provided. All other trains, including the "rapid" trains, and third-class compartments have no sleeping accommodation.

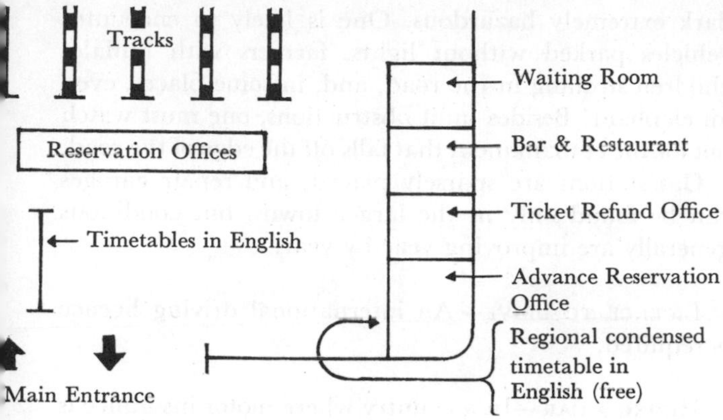

EXTRA CHARGES FOR A BERTH—

First-class berth	100 *baht* ($5)
First-class berth (air-cond.)	150 *baht* ($7.50)
Second-class upper berth	50 *baht* ($2.50)
Second-class lower berth	75 *baht* ($3.75)

Motoring

Driving or being driven in Thailand requires unusually calm nerves. The standard of driving is low, especially outside Bangkok. Probably this has something to do with the fact that drivers are able to "buy" their driving licences instead of spending the time and money to take a driving test.

All main roads and most by-roads are now well paved but on routes used by heavy trucks surfaces are inclined to become uneven and bumpy. Many of the roads in the North and Northeast are built of laterite and become quite dusty in the dry weather. Newer roads have been built on embankments in areas subject to flooding during the rainy season. The lack of street lighting, together with the Thais' lack of road sense, makes driving after dark extremely hazardous. One is likely to encounter vehicles parked without lights, farmers with buffalo, children strolling in the road, and, in some places, even an elephant! Besides unlit obstructions, one must watch out for the embankment that falls off the edge of the road.

Gas stations are sparsely placed, and repair garages can be found only in the larger towns, but conditions generally are improving year by year.

LICENCE TO DRIVE—An international driving licence is required.

HIRING A CAR—In a country where motor insurance is not yet compulsory, one should without exception choose a reputable car rental company. Hertz, the international rent-a-car agency, has offices in Bangkok. Booking may be made through any Hertz office in any country. Another well-established company is the Express Car Rent Co. Ltd., P.O. Box 2118, Bangkok, tel: 57621. Sample rates are:

Small two-door car such as a Datsun Sunny or Ford Anglia: 120–160 *baht* ($6–8) per day

Medium four-door sedan such as a Fiat 125 or BMW 1800: 220–250 *baht* ($11–12.50) per day; air-conditioned, 50 *baht* ($2.50) a day extra

Large air-conditioned car such as a Mercedes Benz 200 or Chevrolet: 400–500 *baht* ($20–25) per day.

All rates are plus 1 *baht* (5 cents) per kilometre over the first 100 kilometres (62 miles). The prices can be bargained over, usually with success if you are renting the car for a week or more.

Hiring a chauffeur with the car is well worthwhile. The

extra charge is nominal and one need not worry if the car is damaged. In Bangkok the major hotels have a hire-car service with reasonable charges. For example, the Narai Hotel charges 40 *baht* an hour for a Mercedes Benz with driver.

ROAD MAPS—Shell and Caltex, the oil companies, both produce good maps of Thailand. The Shell map can be obtained from its office in Patpong Road, Bangkok. Sometimes the map is free, sometimes 5 *baht* is asked for it. The Caltex map is obtainable from the head office on the other side of Patpong Road and from the T.O.T. office free of charge. More detailed maps are produced by the Thai government. Thailand is covered in sections by four maps in Thai and English. The set costs 60 *baht* and is available from the Government Highway Planning Office on the corner of Sri Ayutthaya and Rama VI Roads, Bangkok.

ROAD SIGNS—Direction signs in English are becoming more numerous but one had better travel with a Thai friend or guide who can read the Thai signs.

The Highways Department has inaugurated a simple numbering system for roads. Motorway-type highways have been given single numbers, main roads have double numbers, and by-roads have triple numbers. This is fine except that one is likely to be given a map showing formerly used numbers. Highway 5 is now Highway 4, Highway 21 is now Highway 2 and so on. It can be very confusing, especially as the local people often use the old numbers. Other road signs are mostly international or self-explanatory. A few common ones that may puzzle foreign drivers are shown in the sketches on the following page.

Traffic signal signs.

Bus Services

Frequent services operate on routes from Bangkok to every region and between main provincial towns. Thai buses are suitable for only the hardiest of travellers. They are often converted from trucks and have crude bench seats closely spaced. There is no room inside for luggage; that must go onto the roof. Windows, if there are any, will be open to the dusty, warm air. Fellow travellers will be farmers mostly and, though friendly, can be irksome after the first hour or two, especially if they are carrying chickens, chewing betel nut, or frequently spitting. The drivers adopt a peculiar driving position, sitting sideways to the steering wheel, and they delight in driving as fast as possible. It is quite unnerving when they take both hands from the wheel and make a *wai* reverently, along with all the passengers, as the bus hurtles past a temple.

The fares are about 1 *baht* (5 cents) per 10 km. (six miles). The ticket must be kept at hand as every few miles an inspector will board the bus and check them all, tearing off a corner or making a hole in each one. By the end of the journey the ticket is torn to shreds. There are so many ticket inspectors that one must suppose the inspectors are checking one another's work.

The bus terminals in Bangkok are not central: The Northern and Northeastern Bus Terminal is on Paholyothin Road, towards Don Muang Airport, tel: 71159. The Eastern Bus Terminal (for the Southeast) is at Bangkapi, opposite Sukhumvit Soi 63 (Ekamai Road), tel: 912504. The Southern Bus Terminal is in Thon Buri at Samyak-Faichai, Charoen Sanitwongse Road, tel: 62637. Bus services in Bangkok can be very useful. See pages 154–56 for details.

Subways

There are no subways. The soil is too soft.

Taxis

Thailand has four kinds of taxis—cars, jitneys, samlors, and pedicabs. Whichever is chosen, one must bargain with the driver and agree on the fare before getting in (or on). Picking up a taxi outside a smart hotel or restaurant will make bargaining very difficult, especially for a foreigner. By walking away and hailing a taxi fifty yards down the road 5 to 10 *baht* can be saved on the fare. It is always better to hail a taxi than to accept the offers of drivers or touts that pounce on foreigners at airports, hotel entrances, and railway stations. There is no need to tip. Drivers do not expect it.

Car taxis—These are almost all small, four-door Japanese cars and have yellow licence plates. The cars are fitted with meters but they are never used. By not using the meter the taxi driver can supplement his meagre wages, pocketing part of the fare. The Thais believe that if taxi drivers were made to use their meters then the drivers would demand higher wages and this would result in an increase in taxi fares. The present system works well, as the fares are regulated purely by supply and demand. Since there seem to be far too many taxis, particularly in Bangkok, the drivers will accept a fare for a small profit rather than refuse and earn nothing. Anyway, that is the theory behind the system.*

The easiest way to use a taxi is to have the destination written in Thai (hotel receptionists are helpful) and ask how much it should cost. Then, when a driver sees his

* The same theory lies behind the government system of paying its employees salaries that are not enough to live on. It is accepted that a government official's "perks" will supplement his salary enough to keep his family comfortably. If the system is corrected, the employees will demand higher salaries and the government is bound to increase taxes.

prospective client is well informed, bargaining will become a mere formality. Generally, the minimum fare for the shortest journey will be 5 *baht* (25 cents) and the maximum, anywhere in Bangkok, not more than 15 *baht* (75 cents) per car. The driver will not mind waiting hours for a return journey. He will also not have any change when the time comes to settle the fare.

In the provinces, taxis are shared, so after bargaining and agreeing on a fare one must not expect to be the only passenger. When passing through busy areas the driver will reduce his speed to a crawl, vigorously sounding his horn and shouting his destination through the window to attract more riders. Some foreigners get quite upset by this practice as the driver will pick up more and more passengers until the doors cannot be closed and people are literally hanging out of the car.

Unfortunately, the taxis have plastic-covered seating and in Thailand's climate those cars are like heated ovens. Westerners perspire profusely and consequently stick to the seats.

JITNEYS OR 1-BAHT TAXIS—These are converted Japanese agricultural trucks. Bench seats and a roof are built on at the back to carry eight or ten passengers in comfort (jitneys often carry twice this number). The jitney is a much cooler way of travelling than by car.

Jitneys are not seen in Bangkok except at Lumpini Park, where they operate to and from the outskirts of the city on fixed routes. Passengers may hail the driver and get on or off anywhere en route for a fare of 1 *baht* (5 cents). In the provinces they operate over longer distances between towns and may charge up to 5 *baht* per ride. In Chiengmai they are very convenient, as they will go to any destination within the town for 1 *baht*. As with the shared taxis (mentioned previously), the drivers will

Samlor.

go very slowly through crowded districts and make all kinds of noise to attract more passengers.

Do not bargain with the driver, just get on and watch the other passengers to see how much they pay the driver when they alight. One can then simply pay the same amount. Otherwise, the foreigner may be asked to pay more. (He usually can afford more.)

SAMLORS—These are three-wheeled vehicles converted from motor scooters. Unique to Thailand, they are locally known as "doog doogs," a name derived from the noise of their two-stroke engines. They are also called "honeymoon cabs" because of the cosy seating arrangement.

Samlors were due to be banned from Bangkok in 1965 because of traffic congestion but drivers petitioned the King. As a result, the government compromised by lifting the ban while deciding to issue no more licences. The number of samlors, therefore, is gradually decreasing.

Most of the drivers are poor farmers from the Northeast who work part-time. They are family men and were so grateful to the King for their reprieve that every year, on the King's birthday, they donate large sums of money and blood to the Red Cross as a token of thanks. Over

1,000 of the drivers have also willed their eyes to the National Eye Bank. Their donations are generous since they can earn only about 60 *baht* ($3) a day. Their charitable inclinations do not extend to fare-paying passengers, however, and they drive hard bargains. The Thais use samlors for short rides and pay as little as 3 *baht* (15 cents) but foreigners (especially tourists who want a ride just for fun) will have to pay as much as for a car taxi. Samlor drivers understand only Thai.

PEDICABS—These were banned from the streets of Bangkok long ago but are a popular means of transport in provincial towns.

They are slow, naturally, but a restful and quiet way to sightsee lazily. The fares asked are usually so low that one feels ashamed to bargain too much, especially as the pedicab is propelled by human power. All the same, a minute or two bargaining (with a smile) will establish a friendly relationship, and one can always tip afterwards —it is never expected, and the driver will beam with delight.

Pedicab.

Water Transport

KLONG TAXIS—Ferry boats and speed boats operate very frequent services on the *klong,* crossing from Thon Buri to Bangkok and going up-country from Ta Tien Pier, Bangkok, as far as Bang Pa-In with connecting services to Ayutthaya. Fares are very low. For example, Bangkok to Bang Pa-In is 10 *baht* (50 cents) one way, for a journey of about three hours by speedboat. The long speedboats carry up to seventy passengers.

COASTAL SHIPPING SERVICES—The Thai Navigation Co. Ltd., 712 Hong-Kong Bank Lane, Si-Phya Road, Bangkok, operates cargo/passenger ships on a route between Bangkok and Narathiwat via Ko Samui Island, Songkhla, Pattani, and Tak Bai. From June until September the ships will call at the fishing ports of Lang Suan, Tako, Bohka, Chumphon, and Sapli on the way back to Bangkok. Departing from Bangkok every Wednesday and Saturday at noon, the ships return by the Thursday or Sunday of the following week. A deluxe cabin for two persons costs around 1,920 *baht* ($96) for the round trip. Cars can be transported on these ships too.

HYDROFOIL—Services are planned on the following routes:

Bangkok–Pattaya–Sattahip–Chanthaburi–Trat;

Bangkok–Hua Hin–Prachuap Khiri Khan–Chumphon –Surat Thani;

Surat Thani–Nakhon Si Thammarat–Songkhla–Narathiwat;

Ranong–Phuket.

Enquiries should be made through the Trade and Industry Development Co. Ltd., Mansion 10, 93 Rajdamnern Avenue, Bangkok.

CHARTERING A YACHT—Small riverboats or luxury cruising vessels may be hired from the Atlanta Club, Soi 2, Sukhumvit Road, Bangkok, tel: 57867. The large craft can carry up to ninety passengers in comfort for sightseeing cruises and costs about 2,500 *baht* ($125) for four hours with crew. This size vessel can sleep fourteen passengers in comfort and is fully fitted for sea voyages of several weeks. One can choose to go anywhere around Thailand or further away to such exotic places as Borneo or Bali. Ratcs on application.

Domestic Air Services

Thai Airways Co. Ltd., 6 Larn Luang Road, Bangkok, flys to a surprising number of towns all over Thailand and to Vientiane, in Laos, and Penang Island, in Malaysia.

It also offers air-taxi service. In other words, one may hire a twin-engined, light aircraft—Piper—and ask to be flown to any airfield in Thailand. The Piper (latest model) can seat five passengers and carry 300 pounds of luggage.

8

MEETING A THAI

Your First Encounter

The Thais are good-mannered, gracious people, temperate and conscious of the Buddhist doctrine. They are very proud of their country and it is easy for a foreigner to cause offence inadvertently.

THE WAY TO MAKE A WAI—When meeting a Thai, put the hands together as if in prayer and nod slightly, saying *sawadee* or more politely, *sawadee-krap* to a man and *sawadee-ka* to a lady. Sometimes Thais close their eyes when they nod. The position of the hands is supposed to be quite important. They should be placed in front of the chest when meeting a child, against the chin to greet someone of equal status or a very close friend, raised to the level of the top lip for meeting an older person or someone of senior status, and placed against the forehead when paying homage to Buddha or when meeting the King or a monk. Nowadays, however, Thais will place their hands nonchalantly anywhere in front of the face on most occasions.

The nearest translation of *sawadee* is probably "Greetings." It can mean "hello," "good morning," "good afternoon," "good evening," or "good-bye." Never forget to return the same gesture if a Thai makes a *wai* greeting to you.

A *wai.*

The *wai* position is also used when making an apology and when expressing thanks.

KEEP SMILING—Thailand, often called the "Land of Smiles," is no place for a serious face. When meeting Thais, return the smiles. They are part of the conversation.

There may be times when little irritations occur once too often but it is no use getting angry and shouting. Thais will just stare, bewildered, or simply shrug their shoulders muttering *mai pen rai* (never mind). They always talk in moderate tones, and it is considered ill-mannered to shout or even to talk loudly (a common fault among English and American people when they are speaking to foreigners).

Apart from smiling, saying a Thai word or two, and talking softly, the next best thing to do, since Thais are proud of their country, is to chat about Thailand. However, there is still plenty of opportunity for an unwary *farang* (foreigner) to upset the new acquaintance.

To make more headway—Thais believe that the most sacred part of the body is the head (certain other parts are sacred too), so it will pay to observe the following rules scrupulously:

Never touch a Thai on the head.
Never tap or touch his shoulders.
Never pass things over someone's head.
Back-slapping causes offence.
When seated next to a Thai, do not put your arm across the back of his chair.
Women must never touch or brush against a monk; they do not like women even to talk to them.
Take off your hat when entering a house or temple building.

The feet—Just as the head is thought most sacred, the feet are regarded as the least sacred part of the body. Consequently:

Never touch a person with the foot.
Never sit with the soles of your feet or toes pointing towards a Thai.
When seated, never raise your feet or point at anything with the foot.
Never stamp your feet.
Always remove your shoes before entering a home or temple building (with the exception of Wat Po in Bangkok).

The Status of Women

In the old days, the family system was similar to the Chinese system. Father was the supreme head of the family and the women had no authority at all. They were simply born to serve. It seems that moral codes followed Confucianism, though a husband would often keep "minor wives." In Thai literature the manners and duties of women appear rigid and strict. For example, the wife would watch and serve her husband while he ate and only after he had finished his meal would she be allowed to eat too. Every night, as he went to bed, she would make a *wai* at his feet as a sign of respect.

In the 19th century Thai women became more influential but still today they generally take second place in society, and there are many jobs that are unattainable for a woman. In theory, education offers Thai women an equal chance with men to follow any career. In practice, however, even if a woman became, for instance, a highly successful business executive, she would still have to lower herself to serve her husband at home in order to enjoy a peaceful marriage and to follow convention. Divorce is still rare as women receive no advantage from it.

9

FOOD AND RESTAURANTS

One of the Thais' greatest pleasures is eating, which is understandable in a country where such a wide variety of food is so plentiful and cheap. Thai dishes have a distinctive flavour that comes from the use of coconut, lemon grass, lime, and chillies.

Almost all the restaurants are owned by Chinese Thais. Consequently some dishes are quite similar to the Chinese style, especially in the small local restaurants. You might also find a similarity to Indian and Malay cuisines.

The Thai Palate

Thai people prefer hot, spicy dishes that should be approached with caution. Chillies are added to almost every dish in explosive quantities. However, certain dishes are well worth sampling. The red and green, torpedo-like chillies can be carefully removed from each spoonful (it is as easy as removing bones when eating a fish). If the food is still too hot, add plenty of rice to the dish. This tends to soften the burning sensation. It is surprising how quickly people acquire the taste for such spicy food which is well-suited to the tropical climate.

RICE, RICE, AND RICE—Thais take rice with every meal, at least three times a day. Up-country, an almost solid lump of very sticky, glutinous rice is served with the meal. This is cooked by steaming it in small containers. Restaurants in Bangkok and elsewhere that cater to tourists will serve the non-glutinous rice that is familiar to Western tables. This rice is prepared by slightly undercooking it and then leaving it to "age" in the pot (still covered) in its own diminishing heat. If done perfectly it will be flaky and tender. Cooked a moment too long, it will be sticky and soft, and, if undercooked, the Thais will say it is "too beautiful"—a little too shiny and hard.

Eating Advice

Light breakfasts and snack lunches are suited to the tropical climate. If possible, rest after lunch, in the heat of the day. If the temperature and humidity still drain your energy, a cup of hot China tea is reviving.

Be careful of salads and ice. Also, be cautious of pork. In the hot climate it can easily spoil and then, if insufficiently cooked, can cause trichinosis—parasitic worms in the intestines and muscle tissue.

ICE CREAM—Completely safe is "Foremost" ice cream, readily available in cups at around 2 *baht* (10 cents) each.

DRINKING WATER—Water from the tap may not suit your stomach. In hotels, each guest is supplied with a vacuum jug of water for drinking, and this is passable. In establishments outside hotels, one will be offered Polaris and Fujim bottled water. This is not mineral water; it is just ordinary water, filtered. If one has a delicate constitution, drink only boiled water. Be especially cautious during the rainy season (June to October).

BEER AND LOCAL SPIRITS—Good imported bottled beer

(such as Guinness, San Miguel, and Japanese brands) is readily available, at a premium, in major hotels and bars. The Thai beers named *Singha* and *Krating Thong* are particularly good; they cost 15–20 *baht* (75 cents–$1) a bottle.

As for the locally brewed spirits, frankly, they are best avoided. Crude rice wines, fruit drinks, and a whisky called *Mekong* at 22–25 *baht* a bottle are popular among country folk. Incidentally, the Buddhist precept concerning alcohol forbids "taking that which forms the basis of wrongful temptation." Interpreted in many ways, it is usually taken to mean that while one must not become intoxicated, the precept need not preclude drinking moderately on suitable occasions. Most Thais, although Buddhists, will therefore accept an invitation to a drink at the bar without qualms.

Fruits—With such a variety and abundance of local fruits available at really low cost, the author wonders why hotels generally offer so little variety at such highly inflated prices. While tourists may be offered bananas, papaya, and perhaps pineapple in the hotels, the majority of Thailand's exotic fruits remain undiscovered by foreign visitors, piled high in the markets to be sold to the Thais for whom they are an important part of the daily diet. All tourists visit the Floating Market (see Chapter 14, p. 159), but how many bother to buy and try the produce they see and photograph? Armed with the following illustrated list, there can be no excuse for not exploring the local markets and trying some of these delectable fruits. Nothing, apart from *durian,* will cost more than a few *baht* per kilo, per bunch, or whatever. Even large pineapples can be had for 2–3 *baht*. See "Weekend Market in Bangkok," page 196.

Banana—*kluey* or *gluey*. The word is synonymous with

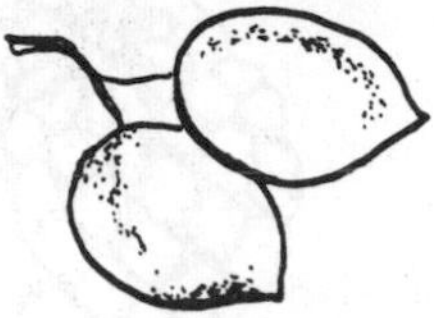

Chinese date *(putsar)*.

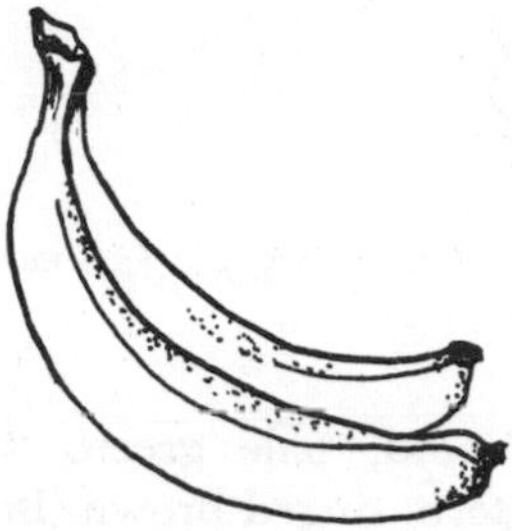

Banana (*kluey* or *gluey*).

"simple," "easy." In Thailand, the banana must be the easiest crop. More than twenty varieties of banana grow here. The most popular are *kluey hom* or "fragrant banana," and *kluey kai* or "egg banana," so called because it is short and fat. These are eaten fresh. If you buy bananas that taste like soap, they should be cooked until they become sweet and sticky. They may be charcoal grilled in the skins (often along the roadside), or fried in batter, oil, or syrup; or they can be made into cakes and used in desserts; also they can be bought like sweets, sliced, sugared, and dried. One cooking variety is called *kluey kheg* or "malay banana."

Chinese date—*putsar*. These are small, plum-like fruits with green skin.

Coconut—*maprao*. Drink the milk fresh. The Thais also use coconut and coconut milk extensively in cooking. Coconut oil is often used for frying. In the south, sugar is made from unripe coconuts. Available throughout the year.

Custard apple *(noi nah)*.

Custard apple—*noi nah*. Round, pale green, thick skin with an artichoke-like pattern, tinged brown. Break it open and eat the white pulp, which is very sweet and cool. Do not eat the seeds. Available June–December.

Durian. Large, greeny-brown, thick, thorny-skinned fruit. The inside has a peculiar, pungent odour that will deter all but the strong-willed from tasting it. The pulp is creamy yellow, sweet, and piquant. The seeds can be roasted. This is the most highly prized Thai fruit and will cost between 60 and 100 *baht* ($3–5) for one. Abundant around late April and May.

Grapes. Recently introduced, they are grown successfully and are not expensive. Juicy.

Guava—*farang*. Shaped like an apple, light green. When ripe it has a strong odour. The Thais have a special way with guava; they eat them sliced, dipped in a sauce made from chillies, salt, and sugar, often using garlic too. January–March.

Jack fruit—*ka-noon*. Large, yellow-brown, thick skin with small, rubbery "thorns." It has an aromatic, sweet pulp. The seeds can be boiled and eaten.

Lansat or *langsard*. Grows in bunches, the size of cherries, yellow. The pulp inside is white and in segments with a few large seeds. It is sweet and succulent. Do not eat the seeds.

Durian.

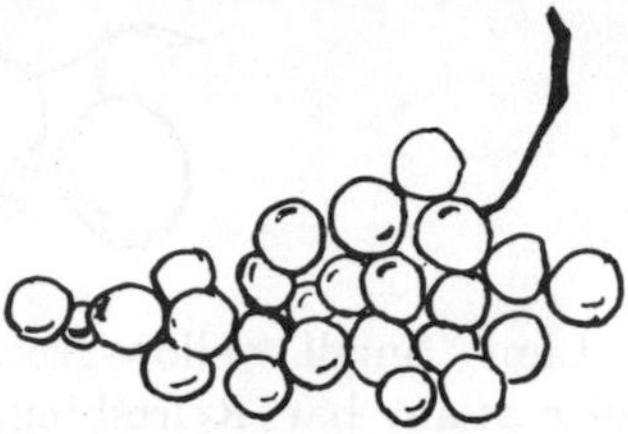

Grapes.

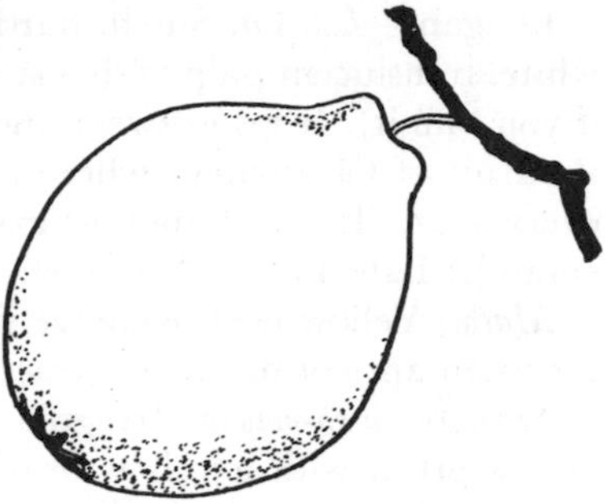

Guava *(farang)*.

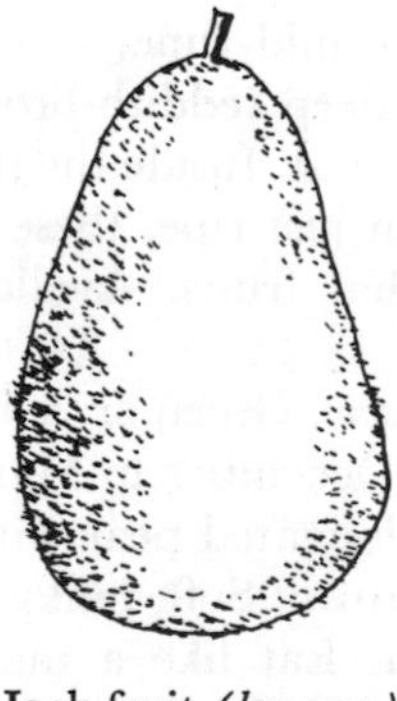

Jack fruit *(ka-noon)*.

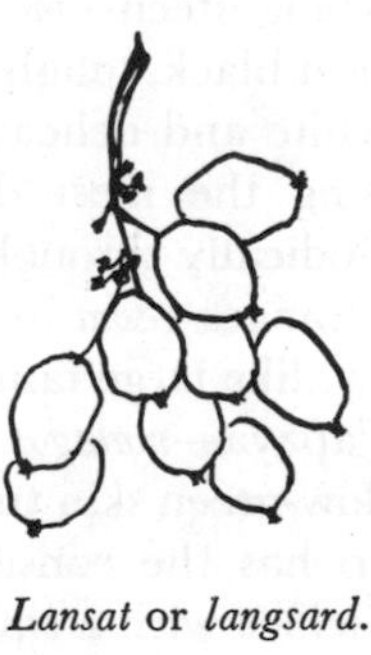

Lansat or *langsard*.

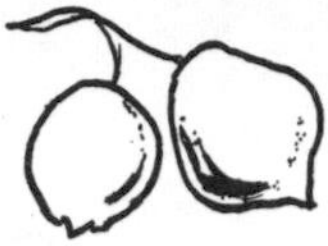

Mafai.

Lime. Small, yellow-green peel. Ask for fresh lime juice at any bar. Refreshing, fortifying, and cheap. It is customary to add a pinch of salt to the drink. One variety called *makroot* (Kaffir lime) is very acid. The leaves and rind are used in Thai curries and other dishes.

Longans—*lam yai*. Small, hard brown fruit with juicy white, translucent pulp with a stone in the middle (bitter if you bite it). It tastes sweet and slightly musty. This is the fruit of Chiengmai, where a *lam yai* festival is held every year. (It is just another excuse for a beauty queen contest.) Late July and August.

Mafai. Yellow peel. Remove skin before eating. Similar to an apricot but more watery.

Mango—*mah-muong*. Irregular egg-shapes; yellow or yellow-green with a yellow-orange pulp inside. Several varieties. Thais eat this in the same way as guava (above). Eaten fresh, it tastes something like a peach. Used in making Thai desserts. Early April to mid-June.

Mangosteen—*mang-kut*. A round, deep reddish-brown, almost black, tough skin. Knife required. Inside the pulp is white and delicately sweet. When just ripe, these are among the most delectable of Thai fruits. Available periodically throughout the year.

Oranges—*som keeo whan*. Just say *som*. Green or yellow, juicy, like large tangerines. Mostly December to March.

Papaya—*malagor*. Like a large, elongated pear with a yellow-green skin turning reddish brown. Soft, pinky-red pulp has the consistency of melon. Eat like a melon. Delicious with a squeeze of fresh lime. All year round.

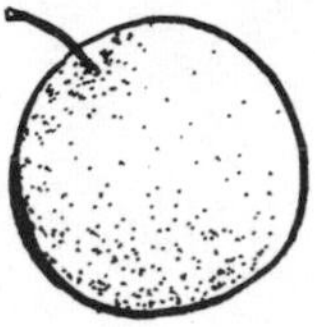

Kaffir lime *(makroot)*.

Longans *(lam yai)*.

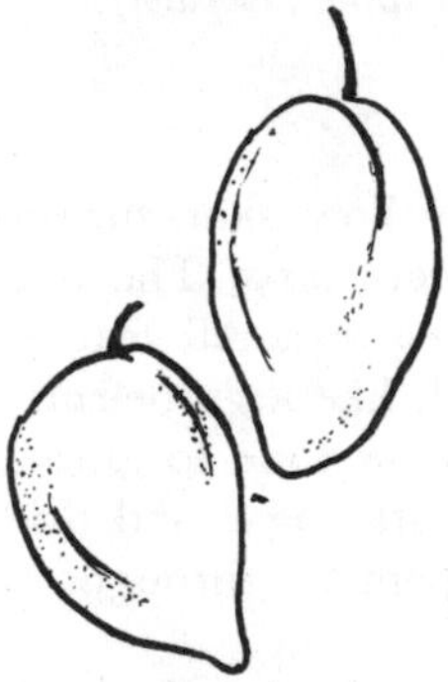

Mango *(mah-muong)*.

Mangosteen *(mang-kut)*.

Oranges *(som keeo whan)*.

Papaya *(malagor)*.

Pineapple *(supparot)*.

Pineapple—*supparot*. Greeny-yellow skin turning to red. Juicy, sweet with slightly acid tang. The best are said to come from Siracha, near Pattaya. All year round.

Pomelo—*som-oh*. Large, round, like a grapefruit with a whitish-yellow thick peel. Similar taste to grapefruit. The peel is sometimes cooked with sugar and dried to make a sweet. Common and popular throughout the year.

Rambutan—*ngow* or *ngor*. About the size of a hen's egg with a deep red, thick, prickly, but soft peel. Very sweet, white, translucent pulp with big stone in the middle. All year round.

Rose Apple—*chom-poo*. Several varieties ranging from deep red to pinky-white. Inside the white pulp is rather like a tasteless plum though some varieties are said to be sweet. January to March.

Sapodilla—*lumut*. Small, reddish brown skin. Juicy brown pulp with plum-like taste. November–December.

Watermelon—*teng-mo*. Large, round, light green variety in January and February. Darker green variety from January to June. Watery, pink pulp. Refreshing.

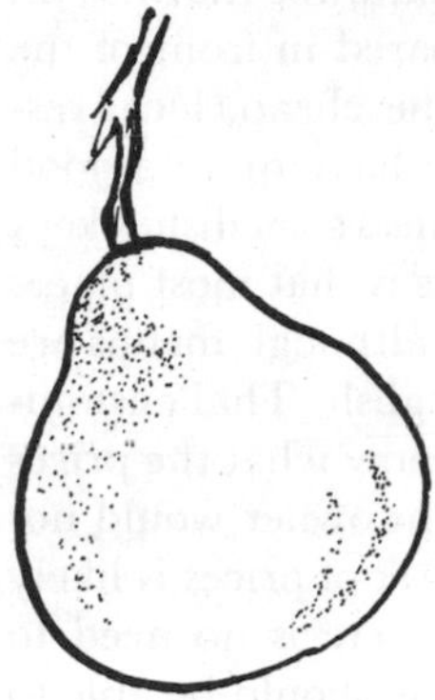

Pomelo *(som-oh)*.

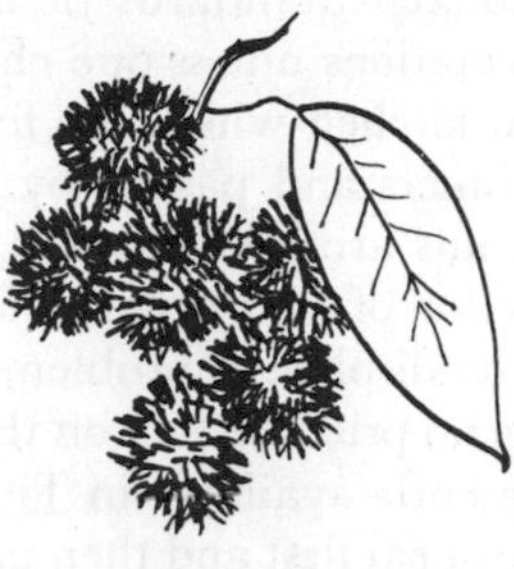

Rambutan (*ngow* or *ngor*).

Sapodilla *(lumut)*.

Rose apple *(chom-poo)*.

Watermelon *(teng-mo)*.

Restaurants

LOCAL—Standards of hygiene may not come up to expectations unless one chooses a restaurant that has an open kitchen where the food is prepared in front of the customers and passers-by. Most of the cheap, local restaurants are open-fronted, and some have quite a good selection of ready-cooked food in spotless steel dishes kept hot on display. A problem for tourists is that most places have no prices shown on their menus although menus are frequently available in Thai or in English. Thai customers just eat first and then pay. They know what the prices should be, roughly, and the restaurant owner would not try to overcharge. A slightly inflated set of prices is likely to be used for foreign tourists, but there is no need to worry—it will never be expensive. One should be able to eat well for 15 *baht* (75 cents) taking soup, a main dish with rice, and something to follow. One may ask the prices when ordering but, it seems, the result is the same.

The usual way to eat is to take a mouthful of rice and then a mouthful from any of the other dishes—in any order—as you like.

On the table, a fork is provided for the left hand and a spoon for the right hand, and, under the table, a spittoon.

LUXURY THAI—These cater to foreign visitors but should not be dismissed as "not the real thing," as the meals are authentic, and Thai people who are rich enough often use these places. Usually, a traditional Thai set meal is served, suitably toned down for first-timers. Thais never suffer a burning sensation when eating their curry. A curry that might seem bland to a native Thai, however, will give the tourist—with his less hardy taste buds—an "authentic" and yet bearable taste sensation. Perhaps the best way to be sure of enjoying this type of restaurant for the first time is to choose one that has a stage show of traditional Thai dancing. The well-established ones are listed in the chapter "Entertainments and Sports" under "Thai Dancing." Some of them have beautiful, ancient style interiors. The meal will cost around 100–140 *baht* ($5–7) per person.

WESTERN-STYLE AND FOREIGN—In Bangkok there is a wide choice of European, Chinese, and Japanese restaurants. Besides these, there will be no difficulty in finding Korean, Indian, Indonesian, Muslim, Mexican, and Vietnamese food. Here is a selection of the author's favourites:

Japanese—Daikoku, Soi Suan Plu off South Sathorn Road. Serves *tempura, shabu-shabu, sukiyaki, yakitori.* Allow 200–250 *baht* ($10–12.50) per person. Lunch, 11:30 A.M.–2:00 P.M.; dinner, 6:00–11:00 P.M.

Chinese—Kinareenava, Thailand's only floating restaurant, on the lake in Lumpini Park in a romantic setting. Serves a wide choice of Chinese food and drinks and some Thai food. In the evening a band plays. Open from 10:00 A.M. till midnight. Allow 30–50 *baht* ($1.50–2.50) per person. This restaurant is popular among local people.

Chinese/Thai—Niyom, near the Sheraton Hotel in Suriwongse Road. Very clean, cheap, and always busy with local people. It has one copy of the menu in English but, if possible, it is better to ask for dishes by their Thai names. Try *cyclops, kau tom* and *pakpun-pa* (pork rolls, rice and hot-sour soup, vegetables), their specialities. Open twenty-four hours a day. Upstairs is air-conditioned. Allow 10–15 *baht* (50–75 cents) per person, without drinks.

French—Chez-Suzanne, near Narai Hotel, on the corner of Silom Road and Dejo Road. Managed by a French lady who personally supervises the cooking. French atmosphere, French prices. Closed on Sundays.

French (but not-so-French)—Normandie Grill, on the top floor of the Oriental Hotel. Luxurious, beautiful dining room overlooking the Chao Phya River. Superb cooking, perfect but inconspicuous service. Good wines available. Jacket and tie required. Reservation advisable. Justly expensive.

Chinese—New Peng Chieng, 111 South Sathorn Road (near the Convent Bridge), tel: 860176. An enormous restaurant serving authentic Chinese dishes with startling efficiency. Seats thousands. Private dining rooms upstairs. Best to go in a group. 50–100 *baht* ($2.50–5) per person.

European—Le Gourmet Grill, First Floor, Montien Hotel, Suriwongse Road, tel: 37060. Interesting menu, imaginative Continental dishes, refined, comfortable decor. Distinguished selection of wine. Allow 150 *baht* ($7.50) per person.

For Other Restaurants—Ask for BAD's (Bangkok After Dark) guide at the hotel reception counter. This is a brochure packed with advertisements and addresses in Bangkok including a list of about one hundred of the best restaurants, each with a reliable outline description. The brochure is up-to-date and free.

Tea Room—Arcade Tea Room, Erawan Hotel, 494 Siyek Rajprasong Road. Open 9:00 A.M.–10:00 P.M.

THAI DISHES—Some districts in Thailand have developed local specialities. These are mentioned in the region-by-region chapters. Here are some of the popular Thai dishes that can be found all over the country:

Khao pad (fried rice). Finely diced pork, crab meat, and/or cooked shrimp are added in generous quantities to cold, cooked rice, then fried and tossed in lard or bacon fat. The distinctive Thai flavour comes from the addition of garlic, fish sauce, and peppers. It is served with chilli

1. Classical dancers in outdoor performance.

2. Motor samlors, the quickest transportation around Bangkok.

3. Monument of Democracy, Bangkok.

4. Street vendors near Pratunam Market, Bangkok.

5. Country girl at her loom.

6. Umbrella making in a northern village.

7. Market stall with Buddhist images.

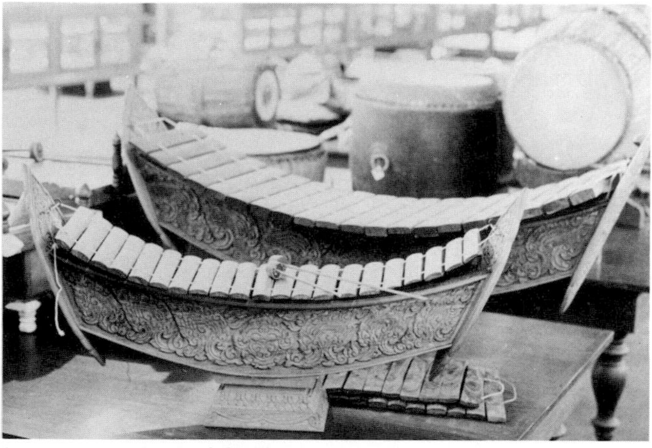

8. *Ranad ek,* classical Thai instrument.

9. A Thai meal: forks and spoons are used, but food is pre-cut.

10. Floating market at Bang Khun Thien on the Chao Phya River.

11. Northern hill-tribe woman.

12. Thai boxing.

13. Elephant race, Surin elephant round-up.

sauces that the customer can sprinkle according to personal taste. Cost: 5–15 *baht* depending on the type of restaurant.

Tom-yum (a hot soup). This has a strange taste that people immediately either like very much or dislike. Basically, it is a spicy chilli and sour soup, served piping hot. It can be made with either chicken: *kai* or *gai*; beef: *neua-sawd*; pork: *neua moo*; fish: *khai plar*; or shrimp: *gung foi*. Its special flavour is from seasoning with lemon or lime juice, lemon grass, magrood leaves (citrus hystrix), galangele (a light-brown root), and finely chopped or pounded chillies. A portion of plain rice with this dish is recommended. Cost: 7–15 *baht* per person.

Gaeng ped (Thai curry). This is, perhaps, the most popular dish among Thais. It usually contains either chicken or beef cooked with chillies, aubergine (eggplant), coconut milk, and various spices indigenous to Thailand. *Gaeng ped* is made with coconut milk; *gaeng pah* is without coconut milk and even hotter. Cost: 5–7 *baht* per portion.

Gung tord katien prick Thai (fried prawn with garlic and pepper). *Gung* means prawn and can be substituted by the word *moo* (pork), *neua* (beef), or *gai* (chicken). This is a popular way of preparing those main ingredients. A mixture of peppercorns, pieces of garlic, salt, and fish sauce is added to the main ingredient chosen, and they are fried together. Eat with rice. Cost: 10–15 *baht* per dish, often enough for two persons.

Ped baikapow neua (fried beef with chillies). The beef (or chicken—*gai*—if you wish) is lightly fried, then a little sugar is added with fish sauce, chillies, and Thai spices, to be fried again together. This dish is very hot but delicious. Cost: 5–10 *baht* per portion.

Khai palo (egg palo). This is similar to a curry but sweet rather than hot. Thai children love it. The egg is first boiled, the shell removed, then it is placed in a saucepan with garlic, pepper, sugar, fish sauce, water, Thai spices, and always a few pieces of pork, then boiled for an hour or two. Cost: 5–10 *baht* per portion.

Hom-mok (steamed fish). Fish, with bones removed, is put in pieces with Thai curry spices and juice squeezed from coconut into a small bowl and steamed for fifteen to twenty minutes. After cooking, a little coriander and chilli may be added, and then perhaps a sprinkle of coconut milk. Cost: 3–5 *baht* per portion.

Finally, for the benefit of thirsty visitors, "Iced water, please"—"*Kaw nam juen noi krap.*"

10

ENTERTAINMENT AND SPORTS

No visitor should miss seeing a performance of Thai classical dancing. In Bangkok, there is also much lively nightlife, but in the provincial towns beyond Bangkok, Pattaya, and Chiengmai, there is practically nothing more than cinemas that generally show old Chinese, Japanese, Indian, and Thai films. Whatever one chooses to do, Bangkok prices compare well with those of European capitals.

Classical Dance Drama

A form of ballet, Thai dance's every movement symbolizes such expressions as fear, joy, anger, love, mockery, and shyness, forming a language of feelings. Thai dance is also rhythmic, precise, and graceful. The costumes are costly and elaborate; heavy brocades are adorned with precious stones, and the faces are covered with masks or thick layers of make-up. The glittering costumes and gestures, the rhythmic swaying, gliding, and bending, and the lilting music are extraordinary and captivating. Performers have to be trained from childhood.

The forms of dramatic dance in Thailand can be summarized as follows:

khon—masked play
nang talung—shadow play
lakon—operatic-style dances
(a) *lakon nai*—performed inside the royal court
(b) *lakon nok*—performed outside the royal court
(c) *lakon chatree* (or *jatri*)—folk form peculiar to the Southern Peninsula
likay (or *likea*)—musical drama in verse

In addition, there are many attractive traditional folk dances and a modern popular dance called *ram wong*.

The recent influx of tourists has brought about a revival and kept alive many of these dances that were almost forgotten. Thai dancing is now actively promoted by the Fine Arts Department through the School of Dramatic Art and the *Silpakorn* (National) Theatre.

KHON (masked play)—The general theme of *khon* is based on the Thai version of the Indian epic, the *Ramayana*, of the poet Valmiki. The Thais adapted the *Ramayana* to such an extent that it is now unique and peculiarly Thai, with many episodes that cannot be found in the original Indian version. The Thai *Ramakian* also reveals adaptations from versions of the *Ramayana* found in Malaysia, Indonesia, Khmer, and Laos, as well as incidental Buddhist overtones. The full story lasts about five hours so that usually only selected episodes are performed.

Originally, all the performers were men (until the 19th century), and all wore masks, but nowadays girls appear and even take male roles, and some characters are not masked. There are four types of roles in *khon*—the monkeys, the demons, the male characters, and the female characters. The masks, especially of the demons, are bizarre and electrifying. The story is recited in an in-

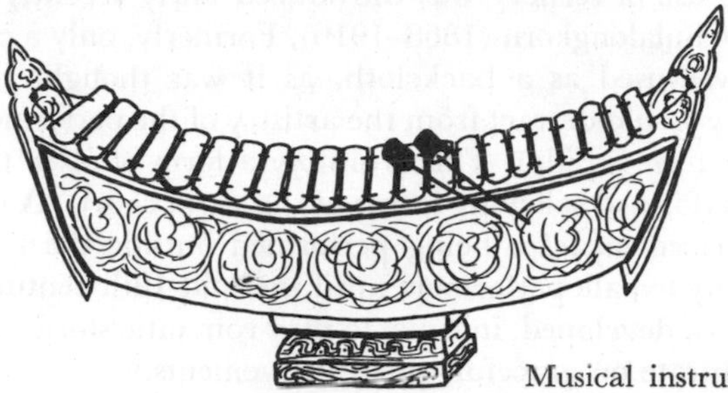

Musical instrument.

toned voice by reciters accompanied by rhythmic music that accentuates the prescribed movements and gestures of the players. Some of the fighting action requires considerable acrobatic skill.

NANG TALUNG (shadow play)—Actors move large, cut-out figures made from ox leather in front of a light to reflect against a screen. All the movements are accompanied by music and recitation. The stories are also from the *Ramakian*. Performances are now rare, but the intricately worked cut-outs are readily available for purchase in the South and in Bangkok as mentioned in the chapter "Shopping," page 108.

LAKON (operatic-style dances)—Allied to the *khon*, the *lakon* differs in that only one or two characters, such as the demon, wear masks, and the other performers may sometimes sing or speak. Even the actor wearing a mask can raise it at times in order to speak.

Traditionally, while *khon* performances are accompanied by recitation, *lakon* performances are accompanied by a chorus with a lead singer. Nowadays, however, this is not strictly adhered to, and facets of *khon* and *lakon* are often combined.

The use of scenery was introduced fairly recently by King Chulalongkorn (1868–1910). Formerly, only a curtain was used as a backcloth, as it was thought that scenery would detract from the artistry of the performers.

Lakon nai (inside). This is simply a form of *lakon* that was performed solely by ladies of the royal court. (A ban was placed on *lakon* being performed outside the royal court by female performers until the mid-19th century.) *Lakon nai* developed, in time, to play romantic stories and concentrate on graceful, gentle movements.

Lakon nok (outside). Originally, this was performed solely by men and was the "*lakon* of the common people," outside the royal court. It lacked the refined techniques of *lakon nai,* being more lively and spectacular to appeal to ordinary folk. *Lakon nok* tended, therefore, to avoid the romantic stories of *lakon nai.* After King Mongkut (1840–68) lifted the ban on women performing *lakon* outside the royal court, *lakon nok* began to have both men and women performers. Subsequently, many features have been combined so that there is often little to distinguish *lakon nai* from *lakon nok.*

Lakon chatree. This developed in the South from a play called *Nora* which features a bird-woman and a folk-tale heroine. Undoubtedly the simplest form of *lakon,* it used to be performed in the open air in comparatively simple costume to the accompaniment of a few basic instruments.

Likay. This is really another form of *lakon* with the main difference being that the performers speak in verse, still accompanied by music. The stories tend to involve historical events such as dramatic political affairs or scenes from court life. They are presented rather like a pantomime. It has also been suggested that Western drama influenced the *likay* (in particular, Shakespeare's plays, translated into Thai earlier this century).

Folk Dances

These are often performed at the end of classical dancing shows in Bangkok and are especially popular in Chiengmai.

The attraction of Thai folk dances lies in their naturalness. Costumes are colourful, sarong-style with long sleeves; hairstyles are exotic, hung with strings of jasmine or an orchid or two; this, plus the pulsating rhythms and, above all, the entrancing beauty of Thai girls, creates a rare, delightful combination that must have pleased many spectators for several hundreds of years.

Originally, they were, and still are, performed at festival times such as at the Songkran festival, Loy Krathong, or at New Year and harvest time. Men and women never come into contact. Movements and rhythms vary but are generally slow and relaxed.

FAWN LEP AND FAWN DUB—fingernail dances from the North of Thailand to entertain the King. Golden, artificial fingernails several inches in length are worn. A variation of this is the candle dance. Instead of employing artificial fingernails, the girls carry lighted candles, and make twisting, whirling, and interweaving movements. This was said to have been originally performed to welcome the menfolk home from the wars.

SUNG SU KWAN—a dance symbolizing taking food to the men working in the fields. It also signifies "respecting order."

TALOONG—a modern dance originating from the South. Performers wear long, flowing dresses and silver shoes.

FAWN PA-MAH—a dance of northern Thailand, originating from the Burmese, that is performed to receive headmen at a reception.

There are, of course, others such as the dances of the hill tribe people which can be seen in Chiengmai. Generally, the northern dances have been influenced by the Burmese, and the southern dances show similarities to those of Malaya.

Modern Dances

Thais love to dance and eagerly adopt popular dances from the West. There is one modern Thai dance, however, called *ram wong,* which everybody knows, just as, broadly speaking, everyone in the West knows the "twist." The *ram wong* evolved from the *ram thone* which used to be danced in the provinces to the accompaniment of *ching* (small cymbals), *krab* (Thai castanets), and *thone* (small drums)—hence the name *ram thone* (drum-dance). The movements and tempo varied, and, as it grew in popularity, songs and popular tunes were adapted to this type of entertainment, which became known as *ram wong.*

Where to See Thai Dancing

THEATRE RESTAURANTS IN BANGKOK—The following listed theatre/restaurants are all good. One should arrive around 7:30 P.M. for dinner at 8:00 P.M., and the shows begin about 9:00 P.M. unless otherwise stated. One sits on the floor at low, teak-carved tables (there is a depression in the floor under the table for legs). They are all air-conditioned.

Amarin Hotel—524 Ploenchit Road, tel: 59840–9. The *Sushada Dining Room* has Thai classical dancing every evening. Comfortable. Smart cocktail lounge. Popular among Japanese tourists.

Baan Thai—No. 7, Soi 32 Sukhumvit Road, tel: 91301–3. (Just behind the Rex Hotel.) Thai-style wooden house. Very comfortable, old-style decor. Four-act show.

Dusit Thani Hotel Sukhothai Restaurant—Saladaeng Circle, Rama IV Road, tel: 86511. Very plush. Opulent decor. Performers dance on a black marble floor.

Maneeya Lotus Room—518/4 Ploenchit Road, Sirinee Building (opposite the Telephone Organization of Thailand), tel: 56412. Plush, brilliant decor. Western or Thai cuisine.

Piman—46 Soi 49 Sukhumvit Road, tel: 912630 or 918107. The author's favourite. The building, a fine piece of architecture, is the only one in existence in the 13th-century Sukhothai style. Very comfortable. The bar downstairs displays some interesting wall paintings and a replica of the first stone inscription of the Thai script made in 1292 by King Ramkamhaeng of Sukhothai (see also p. 45). Elegant decor; very polished show.

Rama Hotel—Silom Road, tel: 31010. Excellent, comprehensive show performed by the Forum School of Dancing. Daily at 8:00 P.M., except Sundays.

Sala Norasingh—Soi 4 South Nana, Sukhumvit Road. Comfortable, old Thai-style wooden house.

Suwanna Hong—Sri Ayutthaya Road, just opposite the Chao Phya Hotel, tel: 514247. Bangkok's largest theatre restaurant, seating up to 500 guests. Spectacular show with a good variety of dances and costumes from many periods and districts. Show compensates for the food. Angkorian period-style decor.

Villa Flora—328 Paholyothin Road, tel: 75025–7. Comfortable, ancient Thai atmosphere. Thai or European cuisine.

OPEN-AIR SHOWS—The following are excellent for photography.

Oriental Hotel—Oriental Avenue, tel: 39920. Show takes place on the lawn at 11:00 A.M. every Thursday and Sunday. Ideal for photography. Forty *baht* ($2) show only. Have drinks on the terrace and stay for the buffet-style lunch in the Verandah Restaurant overlooking the Chao Phya River.

TIMland—near Don Muang (Bangkok International) Airport. Afternoon show includes Thai music, *forn lep* folk dances, classical dances, and other folk dances, partly in open-air, partly on covered stage (see "TIMland" p. 261).

T.O.T. (Tourist Organization of Thailand)—arranges open-air performances in the grounds of the National Museum on Wednesday and Saturday mornings, from November to May. Cost: 30 *baht* ($1.50), tel: 28611–7 for details and confirmation. Ideal for photography.

OTHER SHOWS WITHOUT MEALS

National Theatre (Silpakorn Theatre)—next to the National Museum. The cheapest way to see classical dance drama. See the "Postings" section of the Sunday edition of the *Bangkok Post* for details of performances.

Rama Hotel—Silom Road, tel: 31010. Excellent, comprehensive show as noted above. Daily at 8:00 P.M., except Sundays. 85 *baht* ($4.25) for show and cocktails only.

Nightclubs and Bars

Generally, nightclubs offer a very limited selection of food so the custom is to take dinner first and then go on to a nightclub around 9:30 P.M. The better ones have internationally famous guest stars and polished floor shows. Two of the best are considered to be Sani Chateau and Café de Paris. Not all nightclubs have hostesses.

Bangkok has numerous dance bars with hostesses. Some are smart, some are seamy. Usually no food is served. Prices again are not high. One pays 50–100 *baht*

($2.50–5) an hour for a hostess or dancing partner plus drinks, which are generally reasonably priced. As there are so many of these establishments mushrooming up and frequently closing down or changing hands, it is advisable to ask for a recommendation from the hotel receptionists. Beware of touting taxi drivers—they are out to gain commissions from the less reputable establishments. Every male foreigner is accosted, without exception, by taxi drivers offering girls, boys, massage, blue movies, and so on. The sordid side of Bangkok's nightlife is blatantly open, and the unknowing foreign tourist is vulnerable.

Cinemas

The Thais are cinema-crazy, evident from the gigantic, colourful hoardings at almost every roundabout and from the number of cinemas that exist in Bangkok and are now appearing in every provincial town. Many of the cinemas are air-conditioned, which greatly adds to their attraction.

Besides Thai films, Chinese, Indian, American, and European films are popular. Western films appear surprisingly soon after their release, with sub-titles in Chinese and Thai. Normally, there are five screenings on weekdays, as follows: at 12 noon, 2:15 P.M., 4:45 P.M., 7:00 P.M., and 9:00 P.M. On Saturday and Sunday there is an extra screening at 10:00 A.M. Seats can be booked in advance. See the *Bangkok Post* (daily morning newspaper) for programme details and film reviews. Seats generally cost 10–30 *baht* (50 cents–$1.50).

National Sports

TAKRAW—an ancient and popular game played with a rattan woven ball, called *takraw,* about five or six inches in diameter. It is believed to have originated in Burma many centuries ago.

The object of the game is simply to keep the ball in the air, using any part of the body except the hands or the soles of the feet, passing it from one person to another. There are several variations using teams of seven and a suspended hoop for the ball to pass through. Another form uses a net, rather like a low badminton net.

Takraw is played in Burma, Malaysia, and the Philippines as well. In Thailand, the game is encouraged in schools.

Kite-fighting—Thailand may be the only country where kite-flying has been turned into a sport. The rules used today were formulated in 1905 under the auspices of King Chulalongkorn.

The kites used are called the *chula* (male) and the *pak-pao* (female). The *chula* is, of course, larger, stronger, and has a thicker string. It is star-shaped, measuring about five feet across. The *pak-pao* is much smaller, square, with a long tail. It has barbs to catch the *chula* and a loop to lasso over the points of the star-shaped kite.

The object of the game is for the *pak-pao* to snare the *chula* and force it to the ground. The *chula* can win by causing the *pak-pao* to lose control, perhaps by tangling the string and pulling it into *chula* territory. The fighting manoeuvers require physical strength, lightning reactions, and much practice.

Contests are held from mid-February until May or June in the sky above the Phramane Ground (the site of the Weekend Market) in Bangkok. Reclining chairs are available for spectators.

Thai boxing—This sport developed long ago from combat training. It has become well known throughout the world, and foreigners who watch never cease to be amazed by the strange rules, or rather lack of rules. The

Thai boxing.

boxers may use their fists for punching, their feet and knees for kicking or pushing, and their elbows for jabbing. They may strike *any* part of the opponent's body. This is a great refinement of the boxing that took place years ago. Then, there were no gloves, the boxers' hands and arms were bound with knotted starched cord, and there were even fewer rules. Now, it is less bloody.

Before each bout an interesting ritual takes place. When the boxers enter the ring, wailing music begins from a small orchestra consisting of a Java pipe (which sounds like discordant bagpipes), two drums, and a pair of cymbals. The two contestants, kneeling with hands together, raise their heads and bow to the floor three times to pay homage to their teachers and to pray to the spirits for a victory and protection. Then they perform a strange "boxing dance" emulating their teachers' movements in time to the slow-tempo music. Some boxers tie amulets onto their upper arms. Each boxer wears a *mongkon* (sacred cord) in a loop on his head. These have been "consecrated" by his own teacher and are removed at the end of the rituals.

After a word from the referee, the contestants shake hands, the music quickens, and tension rises as the first round begins. Throughout the bout the drums beat faster and faster, and the Java pipe drones and wails with rising gusto, spurring on the already excited crowd who, in turn, shout vigorously at the boxers who pound and kick each other with ever-increasing frenzy. The boxers, indefatigable, pour sweat and blood.

Five three-minute rounds, with two-minute rests between each, make up one bout. There are two boxing stadiums in Bangkok—Lumpini and Rajdamnern. Lumpini stadium has matches on Tuesdays and Saturdays and Rajdamnern stadium on Thursdays and Sundays. Seats cost from 30–100 *baht* ($1.50–5).

See the "Bangkok Daily" of the *Bangkok Post* for lists of coming boxing events. If you are squeamish you may prefer to watch boxing on the hotel television—in black and white (see also p. 262).

KRABI-KRABONG (sword and pole fighting)—Here is a unique, ancient sport found only in Thailand. It is popular and has been promoted as a national sport by the Ministry of Education since 1936.

It is believed to have developed long ago from games devised by warriors to perfect their techniques in combat and self-defence.

An orchestra, consisting of the same instruments that accompany Thai boxing, plays throughout the performance, and a similar type of ritual and dance takes place beforehand. The performance begins with the two opponents kneeling at each end of the arena—about 8 by 16 metres (approximately 26 by 52 feet), in size. The music starts, and they pay homage to their teachers, bowing to the floor three times. Then, a most extraordinary "dance" called *khun prom* follows, using wooden swords. They dance facing in each direction, demonstrating all sorts of positions with their swords. When the wooden swords are exchanged for the real things the fight seems ready to begin. The music starts again, but instead of fighting they walk past each other with stilted movements, supposedly to study the opponent and to calculate the best method of attack. This is called *dern plaend.* Now, at last, they are ready to fight. Since real swords are used it may be understandable that the fighters have an unwritten code to take it in turns to attack and defend. Also, after a while they agree to end the contest. Nevertheless, it is amazingly skillful, fast, and exciting. (During one performance of *krabi-krabong* which the author attended, between a girl and a man with swords, one tourist fainted with fear for the lives of the battling couple.) One mistake could mean a limb lost! But the Thais have had some 2,000 years' experience since the Mons came to the north of Thailand and introduced the sword. The Mon tribesmen were called *krom dap-song-mu,* which literally means "sword in each hand." Nowadays, it is estimated, about ten per cent of Thais can compete skillfully with a sword. A complete performance of *krabi-krabong* will consist of six pairs of contestants, and various weapons will be used in different combinations such as: sword vs. sword, pole vs. pole, bill vs. bill, two swords vs. two swords, a long pole vs. arm-shields (that can be used as short clubs), and two swords vs. one sword and shield. Surely the most exciting of Thailand's national sports, it can be seen at TIMland, (see p. 262), and at some of the restaurants that have Thai classical dancing shows.

Rural Sports

Normally, tourists will not see any of these activities but they are still practised in the villages.

Cock fighting—The birds, called *ou*, are indigenous to Thailand. They resemble sinewy, scrawny chickens, which is natural, really, since the chicken originally came from this part of Southeast Asia.*

The training is quite cruel but at the same time the owners lavish great care on the birds to keep them in peak condition. After all, prize cocks may be worth up to 10,000 *baht* ($500). They are fed very well with diced pork, rice, and sugar, and training begins when the bird is about eight months old. It is continually washed or splashed with water and then kept in the hot sunlight until it is parched. The gasping creature is then splashed with water again. This is supposed to give the bird a ferocious temperament. Its owner will then teach it to dart away from an attack by moving his hand (gloved of course) in tortuous swift actions.

When the cocks fight they are not allowed to hurt each other—spurs are not attached in Thailand. The audience watches intensely, and the fight is stopped as soon as one of the birds starts to flag. It could hardly be likened to the cruel form of cock-fighting that took place in England until its ban in 1849 and is still seen in Indonesia. Cock-fighting season begins in January, after the harvest.

Fish fighting—A peculiar type of large-finned Thai fish, captured from swamps, vividly coloured with reds and purples, is specially bred for fish-fighting. Only the males are used for fighting. They are so pugnacious that a screen has to be kept between each fish bowl to stop them from banging their heads against the glass.

As with fighting cocks, the fish are well cared for, and a fight is stopped as soon as one of them shows signs of

* Chickens originated from a wild red jungle fowl domesticated about 2,000 years ago. They were brought to the Near East around 1400 B.C. and to the Mediterranean areas around 600 B.C.

flagging. The battle seems to be won on points that are hard to determine, requiring considerable patience and concentration from the audience. It is not always easy to see the fighting as the crowd huddles round the small container. The fish are small too—not more than the length of a matchbox—and their large veil-like fins quiver and sway. Prolonged staring at them may have peculiar effects.

BEETLE FIGHTING—Two horned malc beetles (which are several inches long) are placed within sight of one female beetle (not horned). The "suitors" immediately call a duel that may last several hours. Sooner or later the weaker beetle will be tipped onto his back, denoting the contest's end. Cricket fighting sometimes takes place in the same way.

Sports from the West

Many foreign sports have become increasingly popular in Thailand, and visitors may be surprised by the fine facilities available. Thailand has hosted the Asian Games three times since their inception in 1951. Thais are keen competitors in these and in the S.E.A.P. (South East Asia Peninsular) Games, which include Burma, Laos, Malaysia, Vietnam, and Cambodia.

Popular foreign sports, for which amateur associations exist in Thailand, are track and field, badminton, basketball, boxing (by the Queensbury Rules), cycling, football, golf, hockey, judo, lawn tennis, rugby-football, swimming, table tennis, volleyball, weight-lifting, and yacht racing.

The following may be of particular interest to tourists:

GOLF—Thailand is a golfing heaven with perhaps the best kept and most spacious courses in Asia in beautiful settings, such as the course at Bangphra that spans 7,249 yards between the Gulf of Siam and a lake in the hills. (Bangphra is in the southeast region, a couple of hours' drive from Bangkok.) Some may argue that the course at Hua Hin is more beautiful. One can also find excellent golf courses unexpectedly, in such places as Hat Yai or Phuket Island. Green fees are only 20–40 *baht* ($1–2), and caddies are always available at around the same fee per round. It is not without precedent for the beautiful young girls who serve as caddies to marry the regular players!

Swimming—If you like swimming you will love those cool dips after a long day of sightseeing in Thailand's tropical climate. Very few hotels are without a pool. In Bangkok, there is just one public pool—the Olympic Pool at the National Stadium complex. The beaches around Thailand's coast are ideal for swimming, although many of them have not yet been developed with any facilities. Some that are developed include Bangsaen, Bang Salay, Pattaya, and Hua Hin. The waters are warm, clear, and replete with tropical fish. Sharks and barrucudas are unknown, practically, but jellyfish can spoil the fun during the rainy season at a few places.

Skin-diving—Enthusiasts should experience the coral reefs and rocky island bays around the coast of Thailand. There is no coral to be seen further north than Pattaya. At Pattaya, conditions could hardly be better. One may hire a boat to cross the bay and explore the islands where the coral reefs are situated. The widest reef is only 40 metres (130 feet) or so, but very, very beautiful. Ko Klock Island is a forty-minute ride away. Another fifteen minutes from there by boat are two islands: Ko Sak and Ko Ran. A further forty to fifty minutes westward will bring you to probably the best area for seeing coral—

around Ko Pai Island. The water is most clear here. At Pattaya, corals lie from 2 to 15 metres (6 to 50 feet) below the surface, but the water becomes too murky for enjoyment of the deeper corals.

Other suitable places are found at Bangsaen, where the water is very clear but there is no coral. Phuket, in the Indian Ocean, has unexplored rocky islands nearby where hundreds of varieties of beautiful shells and tropical fish can be found. A few Thais dive in this area.

At Pattaya you can hire all kinds of underwater equipment, including cameras, from the Pattaya Palace Hotel. Otherwise, it is advisable to bring your own equipment. Following the advice of local people, you may wish to use a diving suit, not for warmth but for protection against jellyfish, sea-urchins, and the coral.

The Thailand Sub-Aqua Club arranges excursions to all the best places. Also, Tour Royale, Siam Square, Bangkok, has regular tours operating to Phuket and Ranong—another lovely spot for diving and for beautiful shells.

WATER SKIING—This sport is becoming increasingly popular, especially at the resorts frequented by foreigners, such as Pattaya and Bangsaen. It costs as little as 100 *baht* ($5) an hour after a little bargaining.

YACHTING—The Royal Family and the rich are enthusiastic yachtsmen. Much of the action takes place at Pattaya, revolving round the Royal Varuna Marine Club, which has excellent facilities. Annual and weekend races are organised from here. Small sailing dinghies can be hired at Bangsaen.

11

SHOPPING

Few people may associate Thailand with shopping, yet, for the tourist shopper, Bangkok compares so well with other Asian capitals (including Hong Kong) that it would be worth adding an extra day to one's stay in Thailand to take full advantage of the opportunities. The real bargains lie among locally produced items, since all foreign goods are subject to heavy import duties. The range of Thai products is both extensive and interesting.

Bargaining

Whether or not there is a price tag it is usual practice to haggle over prices. The smiling assistants may insist that their shop has fixed prices, but, if they are Thai, they are susceptible to offers. Many Westerners find that the art of bargaining does not come easily. It is part of the game of shopping in Thailand and should be treated like a game. So haggle with a smile, let the shopkeepers laugh at your "ridiculous" offers, and laugh back at their asking prices. Thais seem to give way more easily to friendly smiles than to deadpan expressions.

Generally, one should expect to achieve a reduction of twenty-five to thirty-five percent on the price asked. However, prices vary considerably so if you are obviously a tourist it is wise to compare prices in several shops.

The Thais have the attitude that if a customer wants something and pays an agreed price for it he should be satisfied. Too often the foreigner feels swindled when he finds another person has bought the identical item—perhaps from the same shop—at a lower price. That is just too bad. Thais will not understand why a price should be adjusted after the buyer and seller have agreed and completed the deal.

If you feel very uncomfortable about haggling over prices (even with a smile) there arc a few fixed-price shops. One is called Thai Home Industries, 35 Oriental Avenue, near the Oriental Hotel, and another, which has a tremendous range of handicrafts from all over Thailand, is the Narayana Phand (pronounced "Narai Pan"), 275–2 Larn Luang Road, which is under government supervision. Department stores have fixed prices too.

Bargain phrases—

How much?	*Tao-rai*
Too expensive!	*Paeng mark*
Can you lower the price?	*Lod raka noy dai mai*
Thank you.	*Korb koon*

Hours

Normal opening times are from 8:30 A.M. or 9:00 A.M. to 6:00 P.M. from Monday to Saturday. Most souvenir shops and shops in hotel arcades, however, will stay open later in the evening, until 7:00 or 8:00 P.M., and on Sundays too.

Delivery Service

It is quite usual for shops to deliver purchases to your hotel as a part of their service, at no extra cost, if asked. The larger and well established shops (and of course the government shop Narayana Phand) will take orders for shipment abroad. Many travel agents also offer shipping services.

Souvenir Suggestions

ANTIQUES AND ART OBJECTS—The area between the New Road and Yawaraj Road, in Chinatown near the Grand Cinema, is *Nakhon Kasem* (Thieves Market), famous for antique shops. Chinese porcelain and Thai bronzes are plentiful, but one should be an expert to know which are genuine antiques and which are fakes. Some of the fakes are so cleverly produced that they are worth buying, especially the carved wood pieces, sometimes studded with coloured glass, and gold objects dulled to look antique. One may take an item to the offices of the Fine Arts Department at the National Museum to have its age verified. Certain objects may not be taken out of the country without a permit.

Bencharong, a multi-coloured porcelain carrying Siamese designs but produced in China from the 17th to 19th centuries, and *Sank'alok,* a brown-and-white pottery made around 500 years ago, are real collectors' pieces that can sometimes be obtained here.

BRONZEWARE—Sets of cutlery, trays, bowls, and other household objects, engraved or plain, are very reasonable. The ancient art of tempering bronze is practised in Thailand. Some of the cutlery has attractive handles made from wood, buffalo horn, and ivory. To prevent tarnishing, bronzeware can be siliconized.

CERAMICS—Thai pottery is unique and attractive. It is often decorated with designs taken from the stone carvings around the temples. Vases, lanterns, wall-plaques, ashtrays, jewellery, and even buttons are easily obtainable.

Something different is Thai Celadon, a reproduction of a valuable pottery created in northern China more than 2,000 years ago. It has an antique-looking, finely-crackled glaze made from following the original Chinese methods of glazing with natural wood ash. Available from Celadon House, 278 Silom Road, Bangkok, the stoneware may also be seen at the company's kilns near Chiengmai.

Cotton—Thai cotton is often overlooked in the rash enthusiasm to buy Thai silk. The colours and designs are unique. It is almost always hand woven and incredibly cheap. Tablecloths with matching napkins, dress lengths with matching beach bags and hats, sports shirts (very cool) and ties, children's clothes, and soft toys are but a few of the cotton products. German and Swiss colourfast dyes are used.

Crocodile-skin products—See under "Skins & Hides."

Dolls—Thai dolls could hardly be described as graceful, but there is something oddly fascinating about their angular postures. Doll-making is a new industry to Thailand that began in the 1950's to provide for the tourist market. The wide and interesting variety needs some explanation.

The most popular dolls are of Thai dancers of which there are basically two kinds—*lakon nai* (inside) and *lakon nok* (outside). The former depict dances that were performed entirely by girls inside the royal court for the King and his guests. *Lakon nai* dolls have the most elaborate, glittering, skin-tight costumes and head-dresses, heavily decorated with "jewels" and spun gold. The latter, *lakon nok,* represent the dancers who performed outside the royal court. There is also a third kind called *lakon chatree* which is quite similar to the *lakon nok* but it is not so easily obtainable.

Other dolls are of the actors or performers of the traditional dance dramas. Bizarre examples are the masked demon *Hanuman,* which has a grotesque white mask, and *Tosakan,* king of the demons, which has a hideous green mask.

These dolls cost around 200 *baht* ($10) each, for there is much intricate hand-work in the elaborate costumes. They are obtainable from Bangkok Dolls, 85 Rajatapan Lane, Rachaprarop Road, Makkasan, Bangkok. This is not an easy place to find so this company will send a car for you if you telephone 72318.

More folksy, less refined, but still attractive dolls are made in Chiengmai. Chiengmai dolls include a curious range depicting the various hill-tribes that live in northern Thailand around the Thai-Burma and Thai-Laos borders, and are of some anthropological interest. The costumes are authentic. All kinds of dolls from throughout Thailand are available at the government-supervised shop mentioned earlier in this chapter.

JEWELLERY—Surely no woman can resist the temptation to buy one or two exotic pieces from the wonderful variety of jewellery found in Bangkok. Certain stones are unbelievably cheap, and they can be set in anything of your own design in just a day or two.

Before buying an expensive item, bargain hard and, if possible, solicit a second opinion from someone who knows something about the stones. A Thai friend can be a great help in getting the prices down. You will find that the stones are very often sold by weight and therefore are cut to retain as much weight as possible, sometimes resulting in a thick, badly proportioned stone. This is worth

Princess ring.

remembering when choosing a star sapphire. For this reason, one with a vivid star may cost less than a heavier, thicker sapphire with a less bright star. But one need not have a very big budget, say 200 *baht* ($10), to enjoy choosing from a wide selection in most of the jewellery shops. The following items are particularly reasonable:

The princess ring—This royal ring has a curious origin, and its nine gems are each said to have mystical influences upon the wearer. Its shape represents a tiered crown. Evolving during the reigns of the first Rama kings, just after Bangkok became Thailand's new capital, it was worn only by the King and a few of his courtiers. The original version, known as the *nopakao* ring, was so heavy, with clusters of diamonds around the nine gems, that it was usually worn on a sash around the waist. It would be transferred to the first finger only for state occasions. Less than a dozen people were officially entitled to wear the *nopakao* ring. Then, in the late 19th century, wealthy people created a similar but smaller nine-gemmed ring without the diamond clusters, and it became more and more popular. This is the princess ring. Its nine gems are:

diamond—symbol of courage

ruby—to bring wisdom, happiness, good health, and good luck, especially in gambling and courting

emerald—to improve intelligence, ensure longevity, and safeguard women during childbirth topaz—to bring wealth and fertility

garnet—also brings good health and happiness, in addition to power, grace, victory, and friendship after quarrels

sapphire—symbolizes truth and affection, and safeguards chastity

moonstone—the Asian love charm believed (in some Asian countries) to have divine properties.

zircon—helps sleep, leads to wealth and wisdom, and wards off evil

cat's eye—believed to house a divine spirit to guide one's footsteps away from depression and financial difficulties

Many of these attributes will actually prove themselves (with a little faith).

Sapphires and star sapphires—Mined in southern Thailand, they vary enormously in colour, quality, and price. It is surprising how many people are unaware that sapphires come in a variety of colours besides blue. The most expensive are white (beware of imitations), then come the clear blue *pailin* sapphires. If you are offered sapphires that have faint lines visible in them, they should be very, very cheap though still beautiful. The star sapphires are probably the best buy in Thailand. The price will vary according to the brilliance of the star and symmetry of the stone. The blue star sapphires are especially beautiful, but a good one will cost 2,000 *baht* ($100) or more.

Rubies—belong to the same species as the sapphire, a mineral called corundum. They vary in colour from a deep crimson or purple to a pinkish rose. Rubies mined in Thailand have a tinge of brown, and the smaller ones, such as those used in the princess ring, are really cheap. Other rubies sold in Bangkok come from Burma and Sri Lanka. Also on sale are blue "rubies" (could they be sapphires?) which are imported raw from Australia to be ground and polished in Thailand.

The tiny red rubies cost as little as 30 *baht* ($1.50) for one carat (about twenty stones), while a red ruby the size of a pea would be almost priceless. The blue Australian "rubies" cost about 200 *baht* ($10) for one carat, around seven times more than the little red rubies.

Topaz—is not indigenous to Thailand and is very expensive. Citrine, a beautiful, yellow-brown stone from Sri Lanka, is sometimes offered as topaz, and it should be cheap.

Other good buys readily found in Bangkok include agate, amethyst, cat's eye, coral jasper, nephrite (Taiwan jade), tiger's eye, turquoise and, especially, zircons, mined in Thailand.

LACQUERWARE—Bowls, small tables, trays, boxes, plates, etc. are very reasonable and have attractive, ancient designs, usually in red or gold on black. Smaller items from about 30 *baht* ($1.50).

MUSICAL INSTRUMENTS—An interesting selection of the traditional Thai instruments is described in the chapter "Entertainment and Sports." They can be bought from Thai Home Industries, 35 Oriental Avenue, Bangkok.

NIELLOWARE—Exquisite inlay work in various colours as well as black goes to create intricate Thai designs on brooches, bracelets, rings, cufflinks, ashtrays, and so on. Considering the amount of silver used and the beautiful workmanship, nielloware is absurdly low priced. Smaller items from 30 *baht* ($1.50).

SHOES—Can be made to measure in two or three days at 250 *baht* ($12.50) upwards. Up-to-date European styles are always on display in Bangkok shops. Silk-covered evening shoes and shoes made from a variety of skins are also available everywhere.

SILK—Now Thai silk is so famous throughout the world that it is taken for granted that every visitor to Thailand will buy a few yards at least. It is sold in every conceivable colour and in lovely, bright patterns on practically every street in Bangkok. Usually forty inches (101.6 centimetres) wide, it is sold by the yard in various weights. A lightweight plain silk costs from 65 *baht* ($3.25) a yard, and heavy weight would be around 100 *baht* ($5) a yard. Printed silk will cost a little more. Modern, colourfast German and Swiss dyes are used. Ready-made items in silk include all kinds of ladies' clothes, scarves, evening bags, purses, shirts, ties, cummerbunds, curtains, and cushion covers. Brocade silk, which is sold thirty-four inches (86.4 centimetres) wide, is also available and is made into decorative evening dresses, stoles, and bags.

One of the reliable shops is The Thai Silk Co. Ltd., (James H. W. Thompson), 9 Suriwongse Road, founded by Jim Thompson, the man who re-started the Thai silk handweaving industry and introduced Thai silk to the Western world just after the Second World War.

SILVERWARE—Intricately worked silver with designs in relief on necklaces, earrings, bracelets, cigarette boxes and cases, spoons, ashtrays, and ornaments is extremely good value. Most of the silverware is made from melted down coins such as the Queen Victoria Indian rupee that contains about eighty-five per cent silver. The decorations usually show mythological creatures or classical dancing.

SKINS AND HIDES—Handbags, shoes, boots, wallets, belts, and similar articles can be bought or made to order from the skins of crocodiles, lizards, or snakes (pythons), or from elephant and buffalo hide. Examples of prices are:

Crocodile-skin handbag—$40–150 (the skin from the stomach of a baby crocodile is most expensive)

Lizard-skin handbags—$15–25

Elephant-skin belt—$3–4

Snake-skin goods are even cheaper.

TAILORING—To be sure of a well-finished suit or dress, you should have at least one fitting and keep an eye on the workmanship at the seams. Made-to-measure is often the same price as ready-made. Men's made-to-measure shirts and pyjamas are particularly worth buying.

WOODCARVINGS—Nowadays the more valuable teak wood is often replaced by the wood of the *mai-daeng* tree which is not quite so hard but has a very beautiful colour and grain not unlike rosewood.

Scandinavian-style salad bowls, forks, and spoons, low tables, and carved trays are lovely. All sorts of other ornamental items and tableware are now produced. They are mostly deeply carved with floral designs. Hand-carved elephants are very popular. One can even buy an elephant *howdah* (seat that goes on top of an elephant), adapted to a handsome lounge chair, but the shipping charge is about as much as the chair itself.

OTHER PRODUCTS—These are hand woven from such materials as banana leaves, palm leaves, rushes, sea grass, rattan, jute, and sisal fibres in unique designs made by combining materials. Products include baskets, handbags, sun-hats, slippers, floor-mats, and similar articles.

Made from paper are mobiles, kites, parasols, and so on. Classical stage masks are made from papier-maché. Also hand crafted are: brass temple bells; traditional shadow-play cut-outs; temple rubbings, mostly from Wat Po, Phimai, and Angkor; oil and watercolour paintings, especially of typical Thai scenes. The widest range of products can be seen at Narayana Phand, the shop mentioned above.

SHOPPING CENTRES AND MARKETS—Local markets and shopping areas of particular interest are mentioned in the topographical information in the Bangkok and Chiengmai chapters, pages 108 and 308.

Part II

VILLAGE AND MONASTIC LIFE

12

VILLAGE LIFE

Nature has freed the rural Thais from the worries of clothing, housing, food, and fuel. All the materials for necessities are provided. Buildings and farm tools are locally made from bamboo, wood, rattan, and earthenware. Cloth can be woven at home from flax. In fact, everything can be made at home apart from one or two steel blades that are bought in the nearest market. For transport, ox-carts lazily provide the means. Food grows with the minimum of effort. Money is of little use. No wonder the Thais are such a carefree, easygoing lot! More than eighty per cent of them are engaged in agriculture, living in villages. Over seventy per cent cultivate rice. In every village, the temple (there is always at least one) plays an instrumental part in day-to-day family life.

The author and his wife were invited to sample this "utopian" life. They accepted, and here follows an account of their stay in a village not far from Chiengmai.

* * *

The winding road, lined with stately *prang* rubber trees, led us from Chiengmai through a rich green countryside, luxuriant with palms and grasses. Houses on stilts with roofs of teak leaves were barely visible through the bush where children played. Soon we turned down a side road, then along a bumpy track through a glade. Precariously, we crossed a fragile wooden bridge and drove past a little monastery, to the banks of the Mae-namping River. The car could go no further.

We walked, following our guide along the riverside path bordered by tall clusters of thick bamboo. Small boats lazily drifted along the waters, pink in the evening sun. The fishermen deftly cast their nets from the bows. Suddenly, an olive-skinned child ran naked from a small house set among lovely, flowering shrubs and roses, darted in front of us, and leapt, landing with a splash in the river. Other children followed and playfully bathed and swam. Further along the path we met our hosts and exchanged the Thai greeting, "*Sawadee*," with *wai*. Going through their bamboo gate we were welcomed by the two daughters waiting at the steps of the house. Politely, they gestured to us to remove our shoes and led the way up the wooden steps into their house, eight feet or so above the ground.

Inside, our first impression was of a lovely teakwood floor, absolutely smooth and shining from its natural oil. While our hosts were bringing water for us from the garden well, we apprehensively looked around the house, wondering where we would sleep. There were very few pieces of furniture—a small table and chairs, a couch, low bed, and a large antiquated radio. One corner contained an altar decorated with flowers and brassy ornaments. Several square cushions, presumably for use in the Buddhist ceremonies held there, were stored next to it in a glass-fronted cabinet. It appeared to be the only glass in the house, for there were no window panes—just slits in the walls with wooden shutters. To complete the decor, every wall had a display of photographs showing the family, several of the sons as monks, and, in colour, a picture of the King and Queen.

Cool water, fresh from the well, was poured for us from

a quaint water jar. It was soft, sweet, and welcome after the afternoon's hot drive. Then, to satisfy our curiosity, we were shown around the rest of the house.

Next to heaps of garlic, piled high to dry, a door led to the kitchen, which was on a verandah that had a slatted bamboo floor. The equipment consisted of a couple of cooking pots, two earthenware water-storage jars, and a brick stove at one end that had to be fed charcoal for cooking. Few utensils were used. Our guide explained that the kitchen, on a bamboo verandah, "needs no drainage since any waste water runs away through the floor, onto the earth below, and disappears naturally. Likewise, any waste food is thrown over the side to feed the chickens."

We looked over the garden at the "free-range" chickens. "That is a 'rice-stack,' " explained our guide, indicating a storage place on stilts with a pointed straw roof. "It is to keep rice-stalks fresh and yellow for 'buffalo gum.' "

"Buffalo gum?" we asked.

"Yes, cows and buffalo love to chew it. It is also used for planting with garlic and onion seeds to keep them moist in the soil."

Near the rice-stack was a pigsty also raised on stilts. To the other side, the guide pointed to a small building with no roof. It was the bathroom and toilet.

Upon asking where we would sleep, we were led through another door to a box-room with a very thin mattress laid on an even thinner straw mat on the floor. The room was devoid of furnishings apart from one chair and a mosquito net hanging ominously from the rafters. The whole family slept around the living room, so normally this would have been the parents' room.

The evening meal—As dusk turned to darkness the resounding, shrill chirping of cicadas became more intense. Kerosene lamps were lit, attracting an occasional moth that inevitably singed its wings. The lamps, set on the floor, cast long shadows and gave a piercing light that strained our eyes. Only those who sat close were properly visible against a background of total darkness. The elders settled down, ready for dinner and an evening of leisure, eyeing us with expectant curiosity. The lamps dramatically accentuated their wrinkled features.

Dinner was served on a thin mat on the floor at one side of the living room. It was quite hard to sit as the Thais do but, having been told earlier that it would be impolite to sit cross-legged and offensive to sit with the feet pointing towards anyone or even with the soles visible, my wife and I made a special effort to sit Thai style. We were half-sitting and half-lying on one thigh with both feet tucked behind, leaning on one elbow to maintain the position. The other hand was left free to eat with.

The women, as previously noted, have a duty to serve the men. In fact, only after the men have finished their meal are the women allowed to eat. We even discovered that guests are supposed to take their meal first, but we could not bear to have the entire family watching us eat, mouthful by mouthful. We insisted they eat with us, which broke the barriers of silence and led to spontaneous conversation. The women trotted back and forth from the kitchen with various dishes, taking care to lower their heads each time they came near us. This intrigued us. Whenever they passed behind anyone they stooped very low indeed until they were almost crawling. Our guide's explanation was simply "It's the custom, you see." (Later we discovered that the woman's head should never be higher than the man's, as a sign of respect and courtesy. Among men, it is a courtesy indicating trust and friendship that evolved from putting oneself in a defenseless position when another man is seated.)

The meal was rich and tasty although simple. There was a dish of curried pork with several small bowls of sauces—chilli, shrimp, and vinegar. Other dishes contained chopped, cooked vegetables, and dried, crisp, salted fish which had an unappetising, dirty grey colour. Each person was served with a generous portion of sticky, glutinous rice. No cutlery was used. We had to pick up a little of the rice with our fingers and press it into an oval lump in the palm, using one hand only. By making an indentation with the thumb into the rice it could then be used to dip and scoop up the meat and sauces. When the ladies did it, it all seemed quite refined. We drank water to bring relief from the chillies in the curry and thoroughly enjoyed the food. Freshly picked bananas, oranges, and grapes followed the main course. By this time it was too late to be told about glutinous rice but our guide was enthusiastic:

"It is steamed in the small bowls so it absorbs only a little water. After a small amount is eaten it swells in the stomach, so the farmers can work for a long time without feeling hungry. It gives us more energy than ordinary rice."

There was no doubt that our stomachs were swelling!

After dinner the men moved across the room, passed round a large tin of rich, home-grown tobacco, and rolled cheroots about four inches long and one-half inch thick. They used young banana leaves to roll them, trimming the ends beautifully by pinching them with the fingers. Some of the men chewed *mieng* gum. This is made by soaking the leaves from a *mieng* tree (rather similar to bay leaves) in garlic juice for "many days." The *mieng* gum leaves are carried, like cigarettes, in the pocket wrapped in a banana leaf and then chewed at whim with a pinch of gritty salt. We tried them but our heavy stomachs groaned. They are an acquired taste.

As we watched the men smoking and chewing we pictured their buffalo chewing the "buffalo gum" and wondered who had introduced the habit to whom?

"They have nothing to do," our guide said. "This is how they relax and enjoy their leisure."

Jungle bath—With our stomachs full of heavy, swelling rice, we asked if we could take a bath and retire. Something was wrong. They had forgotten to tell us to take a bath before dinner. My wife and I insisted, "We must wash at least before going to bed." It had been an uncomfortably hot afternoon. They looked astonished, and we soon realized why. The bathroom, of course, was across the garden in pitch darkness.

Blandly, my wife and I took a kerosene lamp and wandered off down the garden path. Strange noises competed with the shrill warbling of the cicadas. The trees and shrubs were alive with all kinds of creatures from the jungle. In the bathroom we found a large earthenware jar of rainwater and a silvery metal bowl for scooping out the water. The floor was brick with a drain in one corner and for the roof there was only the sky. We struggled against pernicious mosquitoes while wiping the perspiration from our bodies with cold, damp flannels. A toad croaked. Something in the branches above us jumped like a squirrel. Soon we began imagining all sorts of creatures were there in the darkness. A moth flapped its fragile wings against the hot glass of our lamp and, finally, something else winged found a cosy place in my wife's blouse. We fled back to the safety of the stilted house. Within a few minutes we retired, closed the mosquito net, turned out the lamp, and lay down to sleep. The cicadas sang their one-note tune and, despite large mice that pattered and scampered across the rafters above us, we fell to sleep, stomachs still groaning.

The morning after—A sudden tropical rainstorm woke us. Vertical sheets of rain crashed to the ground, cooling the air rapidly. It was 5:10 A.M. when the rainstorm stopped, as quickly as if someone in the sky had turned off a tap. A cock crowed. It was dawn. Tropical birds burst into song. No wonder villagers rise early—this is the best time of the day. We sat by the window, child-like, watching the village come to life, until we were invited to take breakfast. It consisted of pork and marrow soup, a dish of green vegetables, fresh cucumbers, various sauces—and glutinous rice. We had just a cup of tea, explaining that we felt we still had enough energy for the day from last night's glutinous rice.

Looking around the village—After our morning tea we took a stroll with our guide along the riverside path. The houses were in a line facing the river, the older ones made of teakwood and some with walls of interlaced, split bamboo. The wood of the *prang* rubber tree is used more nowadays for building. It is a lighter, softer wood and much cheaper too.

Each family had an enclosure, with fruit trees and a spacious detached house on stilts, surrounded by a bamboo fence. All had a small boat moored nearby or upturned beneath the house for fishing or for transport in the rainy season. Also under each house was a family loom where women weave flax and cotton for their own clothes, a rice grinding stone, small charcoal stove for making rice and coconut cakes, maize seeds for planting next season, and various farming implements. Some houses kept sinewy fighting cocks in bamboo cages. Everywhere, there were chickens roaming almost wild. We asked our guide if they were commonly owned and he replied:

"There are 127 families in this village and so it is like one big family. Nearly every night people gather to make a large fire, and the evening meal is cooked together by the women. Anyone can join in if he feels like it.

"No one need go hungry even if he does no work," I said to egg him on.

"This village produces all its own food—glutinous rice, garlic, onions, tobacco, maize, and vegetables," the guide said. "Of course we have fish in the river and we keep chickens so there are always eggs. Also, there is fruit."

We glanced at the fruit trees, the branches so heavily laden with fruit that thick bamboo stakes had been placed underneath to support them.

". . . we never had a shortage of food."

* * *

Farming

At this point it ought to be mentioned that farming in northern Thailand differs from that in other regions.

Rice is grown everywhere. It is the country's most important crop and has earned Thailand the title "rice-bowl of the East." Less than five per cent of the total is non-rice crops but this pattern is changing.

IN THE NORTH—In addition to the crops listed above (that is, rice, garlic, onions, tobacco, and maize), jute, tea, coffee, sugar beets, and other vegetables are grown, and forestry is a major industry. However, in recent years, the teak forests have become seriously depleted. The Ministry of Agriculture is now revising an old law that provides a fine of 50 *baht* ($2.50) for stealing a teak log. The forests carry the scars of this old law, since teak logs are worth around 10,000 *baht* ($500) each.

IN THE NORTHEAST—Conditions are harsh. Sudden rains bring floods and the soil does not retain moisture. The crop—almost entirely glutinous rice—is uncertain. Many farmers still work a shifting cultivation system, moving to new ground each year. Less than seven per cent of the Khorat Plateau is cultivated.

Fish from the rivers and livestock are important supplements. Even this does not really provide enough food for the whole year, so a farmer will often take seasonal work, perhaps harvesting in another region or as a samlor driver in Bangkok for a few months. But in the Northeast the pattern is changing, following mammoth irrigation projects.

IN THE SOUTH—rubber plantations and tin mining have brought prosperity to a mixed farming area.

THE CENTRAL PLAIN—Almost all the ordinary, non-glutinous type of rice for export comes from here. The glutinous rice grown in other regions matures in only four months so a successful crop is more certain.

IN ALL REGIONS—There is usually only one crop a year, allowing the village people plenty of leisure time while the land lies fallow. Other crops cultivated here and there in relatively small quantities include corn, kenaf, cassava, peanuts, and soybeans. Villages form self-sustaining units and help each other in times of disaster.

* * *

During our walk a man crossed our path holding a three-pronged bamboo spear with a wriggling snake dangling at the end. He smiled gently at us and then proceeded to beat the snake to death.

"We have many snakes here and some are dangerous" our guide commented. "Whenever a villager spots a snake it is his duty to kill it."

The thought of our "bath" last night in the dark, when snakes are most active, sent a cold shiver down our spines. The dead snake was hurled into the river. We strolled on. Our walk took us to a rice-mill where a crude apparatus powered by a small two-stroke engine removed the husks from the rice. The dusty-looking husk powder is kept to feed the cattle, pigs, and chickens.

* * *

Rice Milling

The system of collecting rice from the farms, milling, and marketing is largely controlled by Chinese who have made it a profitable business. The Chinese were the first to commercialize Thai rice.

* * *

And so we spent the day wandering around the village enjoying the peace. Some children played, others were fishing, still others were helping their families. Cows, chewing the cud (or was it "buffalo gum"?), seemed to set the rhythm for the pace of work.

After sampling the local fruits, which were amply sufficient for lunch, we ambled back to the house and drenched ourselves with cooling water in the roofless bathroom under the late afternoon sun. The women of the house bathed in the river.

Water pot.

At 6:00 P.M. the schoolteacher arrived, a jolly, plump fellow who greeted us nervously with "Good morning to you."

We replied, "Good morning to you," and he relaxed proudly and said, "Have a good year."

"Thank you."

We all sat down to dinner. Tonight it consisted of a cauliflower and liver dish, curried chicken, chopped cooked vegetables, and various sauces made mainly from chillies and crushed shrimps with, inevitably, the glutinous rice.

The curried chicken was creamy and piquant, made with coconut milk, shredded coconut, garlic, and peppers strongly flavoured with lime.

The oldest man at the table asked, "How do farmers plough the fields in your country?"

"With tractors," I replied.

"And before tractors?"

"With horses."

"Horses!" Everyone laughed. "Are there no elephants in your country?"

Such conversation continued throughout our meal. Their unabashed curiosity and naive, innocent questions were refreshing. We all had a good laugh at one another.

After dinner some of the men began rolling their cheroots and some chose to chew *mieng* gum. Someone brought out bottles of local spirit. One was called *lau* and cost 20 *baht* ($1). It was yellowish and tasted like crude, fruity whisky. The others were very coarse rice wines. The women also joined us, chewing betel nut which had worn away most of their teeth, leaving a few black molars in cochineal-coloured gums. The light of the kerosene lamps set on the floor made the elder women, with their matted shocks of white hair, look like witches.

We chatted, comparing their village life to life in the

West, and we asked them to explain how Thai villages are administered. "Every village has a *pu yai* (headman)," the schoolteacher began. "The man must be a wise and tranquil person. There is always one in a village who has respect. He becomes *pu yai* and is appointed rather than elected by the villagers. I cannot be headman because I enjoy drinking," he tittered. "Villagers may go to the *pu yai* at any time if they have a problem or to ask him to settle a dispute. Any trouble or crime is reported to him, and he is supposed to report anything serious to the district officer. Actually, it is very rare for police or government officials to intervene in village affairs."

* * *

Local Government System

The central government offices in Bangkok send their instructions to the provincial officer who, in turn, administers his province through the district officers. A district officer is responsible for the local affairs in quite a small area, including several villages. District officers have to depend on the *pu yai*, or headman, of each village for communicating to villagers. The headman of this village received a salary of 80 *baht* ($4) a month and employed one assistant. Money still seems to have little use in daily life.

Education in Villages

"It is still difficult for a child to continue his studies after four years unless his family is very rich," said one of our village friends.

At present, extensive educational opportunities in Thailand are lacking. Villages have neither the facilities nor the incentives to provide a good basic education, and only four years' schooling are compulsory.

In the past, children went to the local monastery to be

taught by the monks. There, they learned to read and write and studied Pali, the language used by Buddhists in prayers and ceremonies. Often the children would live in the monastery and perform menial tasks.

Nowadays, most village schools are still attached to monasteries but are staffed by government-trained teachers. Boys and girls attend together. In order to enter a high school, the child must first reside in a district where one exists. In larger villages, or where there are big monasteries, boys who are too poor to go elsewhere may become novices or may have to serve the monks in return for receiving a higher education. A few monasteries can eventually, through a Buddhist university, bring students to the higher levels of education equal to the other universities of Thailand.

* * *

"*They always return . . .*"—Before we retired that evening we asked if the younger people were finding villages dull compared with life in Bangkok.

"Teenagers from this village naturally go to the city of Chiengmai or even to Bangkok," we were told. "They are full of eager ambition and look for a better life, but there are some bad people in the cities and they get trouble. They always return and settle down near their home."

After going to bed we lay awake wondering how long this oasis of peace and plenty would be allowed to remain untroubled.

* * *

The Future

The increase in population, which is now around three per cent a year, is bound to bring further pressure on the land. In the northeast regions, the United Nations, U.S. government, and Thai government are developing new irrigation projects and artesian wells with tremendous results. More fertilizers will be used, electricity will soon be introduced, and, with constantly improving transport and communications, village life will become more modern. To keep pace, villagers will have to produce more and grow more diversified crops. Trade must increase. Money will become more useful. Health clinics and better schools may follow.

With the exception of health clinics, the author doubts whether any other "improvement" will be beneficial. The only real worry village people have now is illness. People used to go to the monks in the local temple for treatment but now they must pay for a doctor. With an average of only one doctor for every 7,000 persons, the expense is high. The sick often have to wait too long for a medical examination and, if treatment in a hospital is needed, there are both money problems and another long wait.

13

BUDDHISM AND MONASTIC LIFE

Buddhism is the backbone of Thailand as much as Judaism is the backbone of Israel. To understand the art, culture, and people of Thailand, one must first know the history and basic precepts of Buddhism.

The Origin of Buddhism

Many legends and embellishments have clouded the true story of the birth and life of Buddha. Here is an outline of the ascertainable facts:

Buddha's real name was Siddhartha Gautama. Born somewhere between 563 and 556 B.C., he was the son of a ruler of the Sakya people in northeast India. To commemorate his birth, a pillar was placed on the actual spot in 250 B.C. at Lumbini, near Bhairwa, in Nepal. It can still be seen. Following the birth, a seer warned the ruler that his son would see four signs that would change his life: (1) an old man; (2) a sick man; (3) a corpse; (4) a monk. Siddhartha, the seer said, was destined to become either a powerful emperor or an ascetic.

The ruler, who may have hoped his son would become his successor, confined the boy to the palace grounds at Kapilavastu where he lived in luxury, knowing nothing of the suffering and misery in the world. Siddhartha grew up happily, married, had a son, and seemed content. But when Siddhartha was 29 years old he went outside the palace grounds and saw the four signs. The signs showed him the suffering in the world, although the monk may have indicated to him that peace of mind could only be found by living a holy life. He was so affected that he went from one Hindu teacher to another trying to find an explanation to the problems of suffering. Finally, he joined five Brahmins who were fasting in a village. Siddhartha fasted so hard that his body wasted away and he nearly died. The five Brahmins left him in disgust.

After regaining his strength he travelled on to a holy town called Gaya in the State of Bihar, on a tributary of the Ganges. Finally, in the forest at Uruvilva (or Uruvela), near Gaya, he sat down under a *bo* tree and resolved to sit there until "enlightenment" came to him. After a day and a night resisting evil temptation, he became "Buddha"—the "enlightened one." He saw the mystery of existence and the "four truths" that lead to the destruction of suffering and to rebirth and finally to *nirvana* (divine peace beyond this world). Making his way to the Hindu centre of Benares, he met the five Brahmins who had previously deserted him. They were so struck by Buddha's teaching that they became his first disciples. And so Buddhism started to spread.

At about the age of eighty he is said to have eaten poisoned food, whereupon he lay down on his side and passed into *nirvana* (about 483 B.C.). As a result, some statues show him reclining peacefully on his side.

How Buddhism Came to Thailand

Buddhism flourished in India for about a thousand years after Buddha's death, especially during the 3rd century B.C., when King Asoka became a Buddhist and encouraged the teaching of the religion. No doubt the untouchables or Hindu outcasts must have found Buddhism attractive. However, during King Asoka's reign Buddhism divided into two schools of thought, and the disunity that followed may be one reason why Buddhism practically died out in India. Today only .06 per cent of Indians are Buddhist.

Since the split in the 3rd century B.C. the two "schools" have been the "Northern" school, known as "Mahayana," meaning "the greater vehicle," which spread north from India to China and Japan; and the "Southern" school, known as "Theravada," meaning "the way of the elders," or "Hinayana," meaning "the smaller vehicle," which spread south to Ceylon, then to Burma and Thailand. The principal difference between the two is that Mahayana Buddhists regard Buddha as divine and worship him with images, offerings, and prayers. They also believe in heavens and hells through which the dead may pass on their way to *nirvana*. Theravada Buddhists consider Buddha a teacher and try to follow his teachings exactly, preserving the original form of Buddhism. Like Buddha, they are agnostic. Ceylon (Sri Lanka), Burma, and Thailand, therefore, follow the purest form of Buddhism. In Thailand, only a minority are Mahayana Buddhists, and they belong to the Chinese and Vietnamese communities living there.

The Monks

AN IMPRESSIVE EARLY-MORNING SPECTACLE—No matter where one stays in Thailand it is worthwhile to rise at dawn one morning and take a stroll near the hotel. One will surely see bare-footed monks silently pacing the streets to receive offerings. It is an awe-inspiring sight—shaven heads, saffron robes, the metal lids of bowls glinting in the morning sun. They clutch them, almost hidden beneath their robes, looking as if they were pregnant, bringing them out only to receive food from housewives and anyone else who wants to give.

THE ART OF GAINING "MERIT"—Giving food to monks in this way is often misunderstood by foreign visitors. The monks are not begging. They are receiving alms from people who believe they are gaining "merit" for themselves by giving. "Merit" purifies the mind and is said to wash away greed and hatred. By giving, the believer is making a kind of spiritual investment for a better life after re-birth.

Highest "merit" is gained by becoming a monk for life. Some "merit" is won by serving as a monk for a short period from time to time, which is far more convenient. In Thailand, a layman may become a monk and a monk may return to laity at will, unlike a Christian monk who must commit his whole life to a religious order. Other ways of gaining "merit" are by helping to build or repair a temple, showing devotion on holy days, doing good, avoiding evils such as violence, and by showing respect to others when they are gaining "merit."

It is estimated that there are 250,000 *bikkhu* (monks) and more than 20,000 *wat* in Thailand today.

What's Wat?

The reader will find it well worthwhile to study this section carefully before visiting any *wat* in Thailand.

Wat is often translated as "temple" which is not strictly correct since that would define a place of worship dedicated to a god (Buddha is not a god). Another translation is "monastery" which would be correct except that not all *wat** are monasteries. In fact, a *wat* is a group of buildings, usually enclosed by a wall with gateways, that embraces repositories, various halls, galleries, and struc-

* The same form is used for singular and plural.

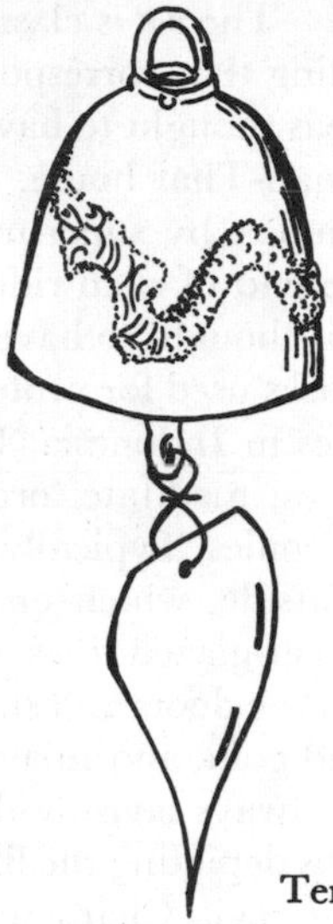

Temple bell.

tures all devoted to the veneration—*not worship*—of the Lord Buddha and to the study and teaching of Buddhism.

What's What in a Wat?

Bot (pronounced "boht" or "boat")—This is the most important and sacred building, immediately distinguishable by eight surrounding boundary stones called *bai sema* (pronounced "by si-ma" or "by say-ma"). These stones mark the sacred area into which, incidentally, no women are allowed. They may be shaped simply or elaborately ornamented with serpents and similar carvings. Sometimes each boundary stone has a canopy for protection from the elements. The stones' purpose is to ward off evil spirits. There is actually a ninth stone buried beneath the *bot*.

WAT ARCHITECTURE—The *bot* is classically a rectangular, one-roomed building that corresponds to the Indian *chaitya* hall. The shape is thought to have originated from the thatched Indonesian-Thai house, and the roof has been made more complex by superimposing one layer above another. At the end of each ridge there is a *chofa* or graceful curl. This is thought to have some connection with the horns and masks used for protection against evil in animistic ceremonies in Indonesia. It is here that the monks meet for services, meditate, ordain novices, and perform all other ceremonies. Typically, it will have thick walls, whitewashed outside, which emphasize the dark orange, green, or violet-glazed tiles of the roof. The beautiful art-work* on the doors and shutters is generally lacquered in black and gold, and inlaid with mother-of-pearl. The interior is always lavishly decorated, usually with storytelling murals depicting the life of Buddha and allegories of victory over evil. Characteristic of the Thai-style architecture are the tapering, octagonal columns, each with a lotus form at its head. These columns are painted red, emblazoned with designs in gold. The older Thai *bot* (and other structures too) had no ceilings. If there is a ceiling, it will also be red with gold designs or gilded studs for decoration. At the west end of the *bot,* opposite the entrance, is an image of Buddha.

* A closer look at the figures painted on the doors and shutters and in the murals will often reveal representations of Brahminic gods. The reason is not a belief in Brahminism. Rather, according to Buddhist myths, the Hindu gods are subordinates and followers of the Lord Buddha. Long ago, the religion of the peoples of Indo-China and Indonesia was either Brahminism or Mahayana Buddhism. The Thais periodically and alternatively followed these religions as well as Hinayana or Theravada Buddhism. Eventually they settled down with Hinayana Buddhism but, of course, the various beliefs have become intermingled. Many Brahminic ceremonies still remain, and the Thais feel no strangeness that Hindu gods appear in their art.

THE BUDDHA IMAGE—The Thai-made images are almost all modelled in stucco or bronze, gilded, cross-legged, with a thick rounded body formed with smooth flowing lines and "synthetized" muscles. The round head has bulging eyes, long earlobes, prominent lips, and hair in regular curls like sea shells, topped by a flame to signify that the Buddha has entered a state of *nirvana*. Raised onto a pedestal that is in the lotus form, the image is designed to be viewed frontally from a lower position. Often the lighting will be dim, highlighting only facial features and giving the figure an air of mysticism. Around the base, which is usually over-richly ornamented, incense and all kinds of offerings are placed in a rather haphazard, muddled manner. This, it is said, accentuates the serenity and peaceful expression of the image, calm and dignified on a plane above the restless disordered world. The image is not an idol; it is not worshipped; it merely symbolizes the great teacher, Buddha, and reminds followers of his doctrine.

It is most important to observe the posture and position of the hands, which convey deep religious meanings. There are four postures:

1. Sitting—usually cross-legged, represents the time when Buddha meditated;
2. Reclining—representing Buddha passing into *nirvana*;
3. Standing—representing Buddha taming the wild elephant sent to extirpate him;
4. Walking—representing Buddha returning to earth after preaching to his Mother and deities in heaven;

and five hand positions:

1. Earth-touching position—this is the most commonly seen pose, called in Thai *bhumisparsa mudra*.

Buddha is touching the earth with his right hand, asking for her to witness the truth of his "enlightenment";

2. Meditation—one hand placed on top of the other, palms upwards, resting in the lap;
3. Turning the Wheel of Law—hands to the breast. Symbolizes Buddha's first sermon in Benares;
4. Peace and Non-Violence—Raised hand with palm facing outwards;
5. Granting Favours—hand turned downwards with palm facing inwards.

Ask any of the Thais to explain more about their faith. They are always willing.

Of particular interest are the Buddha statues of the Sukhothai period (13th and 14th centuries) that have distinctive and strange characteristics. The Thais developed a different style of image representing Buddha *after* "enlightenment"—in a perfect state of mind and body. The faces are oval, and the lines are so relaxed and flowing, with no angular features or masculine muscles, that these images are often said to look rather feminine. In fact, the Thais were aiming to produce an image pure and detached from any physical and terrestrial matter—which is the very essence of Buddhism. Interesting examples are to be found in Bangkok in the National Museum and in Wat Benchamabopitr (the Marble Temple), where there is a Sukhothai-period "walking" Buddha image. Also, in the *wiharn* of Wat Suthat in Bangkok, is perhaps the very finest of sitting Buddhas, mystic and imposing, measuring more than six metres (about twenty-one feet) from knee to knee. It was cast in Sukhothai in the 14th century, in bronze.

WIHARN—The word is pronounced "we-hahn," and is

also spelled *viharn* and *vihara*. The building looks just like the *bot*, except that it has no *bai sema* (boundary stones) around it. A *wat* need not necessarily have a *wiharn*, but, on the other hand, a large *wat* may have several. In northern Thailand the *wiharn* is usually larger than the *bot*, while in central Thailand the *bot* is usually larger. The reason lies in its purpose. While the *bot* is used by the monks, the *wiharn* is used mainly by laymen and for public assemblies. In the North, as there are so many *wat*, each has fewer monks—hence smaller *bot*.

Inside the *wiharn* are more images of Buddha and lavish decorations on the walls and ceiling similar to those in the interior of the *bot*. Often, magnificently decorated cloisters are built around the *bot* and *wiharn* to add reverence and seclusion to the sacred area and the two buildings within. Some cloisters are lined with rows of Buddhas. (The most interesting collection is at the Marble Temple.) Others are decorated with paintings. Usually there are four gateways giving access to this central courtyard, roofed with brilliantly coloured glazed tiles. These highly decorated gateways correspond to the Indian Gopuram of old Buddhist Indian monasteries. In the North, the Burmese influence has resulted in gateways enriched with small *stupa*.

STUPA—The *stupa*, a tall tower, is usually the most noticeable feature of any *wat*. Often a *wat* has a number of *stupa*. There are two types: *chedi* and *prang*. They come in so many various forms that the descriptions below have had to be limited to the basic points only—their origin and their purpose.

Chedi—are bell-shaped, usually white, with a tapering pinnacle above, often decorated by *chattra* or "umbrella" tiers. Long ago, the *chedi* served the purpose of housing a sacred relic of Buddha and were regarded as more important than the *bot*. They originated from central India via Ceylon. As time went by, *chedi* were erected as memorials for holy men and kings and contained their ashes or mementos. Naturally, the *chedi* lost their revered importance, until now they are regarded almost as mere decorative embellishments to the *wat*. Some Thais will say, "It is just a symbol of Buddhism."

Prang—are usually much taller than a *chedi,* with a square-planed, large base, rising into a slender elliptical-shaped mass. *Prang* are much rarer than *chedi* and are found in royal *wat* or palace grounds. A fine example is the highest in Thailand at Wat Arun (Temple of the Dawn) which has virtually become a symbol of Bangkok. *Prang* derived from the corner tower of the Khmer temple, which actually had nothing to do with Buddhism. The Thais borrowed the architectural style to form a new type of Thai *stupa*. They house images of Buddha or sometimes treasure, which is why so many have been pillaged.

MONDOP—This structure corresponds to the *mondapa* of an Indian temple. It is square (cubical, in fact) with a pyramidal roof-structure, in layers, receding and ascending into a tall, slender spire. The older *mondop* were all-brick, rather plain structures with only two or three layers of the pyramidal roofs. More recent *mondop* have highly decorated, wooden super-structures with wood carvings, gilding, and glass mosaic patterns.

The purpose of the *mondop* is to enshrine a sacred object (such as the Buddha's Footprint at Sara Buri, see p. 239), or it may be used like a library or special storeroom to house objects used in religious ceremonies (as at the Emerald Buddha Temple in Bangkok).

SALA—Here and there, set apart from other buildings,

one may see small rectangular structures with pillars and roofs but no walls. These are *sala,* or resting places. Visitors to them can relax in the shade and even sleep—no one will object. Some *sala* are finely ornamented. Most have at least brilliantly coloured, glazed-tile roofs and gilded wooden ornamentation on the gables.

Sala are not only found in the *wat* but also along roads and canals, anywhere that people may want to rest a while out of the fierce heat of the tropical sun. By building a *sala,* one can gain "merit."

HO RAKANG OR BELL TOWER—Every *wat* has one; a simple structure, it has steps up to a small platform, above which a bell is suspended. Very often the structure is two-storied, and a drum is kept underneath. The bell (and/or drum) is used to summon monks to services or to meals. Generally, the *ho rakang* has no artistic appeal. One exception, however, is the *ho rakang* at the Temple of the Emerald Buddha, which is unusually high, pyramidal in form, and decorated all over with porcelain.

HO TRAI OR LIBRARY—This building varies very much in form and size but is usually built high so that the room is well above ground, made of brick, and sometimes in the middle of an artificial pond to keep the manuscripts and books safely away from ants. In the North, the *ho trai* has a ground-floor room built of brick and a first-floor room of wood. Usually, the interior of the *ho trai* has no decoration. There may be several *ho trai* in one *wat.*

PRA SAT—This consists of a square central room from which project three long wings or antechambers and one short wing, or it may have four wings of equal length. The roof and superstructure will be of the same form as on the *mondop.*

The *pra sat* is used either as a royal throne hall (like the Dusit Maha Pra Sat in the Grand Palace) or as a memorial building (like the Pra Sat of the Temple of the Emerald Buddha, which houses statues of past kings).

KUTI OR SANGARAMA—Monks' Quarters. This is a simple building with no special architectural or artistic features, containing a row of small rooms, perhaps with a verandah in front. There may also be similar buildings for schools and pupils' lodgings.

KANBARIEN—Usually to be found somewhere close to the monks' quarters, this originally was where the Buddhist doctrine was taught to laymen. The exterior is not usually impressive unless it is very large—which is rare —when it takes the same form as the *bot* and *wiharn.* Inside is a pulpit. Sermons are given regularly.

THE ENCLOSING WALLS—The surrounding external walls are impressively thick, solid, and high enough to hide all but the gleaming, glazed tiled roofs and pinnacles of the various buildings.

The walls are usually whitewashed, with richly decorated embellishments along the top, ornamental buttresses, and especially ornate gateways guarded by statues of lion-like creatures or grotesque demons. Within these walls only the *bot* and (if there is one) the *wiharn* and their position are planned. They are in line with the gateways. The other buildings are added one by one anytime later on, without, it seems, any thought to an overall, unified plan.

Becoming a Monk (Bikkhu)

In Thailand, one simply chooses a *wat* and asks the abbot. If there is room, the applicant will be admitted.

Foreigners, even if not Buddhists, are welcomed also, but there will be two difficulties. Firstly, a problem of language since Pali (a holy language) is used for chanting sutras and for other observances. Secondly, only two meals a day are taken. Unfortunately, some foreign travellers have abused the overt hospitality of the *wat,* especially in Bangkok, and so some abbots may hesitate to accept a casual foreign visitor. An overnight visitor will be given breakfast and a mat to sleep on. As a matter of courtesy, the least one can do in return is offer a donation.

It is a Thai tradition for a man to become a monk at the age of twenty for a period of three months. This is regarded as a preparation, through religious instruction, for adult life. A Thai man would find it extremely difficult to find a wife unless he had completed his three months as a monk. Some enter a *wat* at a younger age in order to study. As explained earlier, for very little cost or in return for performing menial tasks, it is possible thus to receive a reasonable education.

A *bikkhu,* or monk, is allowed to keep only eight possessions:

1,2. outer and under robes*
3. belt
4. needle
5. shoulder scarf (used for certain ceremonies)
6. razor
7. bowl for food
8. strainer (to save creatures from drowning in his drinking water)

* No one seems to know for sure just how the saffron robe came to be the dress of the Buddhist monks but it has been suggested that long ago the outcasts in India were forced to wear this colour, and the Buddhists chose it as a symbol of their humility and poverty. Furthermore, it is the easiest colour to dye.

When a son becomes a monk he brings "merit" to his parents as well as to himself. Some men enter a *wat* when they cannot find employment, and maybe even to avoid employment. There is no rule to prevent it.

ORDINATION (Buat Naag)—This takes place around Buddhist "Lent" (July–September), a time when large numbers enter *wat* to practise meditation. A ritual is held in the monk's home, attended by parents, relatives, and friends, followed by a procession to the *wat*, where another ceremony takes place, accompanied by much reciting in Pali. Afterwards, gifts are presented to the *wat*.

DAILY SCHEDULE—The times vary from *wat* to *wat*, but the routine is roughly as follows:

About dawn, monks get up and go out to receive offerings of food. Not all monks go out in the morning. Many people—especially members of the monks' families—take food directly to the *wat*.

Breakfast is eaten in silence, without greed.

Monks assemble in the *wat* to chant sutras and recite the teachings of Buddha.

They attend lectures on Buddhist teachings and Pali. There is a period of free time, after attendance at lectures.

The last meal of the day is taken at 11:00 A.M. Only two meals a day are taken, as a full stomach is thought to hinder meditation and clear thought. After mid-day, the monks are not allowed to eat but they may drink.

During the day, if asked, the monks will perform rites such as blessing a house or a new-born child, and attending funerals or weddings. The abbot sends the monks in groups of seven or nine to the family's home, where they chant in Pali. In return, the family will offer gifts of daily necessities.

Around 5:00 P.M., the monks assemble in the *bot* for more chanting.

Buddhist monk *(bikkhu)*.

Monks are allowed considerable freedom to follow their own interests, meditate in solitude, teach, or even to work in a useful occupation.

A BIKKHU'S ASPIRATIONS AND DUTIES—The main aim is to seek *nirvana,* or spiritual enlightenment, which is very difficult to attain. Pali, the holy language, is studied in depth to facilitate understanding of Buddha's teaching. As there is a rule that strictly forbids boasting about spiritual attainments, no one really knows if anyone these days actually reaches the state of *nirvana.*

A novice vows to observe ten precepts and takes more vows progressively until, fully-fledged, the monk is bound by a total of 227 precepts. Many of the rules concern good behaviour and manners.

For Buddhist laymen, the following precepts must always be observed:

Do not kill any living creature.
Do not steal.
Do not commit any wrongful sexual act.
Do not lie.
Do not become intoxicated with alcohol.

For a novice or monk to break any of these five basic precepts would lead to certain expulsion from the *wat,* never to be rescinded. It seems that other rules, if broken, can be confessed, and forfeits will be imposed in the form of extra chores. (Thailand also has nuns, who have shaven heads too. They wear white robes and observe only eight precepts. None is fully ordained.)

The *bikkhu's* duty is somehow to transmit Buddha's teaching to the laity by influence rather than in any formal way. The *bikkhu* is not a mediator between Buddha and mankind in the way that Christian monks are considered to be mediators between God and men, since Buddha is not a God. Therefore, Buddhists neither save souls, forgive, nor condemn. They simply follow Lord Buddha's teaching and believe that each man himself is responsible for his own destiny. They urge Buddhist followers to avoid all evil and to try to purify their minds. Buddhism provides a spiritual strength to the Thais. It is estimated that there are a quarter of a million *bikkhu* and more than twenty thousand *wat* in Thailand today. About ninety-three per cent of the Thai people are Buddhist.

Part III

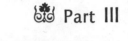

WHERE TO GO AND WHAT TO SEE

HISTORICAL PERIODS

Dvaravati	6th–11th centuries
Srivijaya	8th–13th centuries
Lop Buri	11th–14th centuries
Chiengsaen	12th–15th centuries
Sukhothai	13th–15th centuries
Ayutthaya	14th–18th centuries
Thon Buri	18th century
Bangkok	18th–20th centuries
Constitutional	1932 to present

KINGS OF THE PRESENT (CHAKRI) DYNASTY

Rama I (General Tong Duang)	1781–1809
Rama II (Nabhalai)	1809–1824
Rama III (Nang Klao)	1824–51
Rama IV (Mongkut)	1851–68
Rama V (Chulalongkorn)	1868–1910
Rama VI (Vajiravudh)	1910–25
Rama VII (Prajadhipok)	1925–32
Rama VIII (Ananda Mahidol)	1935–46
Rama IX (Phumiphol Adulyadej)	1946 to present

14

BANGKOK

No other Asian capital has managed to retain so much of its national character and charm. The exotic Orient is here, immediately striking and strange. Bangkok is unique. It is not surrounded by suburbs like other cities. One is either in the city or outside it. Also, it has no city centre. It is just one sprawling conglomeration of buildings, market places, temples, and hotels, criss-crossed by roads and *klong*—naturally fascinating ingredients for any tourist.

Near any hotel there are bound to be street sellers in colourful Thai costume, offering flowers, sweets, or curious delicacies. Then, in the early morning sun, every day, these streets will behold saffron-robed monks quietly pacing with their rice bowls to receive offerings of food from the local people. The monks disappear elusively before the children leave for school and people begin their day's work. Soon the streets fill with traffic roaring and heaving in the heat of the day, desperately fighting a losing battle against the daily congestion.

The city is full of anachronisms. Rooftops and tall concrete blocks are interspersed with glittering, golden *chedi* spires. Bangkok has about 800 active *wat*. The Thais continue their mode of life in the same old way. They have not responded to Western influences like other Asians. The commercialism and materialistic ways of the West are rejected. Thais make good Buddhists but not good businessmen. Their aspirations belong on a higher plane. American and European businessmen may regard them as slow to progress, but the faces of the Thais still shine brightly. Their happiness is infectious, overwhelming visitors who often fall in love with the city. The Thais still greet foreigners with gentle smiles and sparkling eyes. Hotel staff are effortlessly gracious and friendly, and they never hover for tips. This is the mood of Bangkok—inviting, exotic, and friendly.

Gourmets are delighted by the superb foreign restaurants serving dishes from every continent. By night the city swings. Nothing is missing for the night-bird—noisy discotheques, plush nightclubs, comfortable theatre restaurants, ultramodern cinemas, cosy bars, intimate cocktail lounges—and all are reasonably priced. Shopping, too, is highly underrated. There is so much more to Bangkok than its world-famous Floating Market. Similarly, there is so much more to Thailand than Bangkok.

Public Transport in Bangkok

Not long ago Bangkok* was known as "the Venice of the East" for the city was criss-crossed by *klong* (canals)

* The name Bangkok is used by foreigners. Long ago a Chinese trading settlement existed here among groves of wild plum trees. *Bang* means "village" and *kok* means "wild plum tree." Thais refer to the town on the western side of the Chao Phya River, (technically a separate municipality), as Thon Buri, *thon* meaning "money" and *buri* meaning "town." Incidentally, *buri* has the same etymology as "bury" in English, as in Salisbury. The town on the eastern side of the river Thais always called *Krungthep*, which is actually the first word of a twenty-word poetic title spoken to describe the new city by its royal founder. It means the same as Los Angeles—"City of Angels."

and dependent on its water transport. Roads have been built alongside the old *klong* and, especially since the war, with motor vehicles growing more popular, the *klong* have become disused and stagnant. The government encouraged the filling up of *klong*, both to make wider roads and to be rid of the unhealthy waters. In Thon Buri there may still be as many *klong* as roads but on the other side of the Chao Phya River—in Krungthep—there are just a few *klong* here and there alongside some of the roads. It is not possible to build subways because the soil is too soft and so roads remain the only means of transport within the city. Public transport, therefore, is limited to buses.

The buses move fast in spite of other traffic, and they can be very useful to a tourist. Some foreigners find buses less tiring than taxis because there is no need to bargain. The fare is fixed and is only 50 *satang* (2½ cents) for any single journey on any route. Before considering a bus ride one must have a route map. The best one, in Thai and English, is obtainable free from either T.O.T. or from National Outdoor Sites, Ltd. (who produce it), at 212/3 Silom Road, Bangkok, tel: 38564. By following the route numbers on this map, one can find a bus to go anywhere in Bangkok, and, equally important, know where to alight. Without that map there is little hope of arriving at the correct destination. Conductors cannot understand English, and other passengers will simply laugh with embarrassment if spoken to by a *farang*.

The corresponding route and bus numbers are clearly displayed at the bus stops. One should not worry too much about finding the end of the queue. If there is one, it will disintegrate the moment a bus arrives, as the drivers never seem able to stop at the right spot. Route numbers are shown on the front and back of the vehicle. Ignore the numbers on the side of the bus.

Once aboard, grasp something quickly and be ready for the moment the conductor crys *Oo-loy-ee* or blows his ear-piercing pea whistle. The bus will lurch forward violently and tear off to the next stop. The ride will be bumpy, noisy, but thrilling. On Bangkok roads the question of who gives way to whom seems to be determined by the size of the vehicles. Thus, the bus drivers claim their right-of-way almost all the time, ploughing through the thick traffic in unbelievable situations, and negotiating roundabouts with carefree abandon while other vehicles have to screech to a halt to avoid collision.

Wiry conductors, all carrying hinged metal tubes that they rattle and snap viciously, collect the fares, putting coins in and tearing out tickets simultaneously.

The buses in Bangkok serve a population approaching three million, so a tourist is advised not to go near them or even near the bus stops during the rush hours, 7:00–9:00 A.M. and 3:30–6:00 P.M. Surging crowds make getting on and off extremely difficult and the heat doesn't help. The Thais hang on fearlessly to the rails and steps of bus doorways in rush hours.

Be careful at the bus stops near first-class hotels and good shopping areas. They are the favourite haunt of handbag snatchers. Some Thais also have a compelling fascination with gold brooches and necklaces. On the buses, beware of pickpockets, and be especially cautious if you are a lady and are offered a seat. The man sitting next to you may be the "kind" gentleman's accomplice. Also, if you are a lady, do not sit at the back of the bus. It is the custom for monks to occupy the rear seats, and they are forbidden to come into contact with women.

Sightseeing Tours

It is better to take a sightseeing tour by bus or car to see the important sights and to become familiar with the city as quickly as possible. Hotels will be able either to make a booking or to introduce the guest to one of the major travel agencies. Tours are operated daily.

Name of Tour	Fares (approx.)	Times (approx.)	Major places of interest visited
City & Temples Tour	100 *baht*	9:00–12:00 noon or 2:00–5:00 P.M.	Wat Trimitr, Wat Po, and the Marble Temple. (Some agencies include Royal Chapel with Emerald Buddha, too.)
Floating Market Tour	100 *baht*	6:45–11:00 A.M.	By motorboat along *klong* to the morning market place, stopping at Wat Arun and Royal Barges Shed on return.
Grand Palace Tour (Mon. Wed. Fri. —morning only Tues. & Thurs. —morning or afternoon)	100 *baht*	9:00–12:00 noon or 2:00–5:00 P.M.	Coronation Hall, Audience Hall, Ceremonial Hall, Royal Chapel with Emerald Buddha (formal attire required, see p. 167)

The following regular tours are equally worthwhile, but one can easily arrange to do these individually, without a guide.

Name of Tour	Fares (approx.)	Times (approx.)
National Museum Tour	100 *baht*	9:00–12:00 noon or 1:00– 4:00 P.M. daily, except Monday and Saturday.
Klong Katcha —Rural Canal Tour	100 *baht*	2:30–5:30 P.M.
TIMland (Thailand in Miniature)	150 *baht*	2:00–6:00 P.M. daily
NIGHT TOURS:		
Thai Boxing at Lumpini or Rajdamnern Arena	150 *baht*	5:30–8:00 P.M. nightly
Thai Dinner with Classical Dancing Show	About 180 *baht*	7:30–10:30 P.M. nightly

Sightseeing in Bangkok

AIRPORT-TO-CITY DRIVE—Sightseeing really begins from the moment one leaves the airport to drive to the hotel. Even before the plane lands one can see a little of the countryside through the white clouds that hang perpetually over the plains like puffs of cotton wool. Glimpses of the fields reveal a fertile land, rich, green, and flat, ideal for water transport. The paddy fields are cut by long, straight canals that reach into the far distance.

Out of the airport building, the heat seems to melt one's bones. The tropical warmth is soporific. Along the Paholyothin Road (main highway to the city, sixteen miles away), one may notice the lotus plants and water lilies growing in the waterlogged ditch. The water lilies are the ones with leaves floating on the water. Lotus plants grow above the surface of the water and have broader leaves. The lotus is a most valuable plant in Asia. The leaves are used to make bowls for serving Thai curry or for wrapping foods, a medicine can be extracted from the stalks, and the root is a tasty vegetable. Besides, it has a beautiful flower and is of grcat significance to Buddhists.

Also, one can see the ornate spirit houses. Every building has one in its grounds, put into position before construction of a new building begins. It faces the most important room, such as the living room or master bedroom of a home. The Thais believe that a *Chao Ti* (Lord of the Land or Place) lives in the spirit house, and he will ward off any evil spirits that happen to come along. So the Thais make daily offerings to the *Chao Ti*—sweets, fruits, candles, incense sticks, flowers, or anything else that's handy—on a table just in front of the little spirit house.

Nearer the city the traffic thickens. Most of the cars are Japanese but there are models here from all over the world. All the cars are imported, as Thailand does not yet produce its own cars. The import duty on a car is over one hundred per cent so the Thais say when they buy a new car they must also buy one for the government. Coming into Bangkok, one feels that Thailand must be one of the wealthier countries of Asia because so many people apparently can afford that hundred-percent duty.

FLOATING MARKET—The boat ride through the *klong* to visit Bangkok's Floating Market has become a world-famous tourist attraction. Small motor launches seating about ten passengers leave from a pier on the Chao Phya River, next to the Oriental Hotel, early in the morning. Have a very light breakfast and enjoy the various fresh tropical fruits later at the market. Usually it is best to leave from the pier at around 6:45 A.M., or at least before 7:00 A.M., to beat the coach crowds. By hard bargaining it is possible to take a boat for around 40 *baht* ($2) per person. (A Thai can hire an entire boat for about 80 *baht*.)

Along the klong—As soon as the sightseeing boat leaves the pier, bouncing on the choppy, muddy water in a fresh morning breeze, it enters a busy river world among speedy water taxis, houseboats, and cargo barges similar in size and shape to the old Dutch Botta yachts. They weave their way along the fast flowing river. Warehouses and sawmills, with great logs half-submerged outside, line the river banks. The left side is Krungthep and on the right is Bangkok's twin city, Dhonburi or Thon Buri. Thon Buri was the capital of Thailand from 1767–82, when Krungthep became the new capital. The Thon Buri area contains some four hundred *wat*.

After passing under Bangkok Bridge (an unattractive steel structure that can be opened in the middle like Tower Bridge in London), one of the 400 or so temples, Wat Daw Kanaung, can be seen on the right bank. Next to it is Daw Kanaung Klong which leads to the floating market. The *klong* is a photographer's paradise, lined with wooden houses (some on stilts, some set back among the coconut palms), exotic bushes, and tropical flowers. Children dive and swim like fishes around the boats, and the very young will respond to a wave with broad smiles.

In the early morning sun, men and women bathe discreetly in the *klong*. At the same time they may wash their clothes and hair and some even brush their teeth with the murky *klong* water. It seems to act as an oral vaccine against tropical diseases.

The Floating Market area is busy with boats to the point of chaos. Water-traffic police, standing on the roofs of launches, furiously wave their arms and blow their whistles but their efforts are really wasted. There are too many boats to cope with, and the people in the sampans are too busy buying and selling their fruit, paddling about in all directions, crossing the paths of huge, overladen rice barges, "long-tailed" speedboats, and the tourists' motor launches. The floating market has changed in recent years with the sudden influx of tourists. The motor launches disturbed the waters so much that the smaller sampans rocked violently in their wake. The motor boats have literally driven them off the water so now most of the buying and selling takes place on dry land on a concreted open space by the *klong*. Tourists are neatly hustled into the "floating market"—an enormous shopping arcade called the Thai Silk Home Industries Shop, which sells nothing but souvenirs and silk to tourists. At the back of the arcade is a tame elephant, a silk hand-loom, and a Coca-Cola bar. It was inevitable, it seems, that the Floating Market would develop into this. Once, before engines were invented, here was a Garden of Eden. How beautiful and peaceful it must have been!

Nevertheless, the boat ride along the *klong* is certainly worthwhile. Bangkok is still a Venice of the East, and it is interesting to see the fruits and other home-grown produce, and to watch the frantic bargaining. The farmers come here with their produce from the countryside and sell to the merchants who in turn supply Bangkok's population. Some of the fruits are bananas (more than a dozen varieties), rambutans, mangos, mangosteens, jack fruits, pineapples, coconuts (green and shiny), logans, limes, papayas, oranges (three varieties), bitter melons, watermelons, lychees, pomeloes (four varieties), betel nuts (from the areca palm), tamarinds, and durians. Of course, there are others, and the varieties will depend on the season. The boats overflow with piles of fruit as their "lampshade"-hatted owners ply from house to house. Boats and shop fronts are piled high with vegetables and other foods too, such as dried salted fish, garlic, onions, sugar cane, rice, shrimp paste (called *krapi* and used in Thai curry), chillies and peppers, cinnamon, salt, and so on. A few boats have charcoal burners aboard and sell ready-cooked delicacies such as coconut sweets, and some sell coffee. It is fun to try bargaining and to buy a few fruits. Besides, it helps to keep the tourists welcomed. After a short spell at the market area one proceeds along Klong Dan and Klong Bangkok Yai, two delightful canals, to visit Wat Arun.

The little wooden houses have rusty, corrugated iron roofs. In days gone by they were made of palm leaves. However, the houses still look beautiful in the jungle setting, and every home is surrounded by colourful shrubs and flowers—white and pink frangipanis, poinsettias, blossoming hibiscus shrubs, vines and creepers with vivid red, purple, and orange flowers, jasmine, oleanders, and especially bougainvillaeas and orchids that grow wild in profusion in every hue and shade. The scene is magnificent all year round. In front of the houses are wooden quays and piers often made from bamboo. Earthenware water jars are strategically placed around each house to catch the rain from the roofs. If one can peer through a window or doorway, there will be a picture of the King and Queen in every home and perhaps a myna bird in a cage. The most popular family pet here is the gibbon, to be seen on many a balcony.

Among the wild birds, one is likely to see parrots, crows, bulbuls, warblers, sometimes swallows, and always sparrows. The lines of houses are often broken by a brilliantly decorated *wat* set back among spacious grounds. One of them on the left is Wat Rajoros which is very well known among Thais as it was often mentioned in Thai literature and poetry. It is an old *wat* enlarged and redecorated in 1820 by the then Crown Prince, son of King Rama II. The King renamed the *wat* after his son, Rajoros. The last of these *wats,* next to the remains of an old fort on the left hand side, is Wat Arun which is always visited on the way back from the Floating Market.

WAT ARUN RAJVARARAM (Temple of the Dawn)—Also known as Wat Chaeng, this majestic *wat* has become a symbol of Thailand, used on travel posters, seen in films, and depicted in books—an unforgettable sight for tourists. The soaring *prang* rises 217¾ feet and, from

Wat Arun Rajvararm.

afar, is like a tower of jewels, glittering and flashing in the sun. Four smaller *prang* give it an unimpeded, noble symmetry from across the broad Chao Phra River, silhouetted against the sky. At dawn, the sun rises directly behind it to form a glorious backcloth of glowing colours.

The construction of Wat Arun began after Ayutthaya, the old capital, had been sacked by the Burmese in 1767. King Taksin, who had been leading the campaigns against the Burmese invaders, chose Thon Buri to be the new capital of Thailand and decided on the site just south of here for his royal palace. That site is now occupied by the Royal Thai Navy. An old monastery named Chaeng lay adjacent to Taksin's new residence. He ordered it to be enlarged and embellished, and it was renamed Wat Arun. In 1780 the Emerald Buddha was placed here.

But King Taksin's dreams of building a beautiful new capital were short lived, and his military victories were rewarded by misery and misfortune. Tired of fighting, he delegated the leadership of his pressing campaigns to his favourite general, Chakri Tong Duang (Chakri means commander-in-chief), while he remained in Thon Buri to build his palace as he pleased. Shortly afterwards, he became neurotic and thought his courtiers and family were deceiving him in some way. He quickly deteriorated and became insane, saying he was the reincarnation of Lord Buddha and expecting monks to worship him. The new capital was thrown into confusion, and by the time General Chakri returned it was too late. A little revolution had taken place. The army and the people looked to General Chakri to take over as King, and it seems that he simply accepted the proffered throne. The deposed King Taksin apparently expressed wishes to become a monk but, since one could easily leave a monastery at any time, Taksin was seen as a threat, either in or out of the country. The new King was reportedly saddened by his advisors, who saw only one answer to the problem—execution.

The Thais have always had great respect for royalty so, according to traditional form, as decreed by King Trailok in 1450, execution of a royal person had to be performed without shedding a drop of blood.

Some say that Taksin was killed with a sandalwood club by a single blow on the back of the neck. Others say he was put into a sack and beaten to death. Either way, it was not a very nice "thank you."

Anyway, General Chakri became King Rama I in 1781, the first King of the present Chakri dynasty, and he moved the capital from Thon Buri to Krungthep on the opposite bank of the river in 1782. He did this for military reasons as he feared an attack from the West, in which case Krungthep would be protected to some extent by the water. Wat Arun was left unaltered until Taksin's original *prang* was made taller by King Rama II. He added fifty feet to its height and built the four smaller towers. Rama III brought it to its present height in 1842, and his ashes were placed beneath the great Buddha in the chapel.

At Wat Arun, go first to the main *prang*. A close look reveals not a tower inlaid with precious stones but a construction of brick and stucco embedded with fragments of porcelain in a mass of colourful and symbolic designs. One can climb up* three flights of steep, narrow steps to a balcony that gives a rewarding view across Bangkok: the river, Wat Po, Emerald Buddha Temple, the Grand Palace, and so on. Among the multi-coloured decorations one is bound to see the green figures seated on elephants in the niches of the main *prang*. They rep-

* This cannot be done until the restoration work has been completed.

resent the Hindu God Indra riding Erawan, the mythological, three-headed elephant of Thailand. Look for the strange moon god too, riding a white horse in the niches of the smaller *prang,* and for the figures of Kinnari, a mythological creature, half-bird, half-woman. The *prang* is "supported" by curious caryatids and demons.

The four pavilions around the *prang* depict scenes of Buddha's birth, enlightenment, first preaching, and *nirvana.* The *bot* (to the North) was built by King Chulalongkorn (1868–1910) to replace an old one destroyed by fire. The entrance is guarded by two giant demons of frightening proportions.

Regrettably, the *wat* needs restoration, and the beauty of the buildings is at present marred by scaffolding. There seems to be a difficulty in obtaining the porcelain fragments or mosaic tiles needed.

The Fine Arts Department says about 121,000 mosaic tiles will be required for the first part of the restoration. It is searching for manufacturers to duplicate the original porcelain, which came from China.

ROYAL BARGES SHED—Most tours to the Floating Market will include a visit to the Royal Barges Shed. The most interesting and splendid barge is named "Sri Suwannahong." Built in the reign of King Rama I (1781–1809), it is the one used to carry the present King, who sits on the golden, carved dais. The name of the barge is taken from the carved bow, resembling a mythological swan.

The other barge to look for is named "Anantanakraj" and has seven fierce serpent heads carved at its bow. Each of these barges is over one hundred feet long and requires fifty oarsmen. The carvings are exquisitely decorated and richly coloured with gold, red, and green.

Besides these two barges there are more than thirty

Carved bow of royal barge.

others, shorter (except for the Royal Escort barge named "Aneakchatbu Chong"), each having carved prows and vivid painting.

Once a year, thirty-five barges make a grand procession during the Tod Kathin Festival in November (see Chapter 1). The oarsmen wear ancient red costumes and paddle red and gold oars to the rhythm of Thai songs.

THE GRAND PALACE—

Admission—Tuesdays, Thursdays, 9:00–12:00 noon; and 2:00–4:00 P.M.
Mondays, Wednesdays, Fridays, 9:30–12:00 noon.
Saturdays, Sundays, and national holidays, closed.
Entrance fee—15 *baht* (75 cents)

Dress—Gentlemen will not be admitted unless wearing a jacket and tie. Ladies should not wear slacks or shorts. Also, one must wear shoes that cover the toes.

The palace entrance—is on Na Phra Lan Road at the south end of the Phramane Ground through the white-washed brick wall. The Thai-style gateway has two sentry boxes and armed guards standing by, one at each side. The walls, surrounding an area of over one square mile, were built in 1783. They contain the many palace buildings, the offices of the Ministry of Finance, the Emerald Buddha Temple, and the site of the Forbidden City.

One should walk past the guards and go straight along the drive, which is lined with beautifully trimmed, cone-shaped trees, past the Ministry of Finance offices on the right, to the next gateway, a tall, decorated archway reminiscent of Italian architecture. It was especially built high enough for the King to be able to pass through seated upon the elephant howdah or on a golden palanquin. This gateway contains the ticket office and a reception lounge for V.I.P.s. A colourful pamphlet with a brief outline of the palace and the Emerald Buddha Temple is given with the entrance tickets. Keep the tickets; someone will ask to see them again when passing into the temple compound. It is forbidden to use cine cameras but taking still pictures is allowed.

Straight ahead is the Chakri-Mahaprasad Building, a beautiful throne hall and state reception hall built in the Italian Renaissance style and topped by three dazzling, ornate spires and tiered roofs in the old Thai style. At first glance it looks unreal, like a sugar-loaf palace in a fairy tale. It was built in 1882 to commemorate 100 years of the Chakri dynasty and is used by the King when envoys and ambassadors present their credentials. The interior is decorated with portraits of the late kings and paintings showing diplomatic receptions. The Throne Hall is sumptuously decorated with marble, gold, and fine crystal chandeliers. The throne is surmounted by a nine-tiered, creamy-white umbrella—a mark of sovereignty—and has two seven-tiered umbrellas on each side.

Turn right in front of the Chakri building and walk to the gateway in the wall at the end of the inner compound. The small, bushy trees in front of the buildings are ebony. Just to the left of the gateway is the Abhornbhimok, or Disrobing Pavilion, a small, raised platform built against the wall with an exquisite, tiered roof and spire adorned with gold. This was the place where the King would leave his hat and coat before entering the audience hall. The pavilion was built by King Mongkut (1851–68). The platform is the height of his palanquin. This pavilion, together with the Dusit Maha Prasat building, through the gate, are the finest examples of pure Thai architecture in Thailand. A replica of the Disrobing Pavilion appeared at the Brussels Exhibition in 1958.

The Dusit Maha Prasat Building consists of four wings forming a cross with a tall spire at the centre. It was put up by King Rama I in 1789. Visitors can enter and see the intricate decorations and furniture. The walls are hand painted with golden angels and white lotus-flower designs. In the centre of the hall is a high throne inlaid with mother-of-pearl, topped by a nine-tiered, white umbrella. This hall was built as a coronation hall by King Rama I and was used also as an audience chamber. When King Rama I died, his body lay here until cremation, and since that time the hall has been used only for "lying-in-state" of royalty.

Returning from the Dusit Maha Prasat Building past the Chakri-Mahaprasad Building one comes to the

Amarindra Vinichai Hall, one of three main buildings that belong to the MahaMontien group. This group of buildings is used for coronation. Behind the Amarindra Hall is the Paisal Taksin Hall, where the actual coronation ceremony is performed, and behind that is the Cakrabardibiman Hall, which is used as a bedchamber. The Amarindra Hall is the only one open to visitors. This is where the King appears just after being crowned, in his full regalia. The hall, also used for special audiences, is perhaps the most gorgeous part of the whole palace. Its richly coloured walls and ceiling, sumptuous furnishings, and golden thrones are at first glance breathtaking. The most magnificent throne, shaped like a boat, is at the far end of the hall, behind which is a kind of balcony where the King would appear before going to his throne, to the sound of trumpets and the opening of the heavy golden curtains.

Just to the left of this hall is a small pavilion with a marble floor, used for ceremonial bathing of the King, a rite adopted from the Brahmins. Next to this group of buildings, over the fence, is the Borom Piman Palace which houses foreign kings and queens who visit Thailand as state guests. The lovely gardens are used for royal garden parties.

The Forbidden City used to exist behind the MahaMontien and Chakri buildings.

THE EMERALD BUDDHA TEMPLE (*Wat Phra Keo*)—Adjoining the Grand Palace, the temple is enclosed by a whitewashed brick wall. Admission is 5 *baht* (25 cents) but on Sundays and national holidays admission is free. The main entrance is on the Na Phra Lan Road, or one may enter from a small gate at the end of a path leading from the Grand Palace inner gateway.

The temple was built by King Rama I in 1784 to

house the Emerald Buddha and was designed along the lines of former royal chapels in Sukhothai and Ayutthaya. Successive kings each added more buildings. The result is a large compound crowded with many glittering buildings, statues, and monuments. On entering, tourists gaze, momentarily breathless, at the fantastic colour and intricate work. The entire *wat* was carefully restored in 1957 with impressive results, to celebrate the Buddhist year 2,500 (the mid-point of a Buddhist era of 5,000 years). It seems to be the only *wat* never to have been inhabited by monks.

The first building to visit is the *bot*—just follow the crowd. This is a tall building surrounded by a low wall and twelve *sala*. At the south end is a magnificent bell tower. The four entrances are each guarded by bronze lions. Up the first few steps, at the main entrance, is a place to leave shoes. Before entering, have a close look at the three doors inlaid with mother-of-pearl patterns representing mythological animals and flowers. The sound of temple bells is something that will always be remembered by visitors to Thailand. Here, the various tones of the brass-wind bells hanging from the eaves are especially melodious.

Inside the *bot*, a vast, colourful mural spreads across the walls, depicting stories in the life of Buddha, and the lofty ceiling is covered in a red and gold pattern. Of course, the room is dominated by the presence of the Emerald Buddha, seated high on an ornate golden pedestal, beneath an elaborate seven-tiered canopy and baldachin. The image measures approximately 60 centimeters (23 inches) in height; it appears even smaller since it is positioned some 10 metres (32 feet) or more above floor level, dressed according to the season in one of three jewel-studded, pure gold costumes. The King changes the costume himself at a special ceremony at the beginning of each season. Two glass balls hang on either side, representing the sun and the moon. Many small golden Buddha images are placed in front, and there are two standing Buddhas, one at each side of the tall pedestal. A curious item among the odd assortment of offerings on display at the "altar" is an old clock reputed to have been a gift from Queen Victoria.

The story of the Emerald Buddha—According to legend, the figure was made in Ceylon, by the gods. In fact, it was carved from one piece of nephrite, most probably by the Thais of the North, in the 14th century or even earlier. The nephrite, experts have concluded, must have come from southern China.

The earliest known records show it to have been found in a *chedi* in Chiangrai in the first half of the 15th century, when the *chedi* was struck by lightning. The image was golden but the gold flaked off, revealing this green stone image which was believed to be emerald.

When the kingdom of Chiengmai expanded as far as Chiangrai, the King heard about the Emerald Buddha and sent a procession of elephants to bring it to Chiengmai. During the return journey, the elephant carrying the Buddha image suddenly turned towards Lampang. This was believed to be an omen and so the Emerald Buddha was kept in Lampang for the next thirty-two years before it was finally brought to Chiengmai.

In 1552 it was taken to Laos to preserve it from the invading Burmese. It was kept in Luang Prabang and then in Vientiane for a total of 226 years. King Rama I brought it to Thon Buri after conquering Vientiane in 1778. When he established Bangkok as the new capital he built Wat Phra Keo to house the image.

Twelve *sala* or "resting places" are now situated around the *bot*—a welcome innovation to sightseers. After a pause in the shade, walk to the "Pantheon" or *Phra Tepbidorn* just up the steps on a terrace on the north side of the *bot*. The plan of the building is in the form of a cross with a yellow *prang* in the centre of many-tiered roofs. This contains a life-size statue of each of the kings of the Chakri dynasty (all the Rama kings). It is opened to the public only on one day a year, Chakri Day, April 6, when it is thronged with Thais bringing flowers and incense to pay homage to the King's ancestors.

Next to the Pantheon, on the terrace, is a charming little square building with tall shaped roofs in tiers and a spire, all supported by a colonnade. This is a library that houses Buddhist scriptures. The floor inside is solid silver, the walls golden, and the large scripture cabinet is beautifully inlaid with mother-of-pearl.

Just next to this is a tall golden *chedi,* built in 1885 to house a sacred relic of Buddha. Also on this terrace is a large model of Angkor Wat in Cambodia. The model was built by King Mongkut (1851–68), as Cambodia at that time was a vassal-state of Thailand.

In the northeast corner of the compound is another library, called Montien Tham, with a most beautiful west facade. Walking eastwards, one comes to Wiharn Yot, a building elaborately decorated with porcelain in flower designs. This houses the "Manangasila Stone," a large stone, discovered in Sukhothai, believed to have been the throne of King Ramkamhaeng. Further eastwards, in the southeast corner, is the Phra Nak, containing the urns of the ashes of members of the royal family other than kings. One can also see eight *prang* in a line along the east side of the compound, two within the *wat* and six on the outer side of the gallery. These were built by King Rama I to represent eight planets of different colours and also to symbolize various concepts of Buddhist law.

Finally, take a stroll around the cloisters that surround the entire *wat*. The most magnificent, brilliantly restored murals will compel you to stop and linger over scenes depicting episodes in the *Ramakien* (the Thai version of the Indian epic *Ramayana*).

WAT PHRA JETUPON *(or Wat Po)*—This *wat* is popularly known as Temple of the Reclining Buddha and Wat Po, an abbreviation of the name of a former *wat* on this site named Wat Potharam, meaning "Temple of the Bodhi Tree." It covers a very large area just to the south of the Grand Palace and is divided into two sections, the religious buildings and the monks' living quarters, between which runs Jetupon Road. There are, in fact, sixteen gateways, but usually only two are open.

Wat Potharam was rebuilt during the 1780's and 1790's by King Rama I, with various additions and restorations made by King Rama III. The buildings have more muted colourings than Wat Phra Keo (Emerald Buddha Temple) but still, the *wat* is spectacular and photogenic. The following description will trace the route from the gateway in Maharaj Road to the gateway in Jetupon Road.

Straight ahead is the *ho trai* (library) with three *sala* (resting places) all highly decorated with coloured porcelain chips. A little to the left is a school classroom where the *bodhi* tree grows in the middle of the room and through the roof. This *wat* was made into a great place of learning by King Rama III—like a public university. Around the *wat,* one will see other rooms given over to medicine, astrology, and physiology, and one will find scientific illustrations on many of the walls.

Walk now between the classroom and the *wiharn* on the north side to a courtyard with a bell tower. Enter the *wiharn* without removing shoes (this is the only *wat* in Thailand where it is not necessary to remove shoes) and gaze up at the Reclining Buddha. Stretching the entire length of the building, some 160 feet in all, it is made of brick, covered with copper and gold, and pasted with gold leaf in places. The image was built to the order of King Rama III (1824–51) and represents Buddha entering *nirvana*. Walking towards the feet, one passes little altars where the faithful burn incense, donate money, and try their luck noisily shaking tins of fortune-telling sticks. The image's feet are its most interesting feature. The soles have 108 squares, each containing a work of art with mother-of-pearl inlays. They represent the 108 auspicious signs of Buddha around the Wheel of the Law. The toes are all the same size. This *wiharn* also has some fine murals around the walls (if only someone would restore them).

Coming out of the *wiharn*, by the belltower, one is confronted with hawkers and stalls selling all manner of souvenirs, especially cheap jewellery and temple rubbings. (There is another place in this *wat* where one can buy temple rubbings, mentioned below.) Go through the gateway of the east wall, passing another *sala* on the left. This gateway is "guarded" by a pair of humourous, much photographed statues of gentlemen wearing top hats. They are probably Chinese. One is now in the eastern courtyard.

Turn right and one will see a large black *lingam* or symbol of Shiva, decorated by flowers and various offerings brought by women in the hope that Shiva will bring them fertility. On the west side of the *lingam* are four tall *chedi*. The green one in the middle was built by King Rama I and contains a standing Buddha image. At either side are a white and a yellow *chedi*. These two were built by King Rama III, the white one being dedicated to King Rama II. The fourth *chedi*, the blue one behind, is the most ostentatious and was built by King Rama IV. He requested that no successive kings should build any more *chedi* here since he felt that each one would compete to produce an even more elaborate *chedi* and that such competition would be pointless. Thus these four pagodas symbolize the rule of the four Rama kings. There are ninety-five other *chedi* in the compound.

Here and there are *rishi,* small, strange figures in peculiar yoga-like positions on miniature hills of rocks. They represent hermits bound by vows and are said to give inspirational aid to ailing visitors. Also, adding colour and life to the *wat,* are many trees, including papaya and clumps of bamboo, local people selling drinks, fruit, and tidbits such as grilled bananas and squid, cooked on charcoal braziers, and strolling, saffron robed monks.

Finally, visit the red-and-yellow-roofed *bot* which is within two surrounding galleries that contain 394 images of Buddha, all seated. The *bot* is also surrounded by a low balustrade with entrances guarded by bronze lions. On the *bot* wall is a lovely bas-relief frieze depicting scenes from the *Ramayana.* These were brought here from Ayutthaya after the Burmese sacked the city in 1767. Here, one can see young Thais making rubbings. Most of the temple rubbings sold in Bangkok originate from here though many are now produced from wooden carved copies of this frieze. Huge teak doors, inlaid with mother-of-pearl, lead into the *bot* on the eastern and western sides. Inside is a marble floor with two rows of red and gold painted pillars, a brilliantly decorated ceiling, and murals on the walls. The large, gilt-bronze Buddha image, seated on a three-tiered gold and green dais, was brought here from Wat Sala See Na in Thon Buri by the venerated King Rama I, and it contains some of his ashes.

WAT RAJABOPIT—Situated between Fuang Nakhon Road and Asdang Road, off Charoen Krung (New Road).

This is not included on the regular tours of Bangkok but is worth a visit just to see the doors and shutters which are inlaid with mother-of-pearl, and are considered the most beautiful in Thailand. The *wat* was built by King Mongkut (Rama IV, 1851–68) in a style and layout similar to that of the Phra Pathom Chedi in Nakhon Pathom. The *chedi* and galleries are completely covered with shimmering, glazed tiles in beautiful Chinese-style designs, such as flowers and angels. The *chedi* houses a 12th- or 13th-century stone image of Buddha from Lop Buri.

The *bot* at the north side is most interesting. The interior has a gilded arched roof, painted walls, and a marble floor. The exquisite inlaid doors and shutters symbolise the five Orders of Chivalry of Thailand:

The Order of the Crown
The Order of the White Elephant
The Order of Chula Chom Klao
The Order of the House of Chakri
The Order of the Nine Gems

A royal cemetery and small school adjoin this *wat*.

WAT MAHATHAD—Located at the west side of the Phramane Ground on the corner of Mahathad Road and Phra Chan Road and extending behind the Royal Institute, this *wat* is rarely visited by the foreign tourist, yet it is one of the most important in Bangkok, founded many years before Bangkok became the capital. It is a hive of activity.

The original *wat* was rebuilt by Prince Wangna, the younger brother of King Rama I. The Prince became a monk and studied here in the late 18th century. King

Rama I then raised its status to that of a royal *wat,* renaming it Wat Mahathad Sri Ratana, meaning Monastery of the Great Relic. Under royal patronage its importance grew. A Buddhist school in the Grand Palace Grounds was moved here, and it has become one of the most important centres for the study of Pali and meditation. Royal cremations were celebrated here.

The points of interest are not very impressive when compared with other colourful, glittering *wat* in Bangkok. One should quickly take a look at the *mondop* with a golden *chedi.* This is built in the Ayutthaya style and contains the sacred relic. There is also a huge *bot,* probably the largest in Bangkok, and an equally austere *wiharn* which contains cells in which the monks or laity can practice meditation. In the extreme corner of the compound by Mahathad Road and Phra Chan Road is an area crowded with stalls where little statues of Buddha and votive objects are made and sold. At the time of writing there are several gaps in the adjacent fence, leading onto Mahathad Road.

WAT INDRA WIHARN—Also known as Wat In and Wat Bangkhunprom, this *wat* is located on the north side of Visukasat Road at the corner of Chakkraphony Road.

Nobody knows who built this old *wat* which is famous for a great ugly statue of Buddha standing outside. The construction of this monstrosity was begun over a century ago by a man named Somdej Pudtacharn who built the feet and body as far as the navel. An abbot named Po continued the work, and then another and another, but still it is not quite complete. The statue stands 32.9 metres (108 feet) high, 15.8 metres (52 feet) wide and is made of yellow cement resembling a saffron robe. The feet are painted white, and the face is covered with thousands of little gold tiles. It represents the Lord Buddha going out in the morning, carrying a bowl to collect offerings of food from the faithful.

Behind this gigantic concrete structure stands a white tower with staircases that may be climbed for a panoramic view of Bangkok.

WAT SUTAT AND THE GIANT SWING—This *wat,* whose full name is Suthatthepwararam, understandably shortened to Sutat, is situated at the south end of Din So Road, at a square named Si Yaak Sao Chiangcha. The huge red swing is in the square—now a traffic circle—and the *wat* faces it with its *wiharn* easily visible, standing high on terraces to the North. The gate opposite the swing is often closed, in which case one may enter by a school gate from Ti Thong Road. The *bot* is not opened except on a few Buddhist holy days, but at other times, if the man with the key can be found one will be allowed to go in. A donation should be made.

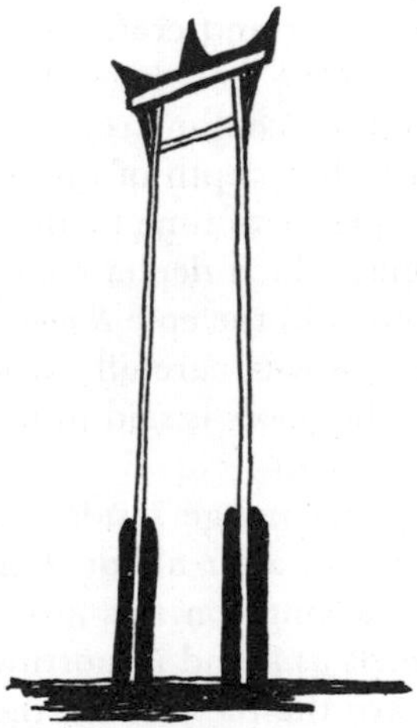

Giant swing.

In 1807 King Rama I (1781–1809) ordered this *wat* to be built to house a large Buddha image then lying exposed in the ruined city of Sukhothai. King Rama I never saw his plan completed, and it was his son, King Rama II, who actually brought the image from Sukhothai to be placed in the *wiharn* and constructed the *bot.* Quite a difficult task it must have been, for the image stands nearly 9 metres (30 feet) high and is probably the largest ever cast during the Sukhothai period. King Rama III later added the monks' quarters and embellishments to complete the building.

The *wiharn* is almost square, surrounded by a gallery containing 160 fine gilded Buddha images. Each of these images contains the ashes of a cremated person and is maintained by the individual family at some considerable cost. Since some of the ashes of King Rama VIII (1935–46) are placed in the huge image inside the *wiharn,* this may have become a fashionable *wat* in which to keep one's ashes. However, the best reason for visiting this *wat* is to admire the five priceless carved wooden doors, a rich example of Thai art and craftsmanship. The doors measure 5.64 metres (18½ feet) high, 1.3 metres (4 feet, 3 inches) wide, and 16 centimetres (6.3 inches) thick, and the carvings reach a depth of up to 14 centimetres (5.5 inches). Allow plenty of time to absorb the intricate details of the designs, which depict scenes in the Himavada forest (mentioned in the epic *Ramayana*) with many animals, birds, and insects carefully worked in among the foliage. One of the doors is said to have been carved by King Rama II himself.

The massive Buddha image inside is called "Srisakyamuni," placed on an altar about 2 metres (6½ feet) high. The strange carvings on this altar-base represent Greco-Buddhist reliefs as found in northwest India. Also worth seeing here are the pictures on the pillars, which show life in Bangkok at the time this *wat* was under construction. As usual, there are murals showing stories of the life of Buddha, but these murals are considered to be particularly fine.

The *bot,* just south of the *wiharn,* is much larger, measuring well over 61 metres (200 feet) long. Only the pillars that surround this building support the four-tiered roof, so the inside is left clear and open. Before entering, do not miss the magnificently decorated black-and-gold-lacquered doors, carefully restored a few years ago. Inside is an image of Buddha cast during the reign of King Rama III (1824–51) together with eighty figures of Buddha's disciples in a variety of colours, each bearing his name on his back. The vividly coloured decorations of the doors, windows, and murals have strong Hindu influences; indeed, many of the Hindu gods and heroes can be recognized in the paintings.

The Opium Box Buddha—One other curious item at Wat Sutat is to be found in a small hall among the monks' quarters. It is the Buddha Sathatamuni, an image 2 metres (about 6½ feet) high, made entirely of melted-down opium boxes. King Rama III ordered this to be cast from the confiscated metal opium boxes following a government ban on opium in 1839 (the wooden boxes were burned).

Metal facsimiles of the King's edict are on display at each side of the image.

The Giant Swing—This originated with the Brahmins. The two pillars (actually teak) are 21 metres (approximately 70 feet) high with a decorative crossbar at the top, all painted red. In Brahminism, this shape is said to represent a jujube tree, and a bowl placed between the pillars symbolizes a river. Apparently the Emperor would watch as entertainers swung to and fro to appease Vishnu, the Hindu diety. Thus, annually in Bangkok, a person representing the King would proceed by palanquin in procession to this spot to ceremonially observe the men swinging, at their peril, as high as possible, watched by thousands of people. Even more strange, as the story goes, the "King" had to sit on one leg with considerable discomfort and could move only after each swinger had caught a purse by the teeth. The purses, atop bamboo poles, were produced only when each man was swinging a full 180 degrees. Since the coup d'état in 1932 this ceremony has never been performed. Some say it was abolished because it did not conform to Buddhist beliefs; others say the new government would not allow a public gathering of several thousand people. (See "Monument of Democracy," p. 195.)

Where to buy your Buddha—Try the shabby, narrow street of small, open-fronted shops leading westward from "Si Yaak Sao Chingcha" (the Square of the Giant Swing). In contrast to the rather dirty, decaying buildings, the shops are packed with beautifully made religious, decorative objects including gold and silver Buddha images, tiered umbrellas, temple bells, altar tables, incense holders, gongs, and "package deal" monk's kits, each consisting of the only eight possessions a monk is allowed (see p. 147).

THE GOLDEN MOUNT AND WAT SRAKET—At some time during a tour of Bangkok, one is bound to see this concrete mount, topped by a golden *chedi* towering high above the sea of wooden houses and modern office blocks. The Golden Mount is 80.5 metres (264 feet) high and well positioned for a good panoramic view over the city if one has enough stamina for the climb. There are 318 steps (the author counted them).

Wat Sraket was formerly called Wat Sakae and the Golden Mount was formerly known as Wat Borombah-

Golden mount.

phot, but all the Thai people called it Phu Khao Tong, meaning "Golden Mount." Eventually, King Chulalongkorn (Rama V) made that its official name. The origin, construction, and importance of this place is fascinating and strange.

Wat Sakae is the oldest part. In fact, there are no records to show exactly when it was built, and all that can be said with certainty is that it was built before 1781 and almost certainly in the Ayutthaya period (1350–1767). It was in that year (1781) that General Chakri, on a mission for King Taksin, returned from his victorious battle against the Cambodians. When he heard the details of the revolution deposing King Taksin (described on p. 164), it is said that General Chakri knew he would become the next king. He then stopped at Wat Sakae to have his hair washed ceremonially, and he called himself Ramathibodi. Thus, here started the Chakri dynasty. The title Rama I was actually given posthumously by his grandson King Nang Klao (Rama III). Wat Sakae was re-named Wat Sraket (*sra* or *sa* means wash; *ket* or *kes* means royal hair) and it became a royal monastery, the site of subsequent royal cremations and ceremonies. The King rebuilt the *wat* and, although it must have been magnificent, it is presently in a poor state of repair compared to other famous Bangkok *wat*. However, some of the buildings are now being restored.

Among the complex of orange, red, and grey-roofed buildings, the *bot,* in a central courtyard surrounded by galleries, is worth a visit. The murals tempt one to linger although some are pretty gruesome. One shows the earth-goddess Thorani washing away the tempter Mara and all his demon followers with water wrung from her hair (see also Thorani Fountain, page 218); another shows the terrible Yomaraja, the King of Hell, inflicting various punishments on the wicked.

The *wiharn,* to the west in the next courtyard, houses a large statue of Buddha some 9.1 metres (30 feet) high, faithfully covered with tiny gold leaf squares. The plinth is highly decorated with golden carvings, coloured porcelain, and glass chips. There are also 163 smaller statues, each dressed with a saffron cloth. The doors are solid teakwood, well carved but not well preserved.

A *bo* or pipal tree grows in the compound. This was raised from a seedling taken, it is said, from the original *bo* tree under which the historical Buddha first attained enlightenment. A priest brought three such seedlings from Ceylon, at the request of King Rama II.

Now walk through the compound of Wat Sraket towards the Golden Mount, past memorial stones and healthy, leafy trees, to the base of the staircase. The climb is not too tiring, as the steps are shallow and, as one ascends, the skyline of Bangkok becomes an eye-level view. Easiest to spot is Wat Sutat and the Giant Swing, then the Marble Temple and the National Assembly Hall. Nearing the top, the sound of Bangkok's traffic diminishes to a dull drone, and the view will inspire any photographer.

Below, the modern concrete buildings of the city are intermingled with colourful temple roofs and *chedi*—grey, white, and gold. Wat Sraket looks surprisingly extensive, with dozens and dozens of old and new Thai-style buildings and monks' quarters. In the distance, like shadows on the horizon, are the Dusit Thani Hotel and numerous water towers. More clearly seen down below is a not-so-pleasant *klong,* bordered by toppling wooden shacks with rusty, corrugated iron roofs. The tinkling temple bells recall attention to the mount. Here at the top are tiny Buddha statues shimmering with gold-leaf squares that pilgrims have pasted on. Fortune sticks are shaken; lotus flowers, gold leaf, and Pepsi-Cola are on sale. To say that people climb up simply "because it is there" would not be far wrong.

The *wat* was built, it seems, for nostalgic reasons as a copy of Wat Phu Kae Thong (Temple of the Golden Mount) in Ayutthaya, the abandoned old capital (see p. 233). King Rama III was the nostalgic soul who ordered the construction to begin, unwisely choosing the site next to Wat Sraket, then a swamp. Inevitably, the building sank. New foundations were built with huge logs driven into the ground but, sadly, they subsided and sank into the swamp in spite of an image of Buddha that had been placed in a hollow in the foundations for "spiritual support." No further work was done until

King Mongkut (Rama IV, 1851–68) ordered a new design of the mount to be built, by which time the old foundations had settled well. The mount slowly grew in size until it was finally completed during the reign of King Chulalongkorn, his son.

Wat Sraket is considered to have the best cremation facilities of any Bangkok *wat.* Traditionally, cremations always took place outside the city walls, and Wat Sraket was the first wat to be built beyond the boundary of Bangkok. Thus, the Golden Mount is used as a memorial, and many inscribed marble plaques can be seen, together with pictures of the deceased.

The Mount is the home of some rare, mummified bodies that are kept in a glass cabinet. One body is of a girl aged about fourteen, and the others are of three old women. Pilgrims place incense and offerings just in front of the cabinet and regard the phenomena as examples of the "transience of life." These bodies were discovered when many coffins were exhumed in order to cremate the remains. These particular four bodies had not yet decomposed and so they have been kept in their present "transient" state for more than forty years.

Lord Curzon and Buddha's teeth—The Mount also houses some of Buddha's teeth, said to be original relics. They were discovered on the Nepalese frontier by an Englishman named William Clacton Pepys. He gave them to Marquess Curzon, then the Viceroy of India. Lord Curzon brought them to Siam in 1899 as a present for King Chulalongkorn (Rama V) when the Viceroy visited Siam on holiday.

In late November the Golden Mount Fair opens, marking the start of a series of temple fairs throughout the city. None is so grand and exciting as at the Golden Mount. The entire building is bathed in a sea of lights so that its outline is visible from afar. Lighted stalls sell novelties and food. Musicians and entertainers amuse the many thousands of visitors.

WAT BENCHAMABOPITR *(The Marble Temple)*—Situated at the intersection of Nakhon Pathom Road and Sri Ayutthaya Road, this temple appears on the back of the 10-*baht* note. Built at the turn of the century of white Italian "Carrara" marble, it is a symmetrical, majestic example of modern Thai architecture that should be near the top of one's list of sights not to be missed in Bangkok. The building is graceful and pleasing with numerous overlapping roofs of golden yellow, Chinese glazed tiles; gables intricately carved and inlaid; windows of stained glass; all simply set among small lawns and shining marble pavements. The interior is equally rich in design and colour but the most inspiring section is undoubtedly the cloister.

The main entrance faces the principal building which is the *bot*. Steps, guarded by two white marble lions, lead up to the magnificently lacquered door. The facing gable (i.e. east side) is carved and inlaid to depict Vishnu riding a *krut* or *garuda*. On the other gables are: south side, the Wheel of the Law; west side, the *Unalom*, a divine symbol representing a lock of Buddha's hair; and on the north side, the *erawan* or three-headed elephant. Tourists are diverted to a side entrance just to the left that leads into the cloister. At this point, however, remove shoes and enter the *bot*.

Inside is an outstandingly beautiful Buddha image, an exact replica of the famous 14th-century Phra Buddha Chinaraj in Wat Phra Sri Ratana Mahathat in Phitsanulok (see p. 343). The walls are of finely stenciled gold and red tapestry, and cross-beams are lacquered in black and gold designs. The whole effect is breathtaking, further enhanced by the gleaming, multicoloured marble floor and stained glass windows. The "altar" is decorated with several small statues (some in glass cases), flowers, candles, and incense. Look, too, for the small statue of King Chulalongkorn, a cabinet containing the Buddhist sutras written on palm leaves, a portrait of King Chulalongkorn as a monk, a Karen hill-tribe drum, and the seat on which the abbot sits to preach.

Return now to the cloister where an interesting collection of fifty-three bronze images of Buddha is kept. Some are original, some are copies. Of particular interest are the large, standing Lop Buri–style image; the image showing Buddha after his forty-day fast, grotesquely emaciated; and the somewhat effeminate walking Buddha in Sukhothai style. The cloisters make a pleasant spot for tired tourists to rest a while. Soft drinks are available from a chest-type refrigerator (donate 2 or 3 *baht* in the box), and almost-tame pigeons come expectantly for food, adding to the peaceful atmosphere. No wonder students come here with their books. The temple kindly provides tables and chairs in the shade.

Leaving by a third doorway, visitors while away more time watching and feeding turtles in the murky canal. In the garden is a *bo* or pipal tree, like the tree at Wat Sraket (see p. 184) belonging to the same family as the tree in India beneath which Buddha meditated and found Enlightenment. This very tree was actually brought from India. The wooden bridge over the canal leads to a small pavilion that houses three enormous drums. Close by is the Song Panuat, a small building once used as a cell by King Chulalongkorn when he was a monk in 1873. This building was moved here from the Grand Palace compound. The interior is decorated with charming murals depicting scenes in the King's life.

WAT TRIMITR *(Temple of the Golden Buddha)*—Located not far from Bangkok (Hualampong) Station in the backstreets at the edge of Chinatown, this *wat* is just off the New Road (Charoen Krung Road) to the right (when coming from the south) from a roundabout with a fountain in the middle. Look for the *chedi* above the rooftops or ask someone. Just say "What try-mitd." It is open 8:30 A.M.–5:30 P.M. daily. Admission free.

The *wat* consists of several large buildings including a fine *bot* with red doors and a crematorium. A driveway, wide enough for tour buses, winds round behind the *bot* to a small chapel reached by ascending a flight of steps to first-floor level. In here, seated upon a pedestal, is the precious image, 5 metres (approximately 16 feet) high, consisting of 5.51 tons of solid gold. It is a brilliant piece of work; the perfect flowing lines, pensive expression, and intricate details make this perhaps the most beautiful Buddha image in Thailand, a priceless work of art. Although it must be over 600 years old it was only discovered, by chance, on May 25, 1953.

Believed to have been cast during the Sukhothai Period (A.D. 1238–1378), the statue was later moved to Ayutthaya. At some time, no one knows when, it was covered with thick plaster to save it from being taken by the Burmese invaders. When Ayutthaya was finally abandoned it was brought to Bangkok, still covered with plaster, placed in a *wat* named "Phya Krai," and forgotten.

Years and years later, this ruined *wat* was torn down to make way for enlargements to the Port of Bangkok. The old Buddha images inside were taken to other *wat* in Bangkok, and a truck delivered one "stucco" image to Wat Trimitr where it remained for twenty more years in a crude shelter in the compound. On that day in May, 1953, it was to have been transferred to a chapel permanently. However, during hoisting and moving, the crane hook broke, and the statue crashed to the ground, damaging the plaster covering. Still no one saw the gold beneath, and the image was left in the open, on the ground in the compound, until the next day. By chance, the night brought violent thunderstorms and torrential rains that spattered mud and dirt from the ground onto the image. In the morning, the abbot went to clean it, and as he scraped away the dirt he spotted gold glittering through the cracks in the plaster. The plaster was soon removed, and this perfect specimen was discovered after more than three centuries. The mind boggles to think how many other forsaken "stucco" images of Buddha really contain statues of solid gold.

OTHER WAT IN BANGKOK—Travellers who enjoy seeking out lesser-known sights are urged to visit the following two *wat* in Bangkok.

Wat Rajapradit—located off Sanam Chai Road with the entrance in Saranrom Lane (opposite the Ministry of Foreign Affairs Offices). This *wat* has very interesting wall paintings inside the *bot,* depicting daily life and festivals in Bangkok during the early 19th century. It was built by King Mongkut (Rama IV) and is fairly small, beautiful, and quiet, a typical Thai *wat* but well kept.

Wat Bovornivet—on Phra Sumein Road facing the old city wall. An inconspicuous *wat* with muted colouring and little of the usual decorative features of Thai *wat.* However, all Thais will have heard the name since this is the very place where the present King entered as a monk in 1956. It was built under the auspices of King Rama III (1824–50) and his son (later King Mongkut) was made the first abbot. He remained so for fourteen years during which time he founded the Dharmayuttika sect of Buddhism, a purer form following the original teachings with none of the legends and Brahmin rites found in other Thai Buddhist sects. The *bot* interior is richly decorated and has some fascinating murals showing foreign life in Bangkok during the mid-19th century. Wat Bovorn School has some 1,500 students from age seven upwards and is recognized as a centre for training teachers and social workers. The *wat* also has a close association with the Mahamakut Buddhist University.

15

MORE BANGKOK SIGHTS AND A WALKING TOUR

Discovering Bangkok

Bangkok is a city of seemingly innumerable sights to excite the senses and stimulate the mind. If the visitor becomes overwhelmed by the glitter of *wat,* he or she might well change the pace by stopping off at the National Museum, a treasure house of Thai antiquity in a particularly tasteful setting.

National museum *(formerly part of the Wang Na Palace)* —The entrance is in Mahathat Road, next to the Thammasat University facing the Phramane Ground. Open 9:00 a.m.–12 noon and 1:00–4:00 p.m. daily except on Saturdays, Mondays, and national holidays. Admission fee is 5 *baht* (25 cents) except on Sundays, when it is free. Currently, there are weekly guided tours of the museum in English starting at 9:30 a.m. on Thursday at no extra charge. This used to be on Fridays, and as the day may be changed again it is advisable to confirm the date and time to avoid disappointment. Photography is not permitted inside the museum; only the exteriors of the buildings may be photographed.

As the National Museum consists of twenty-eight different exhibition halls, it is beyond the scope of a book this length to describe each one fully. The museum

Bronze Buddha head.

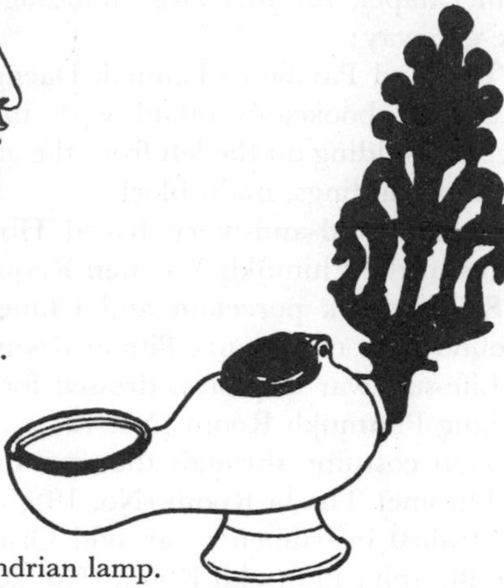

Alexandrian lamp.

houses mainly items of archeological interest and works of art relating principally to the area of Thailand and falling into two main categories, prehistoric and historic, the latter covering works of art dating from the beginning of the Christian era to the present day. Visitors who are especially interested are advised to purchase the forty-page, well-illustrated, official guide to the museum, which includes a large map too, on sale at the small pavilion just inside the entrance to the right. It costs 15 *baht* (75 cents). Incidentally, this pavilion formerly stood in the grounds of the palace of King Vajiravudh (Rama VI), Sanam Chan, at Nakhon Pathom. (Also on sale are colour slides, postcards, and other booklets published by the Fine Arts Department.)

For a brief tour the following are of particular interest:

Phra Buddha Sihing—a smiling Buddha *circa* 13th century, probably Ceylonese. Considered the finest piece of Buddhist art in Thailand. Housed in the Buddhaisawan Chapel, the first large building on the right from the gateway;

The Red Pavilion (Tamnak Daeng) and chair, cabinets, and bookcases inlaid with mother-of-pearl; the second building on the left from the gateway; and, in the central buildings, main block;

Ornate gold-and-ivory Royal Howdahs and palanquins in the Phimukh Montien Room (No. 5);

Sawank'alok porcelain and Chinese pottery, on the ground floor of Vasanta Piman Room (No. 8);

Life-size war elephant, dressed for battle, in the Prisadang Phumukh Room (No. 12);

Thai costume through the ages on the ground floor of Phromet Thada Room (No. 18);

Musical instruments—an odd Oriental assortment in the Burapha Phimukh Room (No. 20);

Royal ceremonial funeral coaches weighing up to twenty tons (no brakes) in a separate storage house situated east of the main complex of buildings (No. 22).

WANG NA PALACE AND THE SECOND KING—The National Museum was originally part of the palace for the Second King or Prince Successor and was built in 1782. The Second King was always a close relative to the King, such as a brother, appointed by the King to aid him. This usually meant dealing with mundane administrative affairs and simply occupying the Wang Na Palace, especially placed in front of the King's palace as a kind of barricade to afford the King extra security. The office was abolished in 1884 by King Chulalongkorn (Rama V), upon the death of the Prince Successor, Phra Pin Klao, the fourth Prince Successor to occupy Wang

Na Palace. The position had caused problems of protocol and raised anomalies in the laws of succession. King Chulalongkorn then ordered three of the buildings to be made into a museum. The other buildings were given to the museum in 1926.

The attractively decorated, colourful old buildings, dotted around the lawns, make the perfect setting for the classical Thai dancing show (see p. 96).

NATIONAL THEATRE *(Silpakorn Theatre)*—Located next to the National Museum at the north end of the Phramane Ground, the National Theatre was rebuilt in the 1960's, following a fire which razed the original building. It is air-conditioned and contains, besides an auditorium, halls for the exhibition of art works. The whole establishment is run by the Ministry of Fine Arts. Forthcoming programmes, which include all forms of classical Thai dance and drama, are published in the English-language Bangkok newspapers. Helpful synopses of the plots are sold at the theatre at each performance.

MONUMENT OF DEMOCRACY—Situated at the roundabout half-way along Rajdamnern Avenue, the monument consists of four tall concrete "wings" around a bowl, topped by a rectangular object said to contain the "Articles of the Constitution." It was actually erected in 1933 by the new military regime to commemorate the coup d'état of the previous year, when the system of government was changed from absolute monarchy to constitutional monarchy.

VICTORY MONUMENT—This tall stone obelisk at a roundabout, close to the city centre along the Paholyothin Road, has a statue of a soldier on each of the four sides at the base. This monument contains the ashes of soldiers who died during the Indo-China war, and is seen on the way from the airport.

WEEKEND MARKET *(Sanam Luang)*—This is held from the early morning of Saturday until dusk on Sunday, every weekend, on the Phramane Ground.

The entire area is covered with stalls under umbriferous canvas roofs and with people, people everywhere. The market is arranged in sections. One should not miss:

The exotic display of flowers and plants for sale along the *klong* to the east of the main market area;

The pet section in the centre, a menagerie of fish, birds, snakes, and various animals, including the most popular, the gibbon, fighting cocks, fighting fish, and flying squirrels;

The miscellaneous section selling everything (but nothing valuable), useful and useless, from transistor radios to stuffed animals and cheap souvenirs.

The other sections sell food and fruits which are as colourful as the flowers, cold drinks, household goods, clothing and material (but not Thai silk), shoes, jewellery, records, and toys. Between the stalls here and there, toothless women with betel-nut-stained lips cook various delicacies on charcoal braziers, oblivious to the heat and bustle.

For the tourist, it is a window to life in Bangkok, an entertaining experience. Beware of pickpockets and always bargain hard.

OTHER LOCAL MARKETS IN BANGKOK—If one is unlucky enough to miss the Weekend Market there are a number of others that a tourist will find interesting and colourful. Strolling around markets is a pleasant way to learn about the local way of life and gain an idea of the general standard of living. Anyway, the exhaustive bargaining is a treat to watch. Most Bangkok housewives try to be at the market between 11:00 A.M. and 3:00 P.M. By 11:00 A.M. the fresh produce should have arrived from the wholesale market (the Floating Market in Thon Buri), and the fresh fish should have arrived from the Gulf of Siam.

Bangkrak Market—situated along the New Road (Charoen Kung Road) about ten minutes' walk south from the main Bangkok Post Office.

This is a large, popular market where all kinds of food, spices, and fruit are sold, as well as general household goods. In particular, one can find a large selection of cut flowers, including orchids that are grown in nurseries in Thon Buri and are bought to be used as offerings in the temples or spirit houses.

Flower Market—located across a canal opposite Thevet Market in the Thevet District by the Chao Phya River.

If one is interested in flowers, hours can be spent here. Shops and stalls sell tropical plants and flowers of all kinds, especially jasmine, roses, and orchids, along a road shaded by flame trees. Many of these dealers also have stalls at the Weekend Market.

Pratunam Market—located along Klong Saen Saep not far from the Erawan and President Hotels, this is an excellent market to visit as one can also combine it with a visit to the adjacent modern shopping centres of Rajprasong and Gaysorn.

At this market there is really everything: electrical goods, fruit, fish, rice, spices, clothing, and so on. Pratunam is particularly noted for good eating at rock-bottom prices. By night, it is packed with local people who come after a hard day's work in the city. The tables of restaurants spill out across the pavement, and stalls offer all manner of Thai and Chinese food. Noodle dishes are supposed to be the best choice. People drink and buskers sing for their suppers. Pratunam is often referred to as the "Poor Man's Nightclub." Nearby is another, similar, all-night eating area at Makkasan Circle.

Sam Yan Market—off Rama IV Road, is one of Bangkok's largest markets, selling a wide variety of food and general merchandise.

Sri Yan Market—along Nakhon Chaisri Road is similar but smaller.

Bangkok has dozens of other markets scattered throughout the city. In fact, by walking in any direction for just a few minutes from any hotel, one is bound to find a market.

CHINATOWN *(including the "Thieves' Market")*—Mainly centred around Yawaraj Road, a broad thoroughfare extending west from the New Road, by Wat Trimitr.

The Chinese predicament—Chinese people inhabited what is now Thailand long before the Thais arrived. The Chinese first settled along the coast, presumably trading. Since the 17th century Thailand has suffered from a shortage of labour. Slavery flourished, and seasonal workers came from the poor regions of Khorat. This was not enough, so the Thais encouraged the immigration of Chinese coolies too. King Mongkut (Rama IV, 1851–68) also sought Chinese immigrants to stimulate the economy by using their trading skills. The result was too successful. The Chinese took control of the agricultural markets, tin mining, rubber plantations, and importing. They ran the shops and restaurants and, as their wealth grew, became more influential in public affairs. Their sagacity brought resentment, and when King Chulalongkorn (Rama V) came to the throne (1868–1910), there was a reversal of government policy and further immigration of Chinese was curbed.

Looking back, the curb was inevitable; the Chinese

had no intention of integrating into Thai society. They set up their own schools, shopping areas, newspapers, and so on, and in Bangkok the area around Yawaraj Road became a ghetto, cited by the Thais as "a den of iniquity, notorious for opium and prostitution." King Chulalongkorn took action to try to confine the Chinese community since its area appeared to be spreading towards the Grand Palace. The King built Wang Burapha, a palace for his younger brother Prince Bhanuband, between Chinatown and the Grand Palace area, to act as a kind of barricade. Ironically, the Prince's descendants sold it, and it is now owned by Chinese, converted to a shopping centre with cinemas, nightclubs, and bath-houses. Well over one million Chinese are resident in Thailand today. Many still keep to themselves, using their own language in private but speaking Thai in public.

Bangkok's Chinatown is fairly extensive. The only way to see it properly is to go on foot. It comprises various sections or streets that each specialise in one type of merchandise, briefly as follows:

Thieves' Market (Nakhon Kasem)—located between the New Road (Charoen Krung Road) and Yawaraj Road near the Grand Cinema.

Once this area was famous for antiques at low prices. These days, one must be really determined to bargain hard and must have some knowledge of antiques in order to recognize the fakes. Antique and curio shops are untidily packed with vases, statues, and objets d'art. Intermingled with the antique shops are restaurants and shops selling tools, kitchen equipment, clothing, and so on. The author found few goods of high quality. Traffic here creates too much dirt, leaving little to attract tourists.

Wang Burapha—is situated just to the east and slightly

south, next to the "Thieves' Market" area. A few bookshops here are worth a visit.

Phahurat Road—directly south of "Wang Burapha," is a market area for material, ribbons, lace, etc. It virtually extends into the "Wang Burapha" square.

Rajawongse Road—stretching from the New Road to the Chao Phya River. Mostly warehouses dealing in materials and clothing. Indian quarter. Unattractive, not worth visiting.

Songwad Road—warehouses for rice, flour, etc.

Sampeng Lane—runs parallel to and south of Yawaraj Road, from Wat Pratuna Kongka as far as Klong Ong-ang. This is the best part of Chinatown. All kinds of goods are sold here, especially gold and silver trinkets. Recommended for inexpensive shopping and for eating at the local Chinese/Thai cheap restaurants. Colourful and busy.

Maha Phrutharam Road—opposite Bangkok (Hualampong) Station. Plumbing goods and tiles.

Yawaraj Road—the home of big trading concerns. Very busy, noisy, wide road. Best seen at night.

New Road (Charoen Krung Road)—many electrical goods, jewellery shops, restaurants, herbal chemists, sweet shops, dentists, etc.

Maha Chai Road—going north from New Road. Wicker wares.

Bamrung Muang Road—furniture.

Statue of King Rama VI—Situated at the roundabout called Saladaeng Circle at the east end of Silom Road, opposite the Dusit Thani Hotel.

Educated in England, King Rama VI or "Vajiravudh" ruled from 1910 until 1925 when he died at the age of forty-six. Among his many achievements are: the establishment of Chulalongkorn University (Thailand's

14. Royal Pavilion, Bang Pa-In Summer Palace.

15. Logging elephants in a northern forest.

16. Heavily laden rice barge on a rural *klong*.

17. Hua Hin Beach.

18. Floating houses on Yom River, Phitsanulok.

19. A "sea gypsies" village, Phuket.

20. The Royal Chapel of the Emerald Buddha, Bangkok, where the sacred jasper image is enthroned.

21. National Museum, Bangkok.

22. Phra Mongkol Bopit, Ayutthaya, one of the world's largest seated Buddha images.

23. Buddha images in the ruins of Wat Yai Chai Mongkol, Ayutthaya.

24. Sacred three-spired pagoda (Prang Sam Yod), Lop Buri, said to be a Buddhist sanctuary built by 3rd-century Khmer craftsmen.

25. Ruins at Ayutthaya.

first) in memory of his father; the setting up of Thailand's Boy Scouts' organization; promulgating a law on compulsory education; and translating many of Shakespeare's works and other plays into Thai. He was also instrumental in Thailand's joining the Allies in 1917. The many garlands of flowers testify the respect the Thais have for this august late King. The statue is in bronze.

LUMPINI PARK—The above-mentioned statue stands in front of the main entrance to this park.

Here, one can find welcome shade and a cool breeze under the umbrella-like trees, but, unfortunately, one cannot escape completely from the noise of Bangkok's traffic. A couple of roads even pass through the park. A stroll around the grounds will reveal more than just trees and grass. The park has an orchestra bowl for open-air concerts, crazy golf, lakes, a Thai-style lakeside restaurant overlooking lovely pink and red water lilies, a clock tower like a Chinese pagoda, football pitches, and Bangkok's only floating restaurant, Kinareenava (see "Western-style and Foreign Restaurants," p. 79). One might also observe people making charcoal and labourers on their haunches cutting the grass with sickles. At night, this is a favourite spot for lovers.

SNAKE FARM—The snake farm belongs to the Science Division of the Thai Red Cross. Formerly called the Pasteur Institute, now known as Queen Saovabha Memorial Institute, it is situated along Rama IV Road, close to the Chulalongkorn Hospital. One should visit either at 2:00 P.M. on Mondays when the snakes are fed, or at 10:00 A.M. on Thursday when the venom is extracted. At other times, the snakes stay in the shade of their dome-shaped "homes" and hardly move. Closed

Saturday, Sundays, and on national holidays. A donation of 5 *baht* is asked for, in lieu of an admission fee.

The Pasteur Institute was founded by King Rama VI in 1913. In 1922 it was moved to the Chulalongkorn Hospital, and the Snake Farm opened in 1923 with its new name in memory of King Rama VI's mother. Its function is to produce vaccine and serum for the treatment of snake bites. Watching the process has a fearful fascination.

The deadly snakes are brought live to this institute, and the catchers are paid according to the size and type of each snake. They are kept in three round enclosures, safely entrapped by a circle of water and smooth concrete walls. One enclosure contains king cobras *(Naja hannah)* which can grow to over twelve feet in length; another contains cobras *(Naja naja)*; and the third holds specimens of banded krait *(Bungarus fasciatus)*, a yellow-and-black-banded snake. These are considered the most dangerous in Thailand, though there are many other poisonous and non-poisonous snakes too. Two rooms contain exhibits of other snakes and display information about the snakes in Thailand.

The king cobras and banded krait are snake-eaters and, because of the difficulty in obtaining suitable live food, they have to be force fed by thrusting pieces of meat down their throats with tongs. At feeding time, the reptile keepers enter the enclosure and wander around among the deadly snakes, seemingly casually. With amazing skill and confidence one man will pick up the slithery creatures, one at a time, holding the jaws open while his assistant feeds each snake with meat, afterwards nonchalantly throwing it into the water where it slinks away.

Making Antivenin Serums—Similarly, the snakes have to be handled to extract the venom, a translucent yellow, viscid liquid secreted through two fangs. This venom is dried to form crystals that can be dissolved in water later when required. The deadly venom liquid is injected, in small specific doses, into horses. Over a period of six to eight months, the horses build up an immunity to a large amount of the poison. Serum is then produced from the blood of these immunized horses. This is the antivenin which can neutralize the effects of a snake bite, but it is only effective if the antivenin is produced from the same type of snake that caused the bite. Thus a cobra serum would be useless in treating a bite from a snake other than a cobra; viper serum treats only viper-bite cases, and so on. At this institute the antivenin serums are also extracted from the Russell's viper (*Vipera russelli*), Malayan pit viper (*Ancistrodon rhodostoma*), and from the green pit viper (*Trimeresurus popeorum*), making six different serums in all.

Venom is extracted from each snake every two weeks. When a snake is ready to be "milked," its poison glands bulge just behind the eyes. In the natural state, the snake venom serves the purpose of killing the prey and assisting digestion. Cobras are considered to be the most dangerous; the victim dies within one to six hours unless treated quickly. However, king cobras produce more venom and therefore could be considered more deadly as the effects of a bite would be even quicker. There is actually no case of a king cobra bite on record in Thailand, so it is the cobras that are feared most. From time to time, nests of cobras are found in Bangkok gardens. They love damp places.

Snake-Bite Treatment—It is unlikely that a tourist in Thailand will have any occasion to think about snake bites and their effects. However, it does no harm to store away some facts on the subject.

If the snake is poisonous a bite will leave two fang

marks and the effects will occur within ten minutes. A non-poisonous bite will leave a row of teeth marks. If bitten, the best course of action is to catch the snake or at least be able to identify it. If it is thought to be poisonous, a tourniquet should be applied immediately to the limb above the bite and released every five minutes. Drink no alcohol. Antivenin serums are distributed to all hospitals and health centres throughout Thailand so that snakebite cases, wherever they are, can be treated very quickly. (In Bangkok go to the Chulalongkorn Hospital, and in Thon Buri go to Shirira Hospital. They are open twenty-four hours a day and have specialist doctors who can identify the type of snake from the symptoms of the poisoning in case the patient does not know.) Cauterization or cutting around the wound to squeeze out the poison are not recommended unless you are lost in the jungle. Besides, the bite may be only mildly poisonous or even harmless.

There is really no need to worry about being bitten by a snake if you take a few simple precautions:

1. Do not move stones or rocks.
2. Do not walk in slippers through grassy places in the evening, or wander off the street in the dark.
3. Avoid passing under dense, shady trees.

Snakes are not aggressive by nature and will never attack a human being unless provoked. They become more active at night.

CHULALONGKORN UNIVERSITY—Situated between the Phaya Thai Road and Henry Dunant Road, the university is next to the Snake Farm, near the Royal Sports Club, which was formerly the School of Civil Servants. In 1916 King Vajiravudh (Rama VI) raised its status to that of a university and renamed it in memory of his father, King Chulalongkorn. Thus it became Thailand's first university. The buildings are grand, representing some fine Thai-style modern architecture. The university has been expanded over the years and now has eight faculties and two affiliated institutes, namely the SEATO Graduate School of Engineering and the Department of Science's Chemical Institute. Both men and women are admitted.

ROYAL BANGKOK SPORTS CLUB—Horse and pony racing take place every Saturday and on some holidays at this club, situated along the east side of Henry Dunant Road. Betting is by totalisator. Bookmakers are illegal. There is a nominal entrance fee.

DUSIT ZOO—Locally called *Kao Din*, which means "Earth Mounds," the zoo is very close to the Marble Temple, along Rama V Road, directly opposite the gateway to Chit Lada Palace, the present residence of the King and his family. This palace is well guarded and surrounded by a moat. Tourists are not admitted.

Admission to the zoo costs 3 *baht* for adults, 2 *baht* for children, plus 1 *baht* for a still camera and 5 *baht* for a cine camera. It is open to visitors every day, even on national holidays, from 7:00 A.M. to 6:00 P.M.

The zoo is unfortunately rather smelly. It contains almost entirely tropical animals, birds, and reptiles found in Asia. Of particular interest is the King's white elephant—a most rare creature—which is not actually white but has two distinguishing features: a soft voice instead of a harsh, trumpeting one, and a very sensitive disposition, hence the broken tusks. In Thai it is called *phra savet aduldejpahana*. The only one known to exist in Thailand, the white elephant is regarded as sacred by Thai Buddhists who believe it to be one of the reincarnations of Lord Buddha. Perhaps this would account for the many monks to be seen strolling in the grounds.

Other rare creatures include a clouded leopard and a banded linsang (like a civet). Both of these animals are on the verge of extinction.

In the middle of the zoo park is a picturesque boating lake, from which there is a fine view of the *National Assembly Hall,* the white-domed building to the West.

NATIONAL ASSEMBLY HALL, Phratenang Anantasamakomb—Situated at the northern end of the broad Rajdamnern Nok Avenue, the building is in the Italian Renaissance style, extravagantly constructed of white marble. Costing $2.5 million, it was designed and built by Italians as a marble throne hall by the order of King Chulalongkorn in 1907 but was not completed until 1915, during the reign of King Rama VI. Since the revolution in 1932, this marble throne hall has been used as the National Assembly Hall.

The interior is brilliantly decorated with coloured marble and murals showing the history of Bangkok. Tourists can sometimes obtain admission by personal arrangement with the officials at the entrance.

THE EQUESTRIAN STATUE—In front of the National Assembly Hall is a large statue of King Chulalongkorn on a horse. King from 1868* until 1910, he was one of the best rulers in the history of Thailand. Anna Leonowens, the English governess made famous through the film "The King and I," was his teacher for several years.

King Chulalongkorn began the modernization of Thailand but he still preferred the old family system

* Sri Suriyawongse acted as Chief Minister from 1868 untii 1882, as Chulalongkorn was only 15 years old when he succeeded King Mongkut. King Chulalongkorn therefore ruled as absolute monarch only from the age of 29.

of polygamy, fathering seventy-seven children himself. He declared freedom of religion and abolished slavery, among his many reforms.

SUAN PAKKAD PALACE AND LACQUER PAVILION—The address is 352 Sri Ayutthaya Road. Open on Saturdays, Sundays, Tuesdays, and Thursdays from 9:00 A.M.–12 noon and 2:00–4:00 P.M. In lieu of an admission fee, a donation of 30 *baht* ($1.50) is requested in aid of a fund to promote fine arts.

The palace consists of a group of six old houses taken from other sites and built on high stilts. Their arrangement enables visitors to pass through each one at leisure to view the priceless collection of paintings, wood-carvings, interesting Siamese furniture dating from the 17th century, weapons, shields, votive tablets, statues, screens, lacquered cabinets, porcelain, and so on. Even if one is not an expert on antiques, it is a fascinating place to visit for its variety and presentation, including such things as a furnished guest room and furnished reception room with no modern touches except for the electric lighting.

Furthermore, there is a most charming and peaceful garden with broad lawns, ponds filled with lotus and waterlilies, and rare, shade-loving plants. Here is the "pièce de résistance," the beautiful Lacquer Pavilion, a masterpiece of Siamese art and architecture. This building used to be at Wat Ban Kling, on the Chao Phya riverside between Ayutthaya and Bang Pa-In. The late Prince Chumbhot had the pavilion transported, re-erected, and restored in this garden as a present for the Princess on the occasion of her fiftieth birthday.

The exact history of this building is obscure but it appears to date from the 17th century and to have been re-assembled from two dilapidated buildings, a *ho trai* (library for storing religious manuscripts), and a *ho khien* (a room with painted murals). The walls are carved on one side with reliefs of a legendary forest named Himavanta and on the other side are decorated with scenes depicting the life of Buddha and the *Ramakien,* produced from gold leaf on black lacquer. A magnificently bound book containing dozens of photographs entitled *The Lacquer Pavilion at Suan Pakkad Palace* is on sale at the office. This gives a most detailed account of the history and murals of this unique piece of architecture.

Another part of the palace is the private residence of Princess Chumbhot of Nagara Svarga, the owner of Wang Takrai, the hill resort described on page 224.

JIM THOMPSON'S THAI HOUSE—The address is 6 Soi Kasemsan No. 2, located down a side street (watch for signposts in English), just opposite the National Stadium, near the Grand Hotel. Open 9:00 A.M.–12 noon, Mondays and Thursdays only. A donation of 25 *baht* ($1.25) per person is requested in lieu of an entrance fee. Proceeds go to the School for the Blind.

James Thompson was an American who became so enraptured by Thailand that he stayed, living frugally in rented properties. Soon he discovered Thai silk and with his business acumen built up a world-famous industry. In other words, he was virtually responsible for re-establishing the art of Thai silk weaving and for turning it into a major export commodity. After about ten years, he built his own house—this one—by combining and reconstructing six old teak houses into one spacious mansion and adding decorative pieces from old palaces, shops, and other houses. The result is a unique and magnificient residence that has attracted newspaper and magazine reporters, and visitors from all over the world.

At first sight one notices that the house has no glass

windows, only shutters. Mr. Thompson preferred a gentle breeze to air-conditioning. Furthermore, he reversed the walls so that the ancient carvings around the windows face outwards. Inside, the walls are covered with beautiful wood paneling and with paintings. Jim Thompson was not only a clever businessman and capable architect but also a keen collector of antiques and objets d'art that he picked up during frequent journeys around the Far East. The collection of beautiful and interesting objects seems endless—statues of Buddha from Burma, Thailand, Cambodia, and Indonesia, some bronze, some stone, some wood, stucco, terra-cotta, and so on; paintings—said to be the largest collection of religious paintings in Thailand (there are some interesting paintings on cotton hung on the stairway); old bookcases, porcelain, chests, screens, glassware—in every corner there is something to catch the eye. From the lofty drawing room the visitor enjoys a lovely view across a lush garden to a *klong* where small boats drift and children play. On the opposite bank are the silk weavers, kept busy by the constant demands of tourists, thanks to Jim Thompson.

Mr. Thompson disappeared mysteriously while on a trip to Malaysia some years ago. His home, which he willed with its contents to the Siam Society, is still maintained and is open for anyone to enjoy as he would have wished. Now five or more years have passed since his disappearance.

A Walking Tour in Bangkok *(approximately 2½ kilometres or 1½ miles)*

Strolling around the city, one has time to stop and look at little sights that would be missed from a sightseeing-bus window. Allow a whole morning or whole afternoon for this walk.

Start from the Royal Hotel which faces the lovely

tree-edged Phramane Ground, the site of the Weekend Market (see p. 192–6), and go across the bridge over the *klong* directly opposite the hotel entrance. Just to the left is the Thorani Fountain, a monument erected by Queen Saovabha representing Thorani, the earth-goddess. According to a Buddhist legend, the water wrung from Thorani's hair washed away the tempter Mara and all his followers while Lord Buddha was meditating. Devout Thais come regularly to place garlands of flowers around the statue.

A little beyond this monument, just to the right, is a row of stalls in the shade of the trees. (The large building behind is the Ministry of Justice.) Walk along here and browse among the books, postage stamps, street hawkers, and fortune tellers seriously at work in the midst of little, huddled audiences.

Next, cross over the road and go right along the pavement that encircles the Phramane Ground and walk for about five minutes in the partial shade of the trees. One will see a war memorial in the form of a white *chedi* on a road island. This contains ashes of some of the Thai soldiers who died during the First World War while fighting in Europe. When adjacent to the pedestrian crossing, next to a path that goes lengthwise through the middle of the Phramane Ground, stop for a moment and take a look at the magnificent skyline to the left, across the green grounds. In the distance the tall *chedi,* golden spires, and colourful glazed-tile roofs of the Royal Palace and The Emerald Buddha Temple glisten above the whitewashed walls of the palace. This is one of Bangkok's loveliest scenes.

On the other side of the road are some grand buildings in the classical Thai style of architecture. The newer one on the right hand side is the National or Silpakorn Theatre (see p. 195), behind which is the School of

Dramatic Arts, run by the Fine Arts Department. Next to the National Theatre is a more decorative group of older buildings. These constitute the National Museum (see p. 192). It has green signboards with gold lettering over the gateway.

After coming out of the museum, turn right and continue walking along this pavement, going past the enormous green-roofed building, The University of Thammasat (formerly called the University of Moral and Political Sciences). Founded in 1933, this is the second university to have come into existence in Thailand. It is surrounded by a rather unusual fence that has concrete pillars topped by "spirit-house-style" lanterns. At the first turning to the right—Phra Chan Road—cross over to the typically Thai-style gateway in the very thick white wall and go through. This is Wat Mahathad (see p. 177). Come out on to the main road again—Mahathad Road, which bounds the Phramane Ground—and turn right, walking past a very extensive, deep-peach-coloured building on the right. It is the Royal Institute, still shown on many maps as the National Library, which it used to be. The style of this building is Cambodian; originally it served as a pavilion from which royalty and their guests could view ceremonies on the Phramane Ground. In 1916 it became the National Library, which it remained for fifty years until the library was moved to its present home in Samsen Road. The Royal Institute houses old bookcases and stone tablets relating to the development of the Thai script. Just beyond this long building is the Prince Damrong Rajanubhab Memorial Library, which houses Prince Damrong's personal collection of books, photographs, and various possessions. Prince Damrong Rajanubhab (1864–1943) was a son of King Rama IV, and this library was built in memory of the prince's services.

Continuing along the Mahathad Road, the next building on the right is the Ministry of Fine Arts or simply Fine Arts Department, behind which is the University of Fine Arts which covers the study of painting, sculpture, Thai architecture, archaeology, and decorative art. If you are interested, walk in; there is often an exhibition of works.

Looking straight ahead from the Mahathad Road (southwest of the Phramane Ground) is the main entrance to the Grand Palace (see p. 167) just across the Phra Lan Road. Walk down the drive, which has a line of beautifully trimmed, cone-shaped trees on either side, to the next gateway, where you buy your entrance ticket.

Next, take the path to the left (if one is facing the gateway) off this drive, which has buildings with wooden shutters on both sides. A little way along is a small Thai-style restaurant where one can choose a soft drink from a glass-fronted refrigerator. At the end of this path is an ornate little gateway that has golden decorations on the eaves of a tiered roof. This leads into Wat Phra Keo or The Emerald Buddha temple (see p. 170).

Coming out of the main entrance one can see a large government building on the other side of the road (Sanam Chai Road). Around the building is a collection of old cannons on the lawns. This is the Ministry of Defence. Next to it is another large government building, the Ministry of Foreign Affairs. To the left of the Ministry of Defence building, across the road behind the petrol station, is the Lak Muang, a sanctuary for the guardian spirit of the city. It is a small building with a spire, decorated with stucco. (Lak Muang shrines can be found in several other cities in Thailand as well as in other Asian countries.)

In front of the Lak Muang there are always crowds of Bangkokians, food and ice-cream vendors, fortune tellers, and lottery-ticket stalls. Also, little birds in tiny bamboo cages are waiting for someone to pay their captors a few *baht* for their release. Some Buddhists believe that buying the birds' freedom is a way of gaining "merit," without realizing that it will also encourage more people to catch more birds. This is one practice Buddhism can do without.

At this point, one can return to the Royal Hotel, the starting point of the walk, by strolling along the east side of the Phramane Ground. Alternatively, if one has the energy, turn right on coming out of Wat Phra Keo and walk along the pavement next to the high temple and palace walls. Continue as far as the small roundabout where four roads converge (about five minutes' walk). There, on the opposite right-hand corner, is Wat Po, or the Temple of the Reclining Buddha (see p. 174). The entrance is a little way along the turning on the right named Soi Wat Po. After walking around this *wat,* take a taxi back to your hotel. If you return to your starting point at the Royal Hotel the taxi will cost between 5 and 10 *baht* (25–50 cents) depending on your bargaining powers. The ride to other hotels may be 10 or 15 *baht,* according to the distance.

16

DAY EXCURSIONS FROM BANGKOK

Places underlined on the map are described in the appropriate chapters dealing with the Southern Peninsula, the Southeast, and the Northeast regions. Although a day excursion to them is possible, it would be advisable to make an overnight stay because of time and distance. Kanchanaburi would also come into this category but, as yet, there are only local-style hotels available. Therefore, most foreign tourists prefer to visit Kanchanaburi, usually combining this trip with a quick look at Nakhon Pathom, in one long day.

The scenery outside Bangkok is full of interest. No tourist should miss seeing the farming and village life up-country where nothing much has changed for centuries, not to mention the historical towns and archeological sites that are as important as Bangkok itself.

Nakhon Nayok

Some 140 kilometres (87 miles) northeast of Bangkok: take Highway 1 (the Paholyothin Road) past Don Muang Airport to Hin Kong at the 94-kilometre mark, then turn right onto Highway 33 (the Aranya Prathet Road) and, before reaching Nakhon Nayok at the 43-

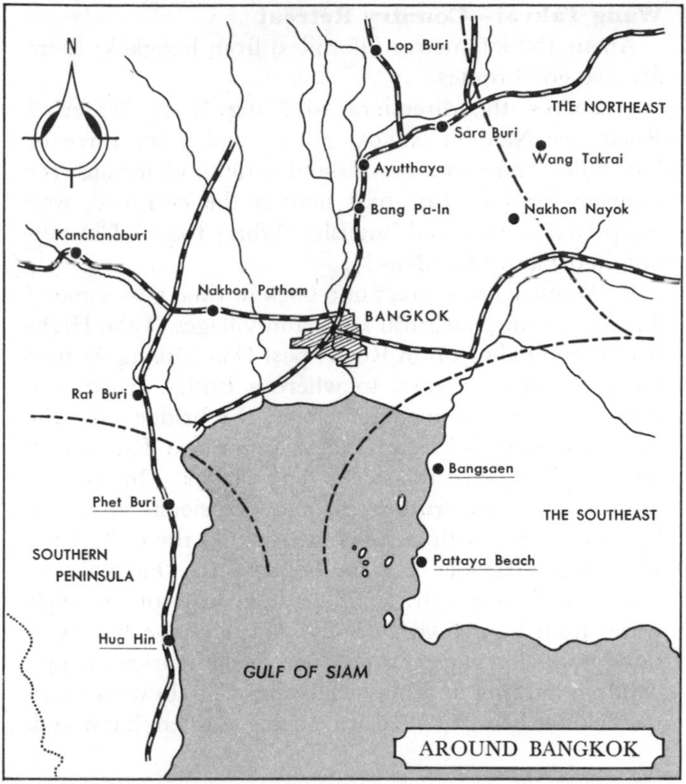

kilometre mark, turn left. This is the Salika Waterfall Road. After 11 kilometres there is a right turn onto the Nang Rong Waterfall Road.

These two lovely waterfalls and the wild surrounding scenery draw visitors from Bangkok in large numbers at the weekends. The Thais love to bathe in the cool streams and pools. The waterfalls may be dry, however, from January until August. You can combine a visit here with an excursion to Wang Takrai.

Wang Takrai—Country Retreat

About 150 kilometres (95 miles) from Bangkok: there are two good routes.

1. Follow the directions to Nang Rong Waterfall Road (see Nakhon Nayok, above) and, after three or four miles, come to a road-island with an enormous tree growing from it. Just past here is the entrance, well signposted in Thai and English: "Wang Takrai, Chumbhot, and Pantib Gardens."

2. Another route takes one back in time past some of Thailand's unspoilt rural *klong* and villages. Take Highway 1 (the Paholyothin Road) past Don Muang Airport for about twenty miles to where a bridge crosses the Rangsit Canal. Immediately over the bridge take the road right, parallel to this canal. It goes via Tanya Buri and Ongarak directly to Nakhon Nayok. On the left are paddy fields, fruit trees, and occasional groves of bamboo dotted with farmers' houses. On the right is the *klong* where people live on houseboats. One will see plenty to photograph: small paddle boats plying their wares from houseboat to houseboat; massive barges in slow procession shipping produce to the market; happy children bathing and playing; water buffalo working in the fields or being washed; rice being planted, harvested,

Barges in procession.

or threshed according to the season; saffron-robed monks wandering around the rural *wat,* and so on. Nothing has been laid on for tourists, who are met only with innocent smiles and affectionate curiosity—no hawkers with temple bells, postcards, and the like. After Bangkok, it is blissfully peaceful. Soon, in the distant haze one can distinguish hills, sometimes purple, sometimes greenish, sometimes touching the scudding white clouds.

Drive through the provincial town of Nakhon Nayok and turn left into the Salika Waterfall Road, leading to the Nang Rong Waterfall Road on the right, which is well signposted for Wang Takrai.

Wang Takrai is open at all times.

Entrance Fee: car 10 *baht* (50 cents) plus 5 *baht* per person.

This is a landscaped estate of about 150 acres situated at the foothills of the Khao Yai mountain range, nestling in a steep valley hanging with lush jungle. Gracious lawns and gardens have been cleverly landscaped along each side of the rushing mountain stream to complement the natural backdrop of vegetation. The estate belongs to Princess Chumbhot, a remarkable lady in her sixties who swims, skis, climbs mountains, and still finds time to plan and improve this beautiful estate that twenty years ago was virgin forest. At that time there was not even a road to Wang Takrai and the Princess, with her husband, used to explore the region on foot along tracks through the jungle where only wild bears, deer, and gibbons had passed before.

Now, Wang Takrai bears the title "Botanical Garden." Strange and wonderful flowers, shrubs, and trees have been brought here from India, Australia, South America, England, Israel, and neighboring Southeast Asian countries. In 1965 the laboriously tended estate was devastated in just four hours by a flash flood. This is a rare phenomenon notorious in the desert areas of the American Southwest where it happens in minutes. In Thailand torrential rain can fall at the rate of two inches an hour and when this happened at Wang Takrai the torrent channelled its way down the mountains into the narrow valley, forming a rushing wall backed by thousands of tons of water. It crashed through the valley, ripping out trees, hurtling rocks and boulders across the lawns and gardens. Within a few years the gardens were restored, and now no one could possibly guess that such a disaster ever occurred here. Precautions have been taken to effect a controlled water course to save the gardens in the case of a similar flood.

TUBING—Wang Takrai is a lovely spot for a picnic or romantic stroll but more active folk may like to try a new sport, invented here by Princess Chumbhot—simply shooting the rapids on a car inner tube. It is very thrilling, though one must be a good swimmer and expect a few scrapes and bruises. There are several sections in three streams for beginners or experts. For a fifteen-minute ride, one must walk upstream for ninety minutes, so you can imagine the speed of the return trip! An inner tube can be rented for a small sum.

ACCOMMODATION AT WANG TAKRAI—Wooden bungalows are available for rent. Reservations must be made at Suan Pakkad Palace, 352 Sri Ayutthaya Road, Bangkok, tel: 70410.

Other facilities—include changing rooms, picnic tables, and a restaurant serving Thai dishes at weekends.

Most noticeable at Wang Takrai is a total absence of litter except in the rubbish bins. Unfortunately, many of Thailand's other beauty spots are sadly spoilt with the remains of picnics.

Ayutthaya and Bang Pa-In

North of Bangkok 88 kilometres (55 miles): take Highway 1 (the Paholyothin Road). Bang Pa-In is off to the left of the 52-kilometre mark. Continuing along Highway 1 to the 66-kilometre mark is another turning left, to Ayutthaya. The drive passes through rich, agricultural areas of the central plain. The northern railway route from Hualampong Station stops at Bang Pa-In and Ayutthaya, taking just under two hours. One should hire a taxi on arrival. Alternatively, there is a regular boat service, though slow, up the Chao Phya River. This is worthwhile one way but you should leave about 5:00 A.M. It is a fascinating journey, as the river is lined with houses, and one can observe people beginning their daily life. One will also pass through a bird sanctuary and lovely jungle growth before arriving in Bang Pa-In at about 10:30 A.M. or at Ayutthaya some thirty minutes later.

Ayutthaya was the capital of Thailand for more than 400 years and, combined with Bang Pa-In, makes a full day of sightseeing that touches the core of Thailand's history and culture. It was founded by King U Thong in 1350 after the Thais had been driven from the north. In the Ayutthaya period, 1350–1767, no less than thirty-three kings reigned over the kingdom. (Many of them were murdered.) The city became one of the most prosperous trading centres in Southeast Asia, inviting Chinese, Portuguese, Dutch, English, French, and Japanese to establish trading settlements. It was on the old trade route between India and China.

Ayutthaya is an island about six miles in circumference created by canals and secondary streams of the Chao Phya River. Here and there map boards of the city show directions to the main ruins and to various other sites of interest.

SIGHTSEEING IN AYUTTHAYA

Wat Yai Chai Mongkol—also known as Wat Chao Phya Thai, the first ruin one sees when driving from Bangkok into Ayutthaya. It is also the oldest building, dating from 1357, when King U Thong constructed it for Buddhist monks who returned from studying in Ceylon. The crumbling, black *chedi* was added later in 1592 by King Naresuan* to commemorate the defeat of the Burmese who had invaded and occupied the city since 1569. The Burmese had constructed Wat Phu Kae Thong or Temple of the Golden Mount (mentioned later) as a monument to their victory, so King Naresuan built this black *chedi* higher than the Burmese monument as a symbol of his power. It once stood over 250 feet high.

Inside the ruin are rows of stark white, life-size Buddha statues, each one with a different face. Many have been well restored and are cared for by worshippers who have had marble nameplates placed in front. They come and offer flowers and incense, and they sometimes dress the figure with a saffron cloth. There must be well over a

* King Naresuan was one of the most heroic of Thai rulers. He was named "Black Prince" before he took power as monarch. In 1569, the prince was captured by the Burmese and taken to Pagan in Burma. The Burmese ruler kept him in his palace and, as the "Black Prince" grew up, the Burmese thought he would make an ideal "puppet governer" for the kingdom of Ayutthaya, which was then in Burmese hands. Naresuan acted the part well until the ruler was convinced of his docile, simple nature and loyalty to Burma and sent him back to Ayutthaya to govern the Thai people. Naresuan had other ideas, however, and when he arrived in Ayutthaya he promptly declared the independence of the Thai people, fought and defeated the local Burmese garrison, and became King Naresuan. No doubt the Burmese ruler was astonished and must have felt pretty silly, to put it mildly.

The Burmese invaded Ayutthaya in a bloody battle through the Three Pagodas Pass. King Naresuan fought a duel on elephantback with the Burmese Crown Prince Upracha and killed him, and Naresuan has been venerated ever since.

hundred images sitting there, peacefully, in the open air. One can also see an enormous torso of a standing Buddha on the *chedi*. The temple seems far from anywhere in the fields but it is still used, and barefooted monks can be seen silently walking among the ruins. Even with their presence, the stillness and quiet are impressive and moving. A new building is being constructed to the rear among magnolia trees.

Wat Panan Cherng—situated on the river bank south of Ayutthaya; it is surrounded by attractive grounds with bushes and hedges trimmed in contorted shapes. At the entrance, sleeping dogs lie in the shade, and an old woman sells lotus flowers and incense. In the doorway to the great hall, which seems to be sagging, prostrate worshippers mutter prayers while other visitors shake fortune-telling sticks. The air is thick with incense. Someone plays music softly on a *ranad ek*.* A massive golden Buddha-image seems to peer down at the people as they enter. It is floodlit and too large for the building. Although in the attitude of meditation, seated, the figure is no less than nineteen metres high. Worshippers, who all look like Chinese, paste little squares of gold leaf onto its base, where the pieces flutter in the breeze.

The image is believed to have been created in 1324, twenty-six years before Ayutthaya was founded. Later, during the Ayutthaya period, the temple building was put up around it. The Buddha is highly revered since, according to legend, tears came from its eyes the day Ayutthaya was sacked by the Burmese. The Chinese community has taken care of this temple for some time and decorated the hall inside with Chinese lanterns. One

* The *ranad ek* is a classical Thai instrument like a curved wooden xylophone with wooden keys.

may walk around the Buddha and see the niches in the walls and the details of the decorations.

The other side of the entrance leads to a landing pier on the Chao Phya River where small boats can be hired. By the pier, facing the river, is a small, Chinese-style temple. Inside is an image of a princess to whom the temple is dedicated. The story behind it is hard to believe. Apparently, King Prachao Sua, who reigned over Ayutthaya from 1703 until 1709, wanted to have a wife with white skin (which is considered very beautiful by Thais). He sent messengers to China to search for a white-skinned lady and, after a time, a beautiful young princess was found. A suitable "arrangement" was made with her father, and she began her great journey to Ayutthaya by ox cart.

After many months, the young princess arrived at Ayutthaya, excited and anxious to meet her royal suitor. She boarded a ferry to cross the Chao Phya River but at the other side the King's servants begged her not to disembark, as the King was not quite ready to receive her. The young girl could not bear to wait a moment longer and walked into the grounds of the palace to see the King. She was shocked by what she saw. The King, a fun-lover, was passing the time with some young maidens in a bath! The young princess was so distraught that she went back to the river and walked slowly into the water until it covered her head. Nobody could save her as it was forbidden to touch royalty. The King, having heard the alarm, had chased after her but caught only a glimpse of her beautiful face—the most beautiful he had ever seen—just before she drowned.

So it is said that King Prachao Sua had this temple built in her memory at the exact spot where she walked into the river. He was haunted by his love for this girl and suffered so much from her loss that he became deranged. It is said that he then demanded a young virgin every evening and, after he had finished with her, he killed her, ceremonially, the following morning. No wonder he is called "Tiger King." This lasted every day for almost one year until he died.

Wiharn Phra Mongkol Bopit—houses the largest bronzed Buddha image in the world. The handsome building is obviously new. It was rebuilt in the 1950's when Field Marshal Pibul Songkram* was Prime Minister. A photograph hanging just inside shows the state of the building and Buddha before repairs began. During the restoration many valuable articles were found buried, and hundreds of little bronze images were discovered inside the Great Buddha. These are now on display at the local Chao Sam Praya Museum (mentioned later). Nobody knows exactly when this Buddha image was made, although it was most probably during the Ayutthaya period. It has been damaged and restored several times. The chapel is usually busy with worshippers bearing incense, flowers, and offerings. The Buddha, absolutely black, towers portentously above them. Its white, haunting eyes, glimmering in the dim light, are mother-of-pearl. One may walk around the inside behind the image.

Wat Phra Sri Sanphet—adjacent to the above chapel;

* Pibul Songkram made substantial efforts to create a friendlier relationship with the Burmese, who had neither been forgotten nor forgiven for invading and pillaging Siam's richest cities. Ayutthaya was the greatest and most prosperous capital, with scores of palaces and temples. Records of the European merchants show that they had never seen such extravagance and wealth before. It was destroyed by the Burmese who took the Thais back to Burma as slaves. Two centuries later the Burmese Prime Minister, U Nu, responded to Thailand's friendly gestures by sending large sums of money for the restoration of Ayutthaya's buildings.

all that remains are crumbling walls and three repaired white-and-grey *chedi*. The site, however, is important. The temple that stood here was within the precincts of the Royal Palace. It was then as important as the Emerald Buddha Temple is today. It used to house a standing Buddha 15.9 metres (53 feet) high which was covered with 263 kilograms (578 pounds) of gold. When the Burmese took Ayutthaya in 1767 they set fire to the temple and peeled off the gold from the image, which was originally made in the year 1500.

Around the temple are three very tall white-and-grey *chedi* which have been restored. They have become a symbol of Ayutthaya. Beneath them, treasures and small images of Buddha were found that are now on display at the National Museum, Bangkok. The temple of the Emerald Buddha in Bangkok has been built in a similar design to that of this former Palace temple.

Royal Ancient Palace—only the ruined foundations of magnificent palace buildings remain, half-hidden among the grasses and shrubs, except for the Tri Muk Building. This building is a replica of the original wooden structure put up by King Chulalongkorn in 1907. It was used by the kings in special ceremonies paying homage to the monarchs of Ayutthaya.

Wat Logya Sutha (*Temple of the Reclining Buddha*)—nothing remains of the temple building but the Reclining Buddha, 28 metres (92 feet) long, still here in the open air: it is a very peaceful spot surrounded by jungle, yet still visited by faithful Buddhists who buy flowers and incense and little gold-leaf squares to paste onto the image. Its head rests upon lotus flowers. No one knows how old it is. It was restored in 1956.

Wat Phu Kae Thong (*Temple of the Golden Mount*)—a great pagoda, 80 metres (262 feet) high, just outside the old town 2½ kilometres (1½ miles) north, apart from any other buildings; it was originally constructed by the Burmese to commemorate the victory of their first invasion of Ayutthaya in 1569. During the reign of King Boromagod in the mid–18th century, the upper part of the pagoda was remodelled to a Thai style. In 1956 the Thai government placed a ball of solid gold weighing 2,500 grammes on the top to celebrate 2,500 years since the beginning of Buddhism.

Visitors can climb the white-and-grey structure up steep steps, but the view of paddy fields all around is hardly worth the effort.

The Elephant Kraal—in olden times used for the capture and training of wild elephants, it is simply a stockade with a fence of teak logs about five feet high, with a special area surrounded by logs inside. The kings used to arrange elephant demonstrations here for state guests.

The elephants were a great asset in the Ayutthaya period. In peacetime they worked in the forest, and during a war they were the beasts of burden. White elephants were highly prized and whenever found were brought to the king. They were so sought after that they were actually the cause of several of the Burmese invasions.

The Ayutthaya Museum, formerly Chandra Kasem Palace—has outside walls more grand than the building, which reminds one of a French château rather than a royal palace of the East. The original building was constructed in 1577 by King Maha Tamaracha for his son, the Crown Prince Naresuan. It was used by him and later kings until Ayutthaya fell to the Burmese in 1767. King Rama IV rebuilt and restored many parts of the palace, which he used during his visits to Ayutthaya.

Now it is used by the Fine Arts Department and the administrative officers of the local government. The gardens are littered with bits and pieces of porticos, heads of Buddha, cannon barrels, and a few odd statues recalling Hindu art. It is more interesting inside and has a display of ceramics, mother-of-pearl inlaid objects, and lovely statuettes. In the second building the shadow-play puppet screens and cut-outs called *nang-yai* are particularly worth seeing.

Open 10:00 A.M.–4:30 P.M. daily except Mondays and Tuesdays.

Wat Rajaburana—vast crumbling ruins of this temple and of Wat Phra Mahathat opposite convey some impression of Ayutthaya's noble past; the ruins are of red brick or laterite, vaguely resembling the Khmer ruins of the Northeast.

The Rajaburana Temple was built in 1423 by the seventh king of Ayutthaya, King Boromaraja II, on the spot where his two elder brothers had been cremated. They killed each other in a duel for succession to the throne. In the late 1950's the Fine Arts Department made excavations and found large quantities of buried treasure, most probably hidden there when Ayutthaya came under attack. Golden figures and jewels were found, as well as many religious objects including thousands of Buddhist votive tablets that were later sold to raise money for the Chao Sam Praya Museum (mentioned below). Also discovered at that time were ancient murals on the walls of the crypt. These murals can be seen by anyone who can find the attendant; he has the key to the door. Even if one cannot find him, a stroll around the crumbling pagodas reveals some fine decorative carvings and relief work.

Wat Phra Mahathat—opposite the Wat Rajaburana mentioned above, these ruins are the remains of a temple constructed in 1384 by King Ramesuan. In the 1950's the government found hoards of treasure buried here. The objects, including a relic of Buddha in a gold casket, are now kept at the Chao Sam Praya Museum.

Chao Sam Praya Museum—displays a large collection of gold and silver votive tablets and thousands of Buddha images in such materials as stone, gold, and crystal. There are also some interesting stone carvings that date back to the 6th and 7th centuries and some fine examples of wooden door-panels carved with remarkable designs.

Open—9:00 A.M.–4:00 P.M. daily except Mondays and Tuesdays.

BANG PA-IN *(Royal Palace and Gardens)*—About 61 kilometres (38 miles) north of Bangkok on the way to Ayutthaya either by road or rail. Admission costs 2 *baht* (10 cents). Open daily except Mondays.

Bang Pa-In has been used as a summer palace for centuries. It consists of a curious variety of buildings in Gothic, Renaissance, Chinese, and Thai styles. Strangely enough, they complement one another beautifully, being nicely spaced about the grounds. The palace originated from the time when Ayutthaya was the capital, during the reign of King Prasad Thong (1630–55). He chose this island as a site for a temple to be built—Wat Chumphon Nikayaram—and, later, had a palace constructed at the edge of a lake which he used as a country villa. This palace has been replaced by the Royal Pavilion (Aisvarya Dib Asana) in the middle of the lake in pure

Thai-style architecture. It is very similar in design and style to the Disrobing Pavilion—Abhornbhimok—at the Grand Palace in Bangkok. The statue inside is of King Chulalongkorn (Rama V).

Bang Pa-In was used as a summer palace by all the kings of Ayutthaya who succeeded King Prasad Thong. After the capital was changed to Thon Buri, and then to Bangkok, it was left unused until King Mongkut (Rama IV) came and stayed. He could make the trip fairly easily by motor launch. King Mongkut built a new palace of two storeys but as this fell into disrepair it was replaced by the present, Renaissance-style, single storey building, the Varobhas Piman Pavilion. This is the only building visitors may enter. Inside are King Chulalongkorn's throne and some fascinating paintings that give an insight to the court life and methods of fighting with elephants in the old days. This pavilion was used for ceremonies of state.

To the north is an elaborately decorated Chinese-style building, Vehas Chamrun. A Chinese millionaire had this built as a present to the King for use as a residence during the rainy and cool seasons. Nearby, on a little island, is King Chulalongkorn's Observation Tower, the Vidur Dasana, especially built just so that he could enjoy the view. Close by, among the lovely gardens, is a memorial stone erected by King Chulalongkorn to his consort Queen Sunanda and their two children, who drowned when their boat overturned on the river, in 1881. Since commoners were forbidden to touch royalty no one attempted to save them. The memorial has a very moving epitaph in Thai and in English.

Apart from the extraordinary collection of palace buildings, picturesque gardens, and serene lakes, the other places of interest here are Wat Nivet Dhamapravat and Wat Chumpon Nikayaram. The former, on an island in the Chao Phra River, can be reached by a cable car. The temple was built during the reign of King Chulalongkorn (1868–1910) and has, unbelievably, a *wiharn* in the Gothic style while the other temple buildings are built in a strange mixture of Western and Thai architectures. The latter, Wat Chumpon Nikayaram, lies outside the area of the palace grounds near an old iron bridge towards the railway station. It has no special point of interest apart from being the earliest building of Bang Pa-In, constructed by the order of King Prasad Thong in the 17th century.

Sara Buri

The provincial capital of the province of the same name lies 104 kilometres (67 miles) north of Bangkok on Highway 1 (the Paholyothin Road).

Apart from going by car, there is a train service from Hualampong Station, Bangkok. The journey takes about 2¼ hours by express or 3 hours by a local train, 55 *baht* ($2.75) first class, one way. There is also a very frequent bus service for hardy tourists starting from the Northern Terminal on the Paholyothin Road, tel: 71159. The fare is 10 *baht* (50 cents) one way.

Sara Buri town is just like any other provincial capital, and the surrounding plains are typical of Thailand's rural scenery, predominantly rice paddies dotted with

Farmers and water buffaloes.

farmers' villages. Sara Buri town was founded four centuries ago by King Phra Mahachakraphat as a centre for troops. It still serves as a communications hub linking the surrounding provinces, though the city centre has been moved near to the railway station. Close to the town are Phra Buddha Bat (Shrine of the Buddha's Footprint), the Pukae Botanical Gardens, and Phra Buddha Chai (Shrine of the Buddha's Shadow)—three attractive, interesting sites, popular among the Thais and Chinese (especially at weekends) but not often visited by foreign tourists.

PHRA BUDDHA BAT—As one turns left off Highway 1, just beyond the small town of Phra Buddha Bat, the *mondop* is immediately prominent, with its golden pinnacle towering over a hundred feet atop a hill named Suvarnaban Bot. The shrine is highly decorated with glittering coloured glass, lacquer, and gold. The *mondop* is reached by three flights of steps, guarded by *naga* or serpents. The climb is arduous, but one is encouraged by the hundred or more temple bells that tremble and tinkle in the wind, competing with the song of birds. At the top, the climber is rewarded not only by the intricate beauty of the building but also by a magnificent, panoramic view across the Sara Buri countryside.

The *mondop* has eight doors, each inlaid with mother-of-pearl, Thai designs. These were placed here in the mid-18th century by King Baromakot, then King of Ayutthaya. Like the rest of the building, these doors were badly damaged when the Burmese ransacked the shrine during a war in 1766. The shrine was also once damaged by fire in the 19th century. After both incidents, faithful worshippers donated more than enough money to restore the buildings, for this shrine has great significance to Buddhists. Many Thais and Chinese Buddhists regard it as the most sacred place in Thailand.

The inside of the *mondop* is also highly decorative and glittering with gold. On the floor is a very beautiful mat made of silver. It weighs 421 kilogrammes (926 pounds) and was donated during the reign of King Rama IV. Pilgrims come here with squares of gold leaf to gild the inside of the footprint on the floor—the reason for the shrine's existence.

Legend shrouds the origin of this holy place but it is popularly believed that the footprint was discovered by a hunter who chased a wounded deer into a wood on this hill. The hunter was amazed to see the deer reappear from behind the bushes with its wounds healed. It sprinted away. The intrigued hunter went into the wood and found a pool of water in the shape of a human foot. Tired, he took a drink and splashed himself with the water, which instantly healed his cuts and sores. His experience was recounted to the King, who had already started a search for the footprint following a report from Thai monks who had made a pilgrimage to the Buddha's footprint in Ceylon. The Ceylonese had told these monks that a footprint of Buddha also existed somewhere in Thailand. This was in the 17th century, during the reign of King Songtham. He had the shrine built over the footprint. The footprint, incidentally, measures five feet by one foot, nine inches, and is eleven inches deep.

Around the Suvarnaban Bot hill are statues of demons, expertly carved and startlingly grotesque. They are to ward off evil spirits. Since the 17th century various kings have added buildings—*wiharn*—that can be seen scattered about the surrounding hillsides. They contain religious articles and images of Buddha in various attitudes. To the north is a *chedi* constructed of marble, erected by King Rama IV in 1860, a reminder that Sara Buri is the only place in Thailand where marble is quarried. Several caves in the district are also considered sacred, and the nearby hills have become a favourite place for Chinese to make their tombs.

Every weekend the shrine is crowded with pilgrims, and twice a year it is packed. The first occasion is when the Chinese celebrate, from the first day of the waxing moon to the first day of the waning moon of the third lunar month—a period of about two weeks that coincides with the Chinese New Year celebrations. The second occasion is during the same period of the fourth lunar month, when more Thais celebrate and the countryside is covered with people camping. Entrance gates are closed at 4:00 P.M.

PUKAE BOTANICAL GARDENS—115 kilometres (72 miles) from Bangkok at a right turning just off Highway 1: this is a lovely picnic spot managed by the Forestry Department since 1940. The gardens have an interesting variety of trees, shrubs, flowers, and herbs mostly from Thailand, Japan, and China. Picnic tables and food and drink stalls are found in the grounds.

PHRA BUDDHA CHAI—about 5 kilometres (3 miles) along the road that turns off Highway 1 at the 103-kilometre mark from Bangkok: it is another favourite spot for Thai and Chinese pilgrims who visit the Phra Buddha Bat. This shrine is centred around a footprint in relief that is believed to be a shadow of Buddha's foot.

Lop Buri

Situated beyond Ayutthaya, Lop Buri is 155 kilometres (93 miles) north of Bangkok and it may be reached by train, car, or bus. The trains run from Bangkok (Hualampong) Station, taking about 3 hours. By car it also takes about 3 hours but one has the advantage of being able to visit Ayutthaya, Bang Pa-In, Sara Buri, and the Pukae Botanical Gardens with ease en route. To take in all these places properly, an overnight stop is worth considering. Hotels in this region will be limited to local-style accommodation, though they seem to be generally improving in standards. The Tanin Hotel, for example, not far from the Phra Buddha Bat (see p. 238), even has air-conditioned rooms and hot water. If one chooses the cheapest mode of travel, bus, allow 4 hours for the journey. After Ayutthaya, the scenery becomes more interesting as one leaves the flat rice plains around Bangkok and approaches a range of hills.

Lop Buri has a long and chequered history that dates from around the 5th or 6th century, when it was founded as a Mon city named Lavo (or Lawo) and existed as such until the 11th century (Dvaravati period), when the Khmers came. Under Khmer rule it flourished, and a rich new style of art evolved that is basically a combination of Mon and Thai arts with the Khmer. This is what has become the famous "Lop Buri–style" art. In the 14th century, following the decline of the Khmer (Angkorian) Kingdom and the consecutive rise in power of local rulers, Lavo eventually came under the control of Thai kings, one of whom re-named it Lop Buri.

The city of Lop Buri continued to hold its importance as an administrative capital, along with Ayutthaya, until 1548. It was razed to the ground then as a strategic measure during a war with the Burmese. From then on Ayutthaya thrived as the capital and rich trading centre, and Lop Buri lay forgotten until 1664. In that year, following a tiff between King Narai and Dutch traders, a Dutch fleet blockaded the Gulf of Siam and even threatened to invade Ayutthaya. King Narai realized how vulnerable his capital was to attack by any major sea power and so he commissioned French architects to build a second capital, away from the sea, where he could take refuge if a war broke out. Lop Buri was the site chosen, so again the city grew, but this time the architecture was a combination of Thai and Western styles. King Narai spent eight to nine months a year there for the rest of his reign (1656–68).

King Narai's successors had different ideas, and thus this regal city was once again abandoned and left to the mercy of the elements for nearly 200 years until King Mongkut (Rama IV, 1851–68) ordered restoration. Most of the buildings had decayed beyond saving, and so new buildings were constructed, retaining their original style as far as possible. King Mongkut then lived there for several years.

King Chulalongkorn (Rama V, 1868–1910) was not so interested in the place but neither was he indifferent. He handed over the royal palace to the local government as Lop Buri Government House. In 1940, the Thai Government built a new town just east of the old city and converted the royal palace into a museum.

SIGHTSEEING IN LOP BURI—This is best done by car, or one can hire a samlor for about 20 *baht* ($1) an hour.

Elephant Kraal—situated just before entering Lop Buri (if coming by car from Bangkok): only an earth mound remains. This lies close to the Pratu Phaniad or old city gate. King Narai staged an elephant hunt here in honour of Chevalier de Chaumont, the French Ambassador to Siam. King Narai so respected this ambassador that he gave him a Thai name and bestowed upon him an honourary military title.

Kala Shrine (San Phragan)—in a large roundabout next

to the railway line on the east side: it is on the road from Bangkok following the Elephant Kraal Site.

The original Khmer laterite *prang* is in ruins. In front, however, is a small temple built in the 1950's. This contains a valuable stone image of the Hindu God Vishnu and a Buddha image belonging to the Lop Buri period (11th–14th centuries). A large old tree in the compound is the habitat of monkeys. Extreme caution is advised.

Wat Nakhon Kosa—just a little way south of the Kala Shrine: a 12th-century *prang,* built by the Khmers, it seems to have started out as a Hindu shrine, later to be converted to a Buddhist *wat* during the Ayutthaya period (14th–18th centuries). It is now in ruins.

Wat Indra—on the west side of the railway track opposite Wat Nakhon Kosa: this is a complete ruin of a temple believed to have been built during the Ayutthaya period.

Wat Phra Sri Ratana Mahadat—on the west side of the railway track a few hundred yards south of Wat Indra: the ruins cover an extensive area with a tall *prang* dominating the present scene. It was built by the Khmers in typical Angkorian style, probably in the 12th century.

Narai Raja Niwes Palace (Lop Buri Museum)—situated west of Wat Phra Sri Ratana Mahadat: the entrance is on the north side, in Rajdamnern Avenue.

This was the palace of King Narai, most likely on the site of a former royal palace. King Mongkut is chiefly responsible for restoring and conserving its original style. Now housing ancient art objects relating to Lop Buri and the immediate vicinity, this museum is open 8:30 A.M.–4:30 P.M. daily, except Mondays, Tuesdays, and national holidays. The many sections of the palace make this the most impressive sight in Lop Buri, and time should be allowed for a walk around the grounds.

Constantine Phaulkon's Residence—situated a little way north from the Narai Raja Niwes Palace: this was built in European style for Chevalier de Chaumont and became the home of Constantine Phaulkon, King Narai's prime minister, a man of Greek extraction. Phaulkon was assassinated in 1688 for political reasons. The remains of the building appear extraordinarily incongruous since the structure is purely Western-style in every detail. Lop Buri market, a busy countrified affair, is very close to this house along the banks of the Lop Buri River.

Phra Prang Sam Yod—returning from Phaulkon's Residence to the Bangkok road, passed on the left, just before crossing the railway track to the Kala Shrine roundabout: it consists of three enormous *prang* joined by two galleries, and is so well known that it is regarded as the symbol of Lop Buri. Its original purpose is a matter of some controversy among archeologists and scholars. Some say it was built as a Buddhist temple, probably in the 13th century, and some say it was built as a Hindu shrine and converted to a temple later. What *is* certain is that it is the finest remaining monument to the Khmers in Thailand. Although the temple is in a ruinous state, one can visualize its richness as it once stood, covered with ornamental carvings and stucco.

Paknam Crocodile Farm

The farm is situated along Taibaan Road, Paknam town. (You need a driver who has been there before.) Open 8:00 A.M.–4:00 P.M. daily. Admission charge is 6 *baht* per person.

The drive passes through busy Sukumvit and then along a very quiet old road by a wide river lined with cedar trees. One passes the Red Cross Convalescent Home, "Sawanganivas" (200–300 *baht* or U.S. $10–15 a day), and eventually along an unpaved road.

The farm is owned by a Mr. Utai, who breeds and raises crocodiles for their skins. Thai crocodiles have six "bumps" in a row across their necks while other crocodiles have "bumps" along the length of their necks. Crocodiles are said still to be living in their natural state in Lake Bueng Borapet in Nakhon Sawan Province (central Thailand) and in some parts of the south. They lay their eggs in large numbers in the sand or dry mud to be hatched by the heat of the sun. At this farm, more than 3,000 crocodiles are kept in concrete walled tanks and fed daily with live fish. The water in the pools has been stained a vivid green by the crocodiles' saliva.

When the crocodiles grow to about six feet in length and at least eighteen inches around the middle—that is, after about three years—they are killed by a sharp stab on the back of the neck. Then, in hardly twenty minutes, they are skillfully skinned. The skins are sold to be made into handbags, shoes, wallets, and so on, and many of these products are available here. Also, stuffed baby crocodiles can be purchased here. The meat is sold to restaurants and to chemists who dry it to make a medicine for respiratory ailments.

Visitors can feed the crocodiles with live fish and watch demonstrations of how to catch a crocodile. Caution is advised, as these are predacious creatures. The mothers will eat even their young.

Phrapadeang Village

The village is south of Bangkok 26 kilometres (16 miles) by river; the trip can be arranged through most

Bangkok travel agencies. A round trip by boat, pedicab, and bus usually takes about 4½ hours.

The boat ride is restful and interesting. The banks are lined with tall palm trees, numerous *wat,* and stilt houses, each with its own colourful spirit house and pier. Navy ships, long barges, sampans, and "longtailed" taxis crowd the waters. One can catch an insight into rural life and see cheerful, smiling faces everywhere.

Phrapadeang was established long ago by the Mons, who fled from Burma during one of the many wars. The language, costume (especially at festival times), and culture are thus slightly different from pure Thai. Tourists usually enjoy a ride by samlor through the town and coconut groves to visit one of the old temples and to see Phra Chulachomklao Fort, the biggest in Thailand.

Rice Barge Tours

Similar excursions to villages and rural markets are arranged by many of the Bangkok travel agencies. Tourists travel in converted rice barges and are offered inducements such as free drinks or dinner on board. Interesting.

Nakhon Pathom—Oldest City in Thailand

Situated in the Central Plain 58 kilometres (36 miles) west of Bangkok: by car or bus, it is a smooth, comfortable ride. From central Bangkok one crosses the Chao Phya River into Thon Buri by the Memorial Bridge. At the second roundabout is a statue of King Taksin. The Pet Kasem Road branches here, to the right, leading direct to Nakhon Pathom past the Rose Garden Resort. The bus service goes from the Ta Phra Terminal in Thon Buri, leaving every 15 minutes. One may also go by train in less than 1½ hours from Hualampong Station, Bangkok.

Village houses and *taln* trees.

The excursion to Nakhon Pathom makes a welcome change from the busy city of Bangkok. One passes through flat rice plains scattered with tall "taln" trees. Some parts are swampy in this rich agricultural area, completely rural and untouched by modern industrialisation. Water buffalo can be seen lazing in the muddy streams. The farmers' cottages blend pleasantly with the surroundings, as they are made entirely of palm leaves with walls of interlaced split bamboo. Bananas, coconuts, watermelons, oranges, and custard apples are only a few of the fruits for which Nakhon Pathom Province has become famous. One good reason for visiting Nakhon Pathom is to see and be able to photograph Thailand's typical rural countryside.

If travelling by road, a stop at the Rose Garden Country Resort is recommended (see p. 255).

Just before entering the city, along the road from Bangkok, there is a little shrine dedicated to "Yai Hom"

—"Grandmother Hom." A small figure of her with a little boy in her arms is visible inside the shrine. She is a victim in a famous Thai mythological story. Briefly, according to the legend, she found the little boy in the jungle and adopted him. When the little boy, Phya Pan, grew up, he became a powerful army commander. To expand his domain, he attacked Nakhon Pathom. He battled on an elephant face to face, or rather trunk to trunk, with the King of Nakhon Pathom, and the King was killed. The young conqueror then entered the Royal Palace, where he found such a beautiful woman that he decided to marry her. Phya Pan was later shocked when he overheard someone saying that this was actually his mother, and that he had killed his own father—the former King.

Distraught, he returned to Grandmother Hom to ask if it could be true. She confessed that a soothsayer who had visited the King's palace when Phya Pan was born had predicted that this son would kill his father. The King had the child taken into the jungle to be left to the mercy of the tigers and snakes. Phya Pan was so furious that he had not been told of this secret that he killed Grandmother Hom in a fit of rage. When he came to realize what awful crimes he had committed he went to the monks to ask what he should do for atonement.

"Build a *stupa* as high as a dove flies," he was told. The *stupa* he built is supposed to be the original one later covered by Phra Pathom Chedi.

VIEWING THE PHRA PATHOM CHEDI—Returning from legend to fact, this is the largest, tallest *chedi* in Thailand, and no one would dispute that it is also one of the largest *chedi* in the world. Its towering spire is overwhelming, especially as the surrounding landscape is so flat. It stands 120.45 metres (380 feet) high. Its dome of brown-

Phra Pathom *chedi*.

glazed tiles shimmers like gold in the sunlight. Wat Chedi is the holiest place for Buddhists in Thailand. It marks the place where Buddhism was first introduced to the country.

At the main entrance there are three wide flights of steps. Level with the top of the first flight are two small *sala*—one on each side. Go up to the top of the steps onto the upper terrace and straight ahead is a tall, gilded standing Buddha, framed by a carved, gilded archway. (This is the north *wiharn*—there is one *wiharn* at each of the four compass points.) The head of this image came from the north of Thailand, and the body was ordered to be cast for it by King Rama VI (Vajiravudh). His ashes are buried at the base of this image, according to his wishes. Streams of pilgrims pass in and out, bowing to the floor and making offerings in acts of veneration.

Now turn left, going around the upper terrace in a clockwise direction. First, one will notice a row of fancy stone bell-towers, all alike, going all the way around. There are twenty-four altogether. Then, on the left, there is a rocky garden with bushy shrubs and leafy tamarind trees. Here, it is peaceful with only the sounds of the sweet-toned temple bells in the wind and the bird songs. Soon one arrives at the east *wiharn.* Inside is an image of Buddha seated beneath a *bo* tree. Just outside, facing this *wiharn,* are steps leading to an enormous *bo* tree which, like the one in the compound of Wat Sraket, Bangkok, is said to have been specially brought here from Ceylon. (This is the tree beneath which Buddha meditated and found enlightenment in the forest at Uruvilva in Bihar, India.) Going down these stone steps, (note the railings, carved and decorated in the shape of *naga*—serpents) there is a small museum to the left and a *bot* to the right, on this outer, square terrace.

The museum is open 9:00 A.M.–12 noon, 1:00–4:00 P.M. daily except Mondays, Tuesdays, and national holidays. Admission by donation, as much as you like. It contains stone carvings and items of archaelogical interest that were found in and around Nakhon Pathom. The *bot* opposite contains a much treasured Dvaravati-style (6th–11th century) Buddha image. Return up these east steps and continue left, to the south *wiharn.*

This *wiharn* contains an ancient stone image of Buddha protected by the seven-headed serpent that kept the rains off Buddha while he meditated in the forest. Just down the south steps, facing this *wiharn,* to the left can be seen a replica of the original *stupa* that is now inside the huge *chedi.* It is interesting to note that without its Khmer *prang* it would resemble the Indian *stupa* of the 3rd century B.C. To the right, there is another replica; this represents a *chedi* in Nakhon Si Thammarat.

Continue now to the west *wiharn*. This contains two chapels, the outer one housing a gilt reclining Buddha image nearly 9 metres (30 feet) long, and the inner chapel with a smaller version accompanied by three disciples kneeling before him. This represents Buddha just before he died. Now continue walking to complete the circle and go through the archway next to the north *wiharn*, into the inner gallery.

The inner gallery also encircles the great *chedi*. The walls are lined with plaques of ancient Khmer script and with images placed in niches. The decorated ceiling, entablatures, white pillars, and numerous moongates of this gallery, with the gleaming golden-brown tiles of the gigantic *chedi* towering into the sky on one side, have an extraordinary atmosphere about them—strange, Oriental, alluring.

THE NOVEMBER FAIR—In this month the grounds of the Phra Pathom Chedi become the focal point of a three-day fair. Thousands of people come from afar, and Nakhon Pathom is packed. It is rather like a glorified market with a prevailing carnival mood helped along by musicians, fortune tellers, entertainers, and various amusements. Yet no one leaves Nakhon Pathom without paying homage to Buddha at the great *chedi*.

HISTORY OF THE CHEDI—The original *stupa* (a replica stands at the south of the great *chedi*—see above) is surmised to have been the very first *stupa* erected in this land. It marks the place where Buddhism first became established in this part of Asia. Scholars have deduced that the site of Nakhon Pathom was once called "Suvarnabhumi," the capital of the Kingdom of Suvarnabhumi which stretched from southern Burma to Annam (now part of Vietnam) and southwards to what is now Malaysia. It is recorded that King Ashoka (India) in the 3rd century B.C. sent two missionaries to Suvarnabhumi to spread the teaching of Buddha. India was already familiar with this region, as many Indians had come here by boat and settled. At that time the city was closer to the sea. Archeological finds in the area include relics such as "wheels of law," inscribed tablets, and carved altars that are dated as pre-143 B.C. The building of the original *stupa* has thus been dated, conservatively, as 150 B.C. This is long before Thais migrated into the area.

The city is also believed to have been the capital of the Kingdom of Dvaravati that existed from about A.D. 500 to 1057, and, according to Chinese chronicles, stretched from Srikasetra (now Burma) to Isanuburi, now Cambodia (Khmer Republic). During the Suvarnabhumi and Dvaravati periods, the *stupa* must have been restored and repaired many times.

In A.D. 1057 the city* was vanquished by the Burmese, and the inhabitants abandoned it for about a hundred years. Then Nakhon Pathom was again abandoned because the river Chaisri and access to the Gulf of Siam were silting up. The Phra Pathom Chedi fell into disrepair and was left, almost forgotten, for hundreds of years at the mercy of the encroaching jungle.

Although a few religious devotees must have continued to come on pilgrimages and a new city named Nakhon Chaisri† was established nearby in the mid-16th century, it was not until the 19th century that the decaying Phra Pathom Chedi was restored. Prince Mongkut, while a monk, made several pilgrimages to the *chedi*. It was a tortuous, fairly dangerous journey from Bangkok in

* Recorded as the city of Thaton in Burmese history but since proved to be Nakhon Pathom.

† A town actually situated on the Tachin River in preparation for a Burmese invasion.

those days, travelling for several days by boat through dense jungle. The Prince firmly believed that this monument was worthy of restoration, but as his elder brother, King Rama III (1824–51), disagreed, the Prince had to wait until he became King himself.

On Mongkut's accession to the throne in 1851, at the age of forty-seven, he had already spent twenty-seven years as a monk. With great determination, he immediately set about building a larger *chedi* to cover the original one. Hampered by a collapse after a heavy rainstorm, the building of the present *chedi* (redesigned) got under way in 1860. King Mongkut also ordered the construction of the four *wiharn,* the restoration of several other structures, and the building of Nakhon Pathom Palace to the east of the *chedi*. Unfortunately, he died before the work was completed.

His son, Chulalongkorn, who succeeded him in 1868, continued the work according to his father's wishes. He even raised the height of the spire. He, too, died before all the work was complete and never saw the *chedi* covered with the brown glazed tiles.

The *chedi* still remained isolated in the midst of dense jungle, and it was not until the railway was built in 1900 that the town began to come to life again. The nearby town of Nakhon Chaisri was moved to create a new town, Nakhon Pathom.

SANAM CHAN PALACE—Consists of several buildings in spacious grounds just about 2 kilometres (over a mile) to the west of Phra Pathom Chedi, along a wide road named "Rajdamnern" (meaning King's Avenue), and over a *klong*.

This was built for Vajiravudh (King Rama VI, 1910–25) as a country retreat, and the buildings are now used as local government offices. The only building of note is the one in a mixture of Thai and European architecture. In front is a statue of the King's favourite dog, named Yaleh. This building really looks like something pictured in a children's fairy tale book.

In the middle of the lawns facing this building is a small Hindu shrine known as the Vikanesuan Shrine dedicated to Phra Kanes, god of the arts. This god is believed to have the power to overcome every obstacle, and so King Rama VI had the shrine built for the actors who used to perform his plays here.

WAT PHRA GNAM—Near the railway station, Wat Phra Gnam was built during the reign of King Rama V (1868–1910). This *wat* is on the site of a mound believed to have been the base of a huge ancient monument.

WAT PHRA PATHOM—About 3 kilometres (2 miles) east of Phra Pathom Chedi, this *wat* has a white *prang* on a high square mound believed to have been the site of an ancient temple. In fact, fairly recent archeological excavations here have uncovered artifacts and foundations believed to be about as old as the original Phra Pathom Chedi.

WAT PHRA MERU—A few minutes' walk southeast from the Phra Pathom Chedi.

This contains a collection of stone Buddha images, each about 16 feet or 5 metres high.

FOOD AND RESTAURANTS IN NAKHON PATHOM—Only Thai restaurants (and local-style hotels) are to be found in this vicinity. The Rose Garden en route from Bangkok would be a better place to eat (or stay). In Nakhon Pathom, the Sirichai Restaurant opposite the main (north) entrance of Phra Pathom Chedi is fairly good.

In this province and especially in town, one can see pieces of thick bamboo sold by the roadside. These contain sticky rice and coconut—a delicious combination—and are cooked over a charcoal brazier. They cost around 2 *baht* each (to foreign tourists) and are well worth trying. Just split the bamboo and there it is!

Suan Sampran—Rose Garden

This luxurious country-club-style resort is less than an hour's drive from Bangkok at 32 kilometres on the Pet Kasem Road. That is about 20 miles along on the highway to Nakhon Pathom.

Open: 6:00 A.M.–8:00 P.M. weekdays
6:00 A.M.–9:00 P.M. weekends and national holidays

Entrance fee: Car: 5 *baht,*
Adult: 5 *baht*; child: 2 *baht.*

The grounds and gardens cover fifty-two acres, beautifully landscaped, alongside the Nakhon Chaisri River in the midst of lush tropical vegetation. Here, roses grow in hundreds of thousands, in fifteen varieties including an unusual "stone rose" that looks rather like a cactus. Most tourists call here to stroll for an hour or so on the way back to Bangkok from Nakhon Pathom. Few people realize that there are very clean, comfortable accommodations and scores of amenities hidden among the trees and parkland. An air-conditioned hotel and seven traditional-style Thai bungalows are situated beside a large lake. Each bungalow is well secluded, with garage, air-conditioning, bathroom, refrigerator, and telephone for twenty-four-hour room service. They cost from 350 *baht* ($17.50) to 650 *baht* ($32.50) a night. A hotel double room is about 200 *baht* ($10) a night. Boats can be hired at the lakeside. There are two swimming pools, one for visitors and one for overnight guests, five restaurants serving Thai, Chinese, and European dishes, a playground for children, a bowling alley, and a miniature golf course. Speedboats on the river are available for hire, together with all types of skis for novice and expert water skiers. In addition, rice barge trips and early morning river trips in small boats can be arranged to see a rural floating market and the Thai village life. There is a new eighteen-hole golf course laid out on the other side of Pet Kasem Road. The Rose Garden becomes crowded at the weekends as Bangkok businessmen come here to play golf and leave their families across the road. If possible, go there on a weekday and, ideally, during May, June, or July when the roses are at their best. The roses are sold for about half a *baht* (5 cents) each and in large quantities to hotels and flower shops in Bangkok.

Suan Sampran resort is owned by the former mayor of Bangkok who, at the time of writing, has entered a monastery as a Buddhist monk. The resort opened in 1968.

Kanchanaburi (Kwai Bridge)

Kanchanaburi is accessible by rail from Thon Buri but the train schedules preclude a day trip. Besides being very cheap, this train passes through some lovely wild country. The station at Kanchanaburi town is about 3 kilometres (nearly 2 miles) from the Kwai Bridge. It is more advantageous to make the trip by car; this can be easily arranged with a Bangkok travel agency. The drive takes 3 to 3½ hours one way, but a visit to Nakhon Pathom is usually included (see p. 246) from where an excellent four-lane road (Highway 4) takes one most of the way to Kanchanaburi town, passing lotus-filled dikes, through flat rice plains, banana plantations, fields of sugar beet, and numerous coconut palms. From Kanchanaburi town to the Kwai Bridge the road goes through a busy fruit and vegetable market and leads into a narrow, winding country lane, passing houses and fences made entirely of bamboo. The town is approximately 133 kilometres (85 miles) west of Bangkok.

THE BRIDGE OVER THE RIVER KWAI—has become a world-famous phrase since Pierre Boulle wrote his best-selling book with that title, which, in turn, became a film. Today this bridge is regarded as a memorial to the men who died during the construction of the notorious Thai/Burma railway. The Japanese, who occupied Thailand during the Second World War, aimed to build a railway from Thailand for use as a military supply line to Burma. They used American, Dutch, British, and Australian prisoners-of-war as virtual slaves, forcing them either to work or die, in the most intolerable conditions. Indian, Burmese, Malaysian, Indonesian, Chinese, and Thai labourers also worked on the project, bringing the total labor force to 60,000 men.

Construction started in October 1942 on the new line, stretching from Nong Pladuk over flat country as far as this river, which is actually called Kwae Yai (Big Kwae). For most of the year the river, though wide, is fairly shallow and can even be waded across, but when the monsoons come it becomes a dangerous, fast-flowing torrent of foaming, muddy brown water, inhabited, it is said, by crocodiles. Of course, the area is malarial, and visitors staying overnight should sleep under mosquito nets and take all other precautions. The dense jungle is not only lush and beautiful but also unyielding and inhospitable. The railway line continued through it to the river Kwae Noe (Little Kwae) which it traversed, precariously clinging to the banks that were often just sheer rock face. Finally, the line penetrated what seemed to be "impenetrable and impassable" jungle and mountain terrain, eventually to join the Burma railway line at Thanbyuzayat. In all, it measured 415 kilometres (257 miles) with about two-thirds of the line in Thailand. Dubbed "Death Railway," it is said to have cost one life for every sleeper laid, or more than 9,000 altogether.

Much of the line was unsafe and therefore dismantled by the Allies after the war, but the section crossing the steel span bridge is in daily use. Near this bridge a diesel engine and a steam engine are on display. Used during the laying of the track, the diesel has two sets of wheels that enabled it to run either along a road or on a railway line. The steam locomotive was used along this line for military transport.

CHUNG KAI OR HOSPITAL CEMETERY—Also by this bridge is a refreshment stand where boats can be hired for around 30 to 40 *baht* per hour to cross the river (15 to 20 minutes). From there one can take a 1-*baht* taxi to this cemetery on the right bank of the river Kwae Noi.

DONRAK CEMETERY—This is the larger of the two cemeteries, situated about 2½ kilometres (1½ miles) from the bridge. The stark simplicity is striking. A large white cross stands in the middle, and neat rows of white stone slabs, each engraved with the name of an Allied soldier, stretch across the lawns. All who lie here are Dutch, Australian, or British. The Americans removed their dead to a cemetery in Hawaii.

THE DISCOVERY OF NEOLITHIC MAN—When the line had reached the banks of the river Kwae Noi, while the POWs toiled in the searing heat, one of the prisoners suddenly recognized a stone among the rubble that was once a tool of Neolithic Man. The prisoner was Dr. H. R. van Heekeren, a Dutch archeologist. He survived the war and was able to return home to compile a book about his first and subsequent discoveries in the area. The interest that followed his publication eventually led to several archeological expeditions in 1956 and later. Thousands of important artifacts dating from 5,000 to 10,000 years ago were excavated, including tools, coffins, and ceramics, as well as bronze sculptures from the 15th and 16th centuries. Visitors keen on archeology should travel initially to the site at Wang Po (accessible by rail from Kanchanaburi town). Kaeng Lawa Cave nearby, the home of Neolithic Man, was discovered in 1961. The National Museum in Bangkok also holds many of the finds.

For the adventurer/explorer—There are trips to be made from Wang Po by boat (about ten hours) to the Saiyok Waterfall set deep in the jungle. Make the journey between June and October, when the monsoons fill the river sufficiently. From here a further two days' trek by boat and elephant (hired from local villagers) to the Thong Pha Phuni District near the Thai/Burmese border passes through almost virgin tropical forest, now a last refuge for the wildlife that has escaped from the increasing areas under cultivation.

Rat Buri (or Ratchaburi)

Situated about 110 kilometres (66 miles) from Bangkok, south of Nakhon Pathom, along Highway 4, Rat Buri is about 2½ hours by train or car from the capital.

One of Thailand's oldest cities, with historic sites that date back 2,000 years, Rat Buri is the centre of the earthenware water-jar industry. (Every household in Thailand seems to have at least one of these pots for collecting and storing rainwater.) Thousands upon thousands of jars are stacked beside the Mae Klong River ready to be loaded and transported to the markets up and down the country. Their ruddy brown glaze shimmering like a sea of lights, the pots are a curious sight.

SIGHTSEEING IN RAT BURI—Visitors should stop at the Wat Khao Wang (Palace Hill Monastery). Originally an old monastery named Wat Sathanat existed atop this hill. King Rama V (Chulalongkorn) ordered it merged with a nearby *wat* and then built a palace on the site. The palace later reverted to the *wat,* and the complex took its present name. Less than 150 feet high, the hill's summit can be reached by car. Tall *chedi* and some rather dilapidated temple buildings are all that remain. The site's attraction lies in the peaceful surroundings, woods, blooming flowers, gentle breezes, and twittering birds.

WAT MAHATHAT—A *prang* 107 feet high, with four smaller *prang* around it, stands as a majestic monument to the Khmers who ruled this land long ago. Erected by them about 600 to 700 years ago, the *wat* has carvings on its crumbling walls that are worthy of note, as are the wall paintings that have been dated as 15th century.

CAVES OF KHAO NGU—Ngu (Snake) Hill belongs to a small range of hills about five miles northwest of Rat Buri. Devout Buddhists make pilgrimages to the Thom Russee (Hermit's Cave) to pay homage to two large Buddha images—one carved in the north wall and one in the south wall. They are believed to have been sculptured at about the time the first Buddhist missionaries came to Thailand, in the 3rd century B.C. The smaller images were most likely made during the Ayutthaya period (1350–1767). The ancient hieroglyphics inscribed below one of the images have never been deciphered. Khao Ngu (Snake Hill) Cave is nearby but would be of interest only to keen herpetologists.

Other caves in the vicinity are Chomphol Cave in the district of Chombung, about fourteen miles further north-east, and Khao Bin Cave, near a forestry station about nine miles from Ngu Hill, off the road to Chombung. Visitors should definitely employ an experienced guide. Chomphol Cave has an opening in the roof and is "forested" with stalagmites and stalactites. It is eerie and dank. The Khao Bin Cave, also dank, is more exciting but also dangerous. The pitch-black labyrinth extends over an estimated three acres.

TIMland—Thailand in Miniature

From Bangkok, go along the Paholyothin Road towards Don Muang Airport. At Bang Khen Station, turn left along Ngamwongwan Road. TIMland is about 5 kilometres along this country lane, past an awesome-looking prison. It is only ten minutes' drive from the airport. Admission costs 100 *baht* ($5) per person.

If one has only a day or a few hours in Bangkok, TIMland is the place to go. It is a twenty-acre park owned by a former forestry official named Mr. Term Tabtimtong. After the war, he began planting teak trees and cultivating a living Thai folk museum by inviting farmers and craftsmen from villages to live and work on his land. His idea was to preserve the heritage of Thai village industries. Over the years, this project developed and expanded into something unique. His friends urged him to open the park to the public, which he did, adding a theatre and arena for displays of Thai dancing and sports, working elephants, an aquarium, and other attractions to amuse the tourists.

One should arrive after lunch and wander around the "Product Display" section to see such things as rice threshing, silk spinning and weaving, pottery making, and paper umbrella and lacquer craft, before the show begins at 3:15 P.M. The programme is as follows:

3:15 P.M.	*Forn leb* fingernail dance of northern Thailand
3:20 P.M.	Demonstration of elephants at work
3:30 P.M.	Thai classical dancing, folk dancing, and music
4:00 P.M.	Thai boxing, cockfighting, snake feeding, sword and pole fighting
4:50 P.M.	Demonstration of elephants at work for latecomers

The visitor sees many aspects of Thai village life and crafts, all set out like a stage show and specially presented for easy colour photography. The indescribable atmosphere is best illustrated by quoting the Master of Ceremonies as he instructs the hordes of tourists watching the elephants hauling a teak log:

"O.K. now everybody, get your cameras ready" . . .

Elephant at TIMland.

(pause) . . . "O.K. cameras set ?" . . . (another pause) . . . "O.K. Jumbo, let it go!" As the elephants dutifully heave the teak logs—smooth and shiny from daily use—into a pond, making a huge splash, hundreds of cameras click simultaneously. So the show goes on. The majority of tourists enjoy it.

For the insatiable photographer, Mr. Tabtimtong has bought eleven performing elephants that demonstrate hunting, working, fighting, and racing, and then make a parade, all at Hua Mark, in the suburbs of Bangkok, about eight miles from town off Sukumvit Road on the left. Performances at 9:30 A.M. and 11:30 A.M. daily.

17

THE SOUTHEAST

Thailand's Riviera

The east-coast resorts are inviting, with spacious bays backed by lush, rolling hills. These are the places to enjoy sports or country quiet. There are miles of sandy beaches, fringed with palms and brushed with balmy breezes—some fashionable enclaves with super-modern hotels, others lonely and empty. The region is fertile and prosperous, the people friendly and good humoured. Glorious sunshine, calm waters ideal for skin-diving, yachting, water skiing, or just lazy bathing; exotic offshore islands, sleepy fishing villages, fresh tropical fruits and seafood—it sounds almost too good to be true. Weekend after weekend Bangkok residents invade the quiet and space of this "riviera." At other times tired tourists are left to toast in peace on the uncrowded beaches.

ACCESS—Good, well-paved, but generally narrow roads make it easy to drive to all the places mentioned below. There is no other means of transport to this area but one can travel as far as Pattaya by air-conditioned coach from Bangkok. There is also a local, provincial bus service that goes as far as Trat.

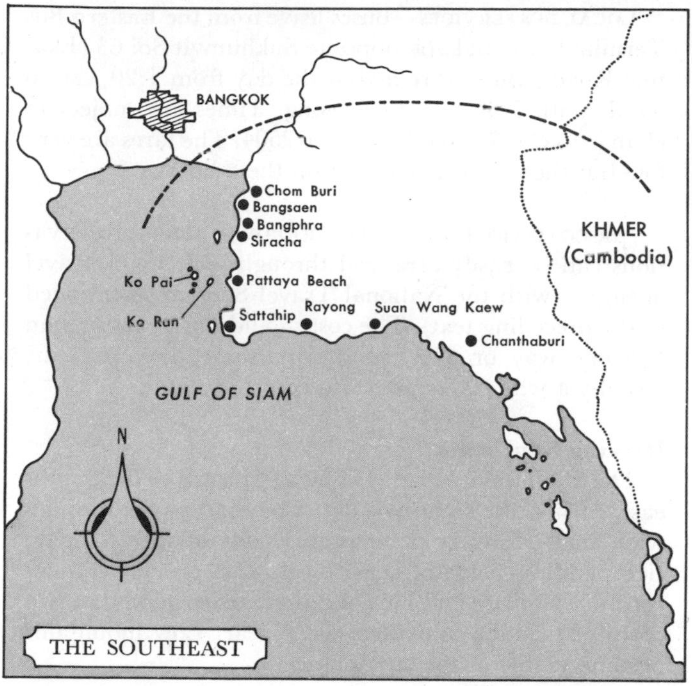

AIR-CONDITIONED BUS SERVICE—This is operated by the National Travel Service, 585 Rama VI Road: telephone 54575, 55486 for reservations.

Bangkok to Pattaya departing three times daily from:

Dusit Thani Hotel	at 9:00 A.M., 1:00 P.M., 5:00 P.M.
Rama Hotel	at 9:15 A.M., 1:15 P.M., 5:15 P.M.
Narai Hotel	at 9:30 A.M., 1:30 P.M., 5:30 P.M.

Pattaya to Bangkok departing three times daily from:

Pattaya Palace Hotel at 9:00 A.M., 1:00 P.M., 5:00 P.M.

The fare is 60 *baht* ($3) one way (30 *baht* for children)
100 *baht* ($5) round trip (60 *baht* for children)

Local bus services—Buses leave from the Eastern Bus Terminal at Bangkapi, opposite Sukhumvit Soi 63 (Ekamai Road). Buses throughout the day from 4:20 a.m. to Trad, until 5:35 p.m. to Rayong. Times are subject to change so check directly—tel: 912504. The fares are very low but there is little comfort on these buses.

Air-conditioned chauffeur-driven car—Reservations can be easily arranged through your hotel, travel agent, or with the National Travel Service (mentioned in the preceding text). The cost should not be more than $25 one way or $40 round trip (same day) per car. Usually a white Mercedes is used.

Driving Southeast

The Sukhumvit Road (Highway 3) leads to the Southeast. At first the scenery is flat. The road passes through wide fields of silvery pampas grass, dotted with poppies, rice paddies, fields of sugar beet, and groves of small coconut. Climate and soil conditions are so good that two crops of rice are cultivated every year. Low mountains become visible in the far distance.

Chon Buri (also known as Cholburi)

Ninety-four kilometres (59 miles) from Bangkok; the modern concrete blocks are new apartments and factories, destined to become part of a new industrial complex using Siracha as its seaport. Previous generations have lived a more peaceful existence, depending mainly on fishing. Along the shore there are hundreds, if not thousands, of stakes placed by the fishermen to form fish traps and to catch the mussels that attach themselves in clusters. The mussels, both horse mussels and sea mussels, are used for feeding ducks. Chon Buri is famous for asparagus that grows in only six months. Tapioca, peanuts, pineapples, and other fruits are also cultivated in this area.

Bangsaen Beach Resort

One hundred and four kilometres (65 miles) from Bangkok, the road from Chon Buri, now a four-lane highway, winds among the hills just out of sight from the sea. Bangsaen is well signposted at a turning to the right. It is a beautifully clean resort with a beach of white sand separated from the hotel and bungalows by a promenade lined with coconut palms. The lawns and gardens are delightful, and to complete the view there is a small island across the bay. The sea is clear and ideal for all water sports. Water skiing, sailing, and fishing trips can be arranged on the spot. Among the gardens are a large, fresh-water swimming pool and a children's pool. An ideal spot for a family with car, Bangsaen is usually busy at weekends but not overcrowded.

SIGHTSEEING AROUND BANGSAEN—One should not miss the lovely view from Sammuk Hill, a five-minute drive from the hotel. It overlooks the bay, attractive weekend villas that belong to rich Thais, and the fishing village of Ang Sila, 6 kilometres (4 miles) north of the beach. Ang Sila literally means "Stone Basin"; it is so named because of the granite found here. The villagers have turned the granite to good use. Strolling through the streets one hears the tap-chip-chick of stone carving going on behind the little wooden houses. Traditionally the local residents have made pestle-and-mortar sets in every conceivable size, rice-grinding stones, and statuettes. Recently, they have turned their skill to producing quasi-Japanese *toro* (stone lanterns) that are not really sensible souvenirs for air travellers but, nevertheless, are excellent value at only about 300 *baht* ($15).

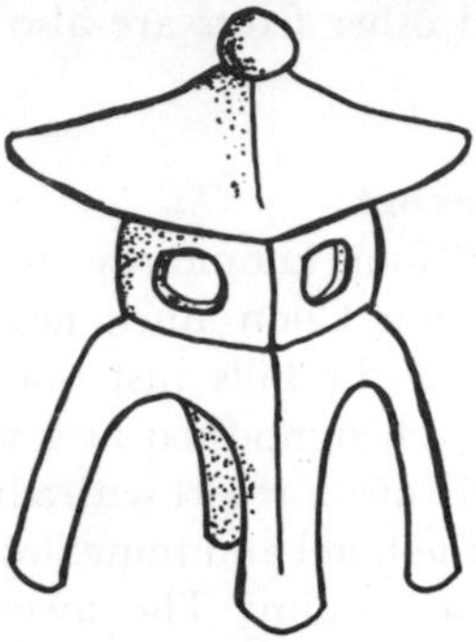

Stone lantern *(toro)*.

ACCOMMODATION AT BANGSAEN—The hotel and some 150 bungalows are spread over an area of 190 acres among the lawns and gardens that face the beach. They are managed entirely by T.O.T., who must be commended on the cleanliness, service, and excellent cuisine. Thai, Chinese, and European dishes are available. Among the many facilities is an air-conditioned convention room. The bungalows are one- two- and three-bedroomed, each with a refrigerator, telephone (for room service), lounge, and bathroom, but they are not air-conditioned. Rates are very reasonable and cheaper from June until November. Bookings have to be made through T.O.T., Mansion 2, Rajdamnern Avenue, Bangkok, tel: 24641–2.

Bangphra Golf Course

From Bangkok 112 kilometres (70 miles), the turning is well signposted to the left, just a few miles beyond the Bangsaen turning along Highway 3. It is a pleasant fifteen minutes' drive from Bangsaen Beach, past fertile farmland and along the banks of a water reservoir surrounded by hills and coconut plantations. The Chinese gateway on the way is the entrance to a Chinese millionaire's private cemetery.

The golf course is dotted with mango, flame trees, and palms set among wooded hills and within sight of the Gulf of Siam which brings cool sea breezes. It is magnificent, 7,249 yards of fairways in a challenging layout (surely one of the longest courses in the world). A non-member public course, it has eighteen holes for a par seventy-two. The green fee is only 20 *baht* ($1) but double at weekends and national holidays. Seventy per cent of the clients are Japanese—always serious and keen. Of the others, one wonders how many came just for the companionship of the pretty, yellow-coated girl caddies.

ACCOMMODATION AT BANGPHRA—Many golfers choose to stay at Bangsaen Beach or to leave their families there happily for the day. Both places are under the management of T.O.T. Unattached golfers may prefer the ultra-modern, air-conditioned motel that overlooks the links. The hotel is being enlarged, and a new swimming pool is under construction for "after-game" dips. Other existing amenities include a bar, restaurant, changing rooms, and a golfers' shop.

Siracha

This is 116 kilometres (72 miles) from Bangkok; turn right off Highway 3 just a couple of miles beyond the turning for Bangphra golf course.

Siracha is due to be developed into a modern seaport. At present it is a muddy bay with a picturesque fishing harbour. There is a small island across the harbour. It is a popular spot among Thais, and there are plenty of very cheap hotels. The shore around here is teeming with sea creatures that are best seen when they are most active, at night, with the aid of a flashlight. All kinds of mollusks and swarms of tiny crabs, some the size of a grain of rice, scratch and scurry at the edge of the waves in search of plankton. Siracha is also the site of sawmills, a plywood factory, and an oil refinery.

Onward to Pattaya

The drive along Highway 1, now a single, two-lane road, begins to wind through jungle-covered, rolling hills. Here and there, one catches a glimpse of Thai-style wooden houses on stilts set back among the bush. Some are roofed with coconut palm leaves that blend well with the surroundings. Others have been "modernized" with roofs of corrugated iron, now rusted. The road continues through fields of swaying pampas, groves of mango trees, coconut palms, and clusters of very tall bamboo. A large institutional-type building on the right, set behind spacious lawns, is a university for Thai monks. An impressive building, it gleams white with twirling decorated eaves imitating the temples. From time to time saffron-robed monks stroll leisurely across the compound. Further on, one flashes past entrances to grand villas along the coast. Here, a new mosque is being built, and there is the Siam Country Club. Several small, signposted turnings to the right lead to Pattaya Beach along short, narrow roads.

Pattaya Beach Resort

This resort is 147 kilometres (92 miles) from Bangkok; allow three hours for the drive.

Before Pattaya developed into a tourist resort it was a sleepy fishing village. Even today, fishermen can be photographed casting their nets from small boats that skim along inshore. But for these fishermen times have changed. Many have turned to the more profitable occupation of renting their boats to take rich foreigners

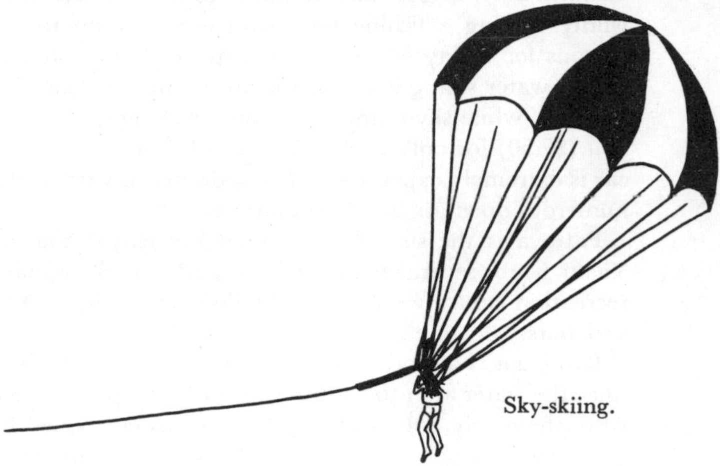

Sky-skiing.

across the Gulf of Siam for a picnic on one of the outlying islands, or for a trip to a coral reef, or a fishing excursion during which the crew will produce a charcoal burner and cook a lunch aboard, using freshly caught fish.

Pattaya has everything for luxurious recreation. The beach stretches for miles around the edge of Pattaya Bay, dotted with coconut palm, flame trees, and, in front of the hotels, sun-shades woven from palm leaves. Apart from cruising with the fishermen, swimming, or strolling along the sands, here are some of the other facilities and activities that one can enjoy: deep-sea fishing; underwater photography; sky skiing; scuba diving; water skiing; horse riding. See also the section on skin diving in the chapter, "Entertainments and Sports," page 106.

All necessary equipment and/or instructors are available. Pattaya is also the starting point for tours to the jungle to see the elephants at work, to the Bangphra golf course, or to Rayong, a quieter seaside, and to Chanthaburi to see the sapphire miners. Costs vary wildly. Hiring a fishing boat with crew for up to ten persons for a day is absurdly cheap at about 200 *baht* ($10); water skiing is reasonable at about 100 *baht* ($5) an hour, while sky-skiing seems rather expensive at 150 *baht* ($7.50) for only twenty minutes. Hiring a self-drive car is extremely expensive. So, too, do prices vary at the numerous open-air beach restaurants.

Pattaya is the site of the fashionable Royal Varuna Yacht Club, several deluxe hotels, and a U.S. military recreation centre with its usual following of night clubs and bars.

Bangsaen is a more suitable resort for young children since the water at Pattaya Beach becomes deep very soon. Also, the lovely, soft white sand is sometimes spoiled by the horse and pony dirt. (It should be only a matter of time before the local hotel proprietors realize that beaches can be *either* for bathers *or* for horse riders but not for both!)

Accommodation at pattaya—Besides numerous hotels there are villas, cottages, bungalows, motels, and even a boatel. Some are close to the beach and a few are on the beach. If one rents a house or bungalow it should be furnished with all necessary cooking utensils including a stove and dishes, a refrigerator or icebox (ice can be delivered daily), and bedding. Shopping for food such as tea, bread, biscuits, and tinned food should be done in advance, in Bangkok. Fresh fruit and fish are available locally. A small accommodation would cost from about 100 *baht* ($5) a day. Three of the luxurious hotels are the Nipa Lodge, built around a well-established tropical garden, the Pattaya Palace, and the New Ocean View Hotel. Rates are generally reduced 10 per cent from

June until January (off-season) and sometimes from Mondays to Fridays. Weekends at Pattaya are crowded.

Sattahip

175 kilometres (110 miles) from Bangkok, Sattahip and U Taphao are sites of U.S. military bases. Asia's largest airport is at U Taphao.

Driving to Rayong

This is 180 kilometres (about 112 miles) from Bangkok using the shortest route—a new road via Ban Bang and Ban Khai; one should turn left at Chon Buri instead of taking Highway 3, which follows the coast. Coming from Bangsaen or Pattaya one may either follow Highway 3 via Sattahip and U Taphao (but beyond here the drive passes through rubber plantations, away from the sea) or, alternatively, take a slightly shorter route, using another new road from Ban Amphoe to Ban Chang, cutting off the Sattahip peninsula. The latter route passes through more enjoyable scenery—verdant rolling hills, occasional rubber plantations, and prosperous settlements. The mighty, towering, white-trunked trees are *mak* gum trees. In this area the people are dependent mostly on sugar and rubber plantations. They make sugar from undeveloped coconuts by simply cutting them open, collecting the juice, and stirring it in a heated saucepan.

Rayong, Province of Secluded Beaches

Looking for a deserted, unspoiled sandy beach? This is the main attraction of the province of Rayong. There are numerous bays where the sea is clean, the sand soft and gleaming white, and the beaches shaded by naturally grown palms. Lovely, too, is the backdrop of wooded hills and forests of bamboo, interspersed with rubber plantations and fields of tapioca. Sometimes one meets local fishermen who greet visitors like long-lost friends. For a few dollars they will take people across to Koh Keo Pisadarn Island, a little tropical paradise not far offshore. There, one finds more white sandy beaches and more palm trees, all peaceful and picturesque. An ideal spot for skin diving, the island has a population of only twenty-six. They spend their time fishing and shipping the white sand across to the mainland to be sold for making glass. Although Koh Keo Pisadarn is one of many islands off the coast of Thailand, it is well known as the place where the famous Thai poet, Soonthorn Poo, composed his work.

Further along Highway 3, 28 kilometres (about 18 miles) beyond the town of Rayong (the provincial capital of the same name) is a signposted right turning to Suan Wang Kaew. It is a beautiful resort where new bungalows have been built along the beach and on the hillsides facing the sea. Plans are in hand to construct a new hotel, tennis courts, swimming pool, and a golf course too. It is rather like Pattaya ten years ago. Nearby, along the narrow coast road westwards, is a lovely Forestry Park of Caserina tress. The reservation, kept by the Forestry Department, is a good area for picnics. The road leads onto Highway 3, making an alternative back route to Suan Wang Kaew.

Going back to Highway 3 again and continuing about 13 miles eastwards beyond the turning for Suan Wang Kaew, there is a small turning right, leading to another beauty spot, the Laem Ma Ping Peninsula, also ideal for swimming or picnics.

ACCOMMODATION IN RAYONG PROVINCE—This is limited to a few local-style hotels. In the provincial capital of Rayong both the "Rayong Otani" and the "New Asia" are adequate and clean. More attractive are the newly constructed bungalows and modern accommodations being built at Suan Wang Kaew, which is developing into a comfortable seaside resort.

Chanthaburi, an Eminent Old Town

This is 324 kilometres (202 miles) from Bangkok. (See preceding text, "Driving to Rayong," for the alternative routes.) In addition there will be a new route, Highway 317, running from thc north of Chanthaburi through mountainous terrain to Sa Kaeo, on the main highway that comes from Bangkok via Nakhon Nayok to Cambodia via Aranyaprathet on the frontier.

Chanthaburi* is a noble town with a grand history, a grand palace, and a grand atmosphere reminiscent of the old colonial towns in the southern states of the U.S.A. Much of its charm comes from its location. The town undulates across a broad valley cut by a winding river. It throbs with activity, just as any town would where fortunes can be made overnight, and merchants compete fervently for business. Chanthaburi is the mining and marketing centre of the sapphire industry in Thailand. This alone would be enough to keep the town rich, but sapphires merely augment its prosperity. Chanthaburi is renowned as the country's richest fruit-growing region, producing a wide variety of interesting, indigenous Thai fruits. To supplement this natural wealth there are luxuriant rubber plantations. By Western standards the workers may have piteous incomes but practically all the rubber tappers and fruit pickers have their own motorcycles (usually Japanese). They work only mornings. In other words, everyone can afford both the money

* Chanthaburi is the name both of the province and of its provincial capital.

to buy the right to dig a plot of gem-bearing land and the time to try his luck in the scramble for star sapphires.

SIGHTSEEING IN CHANTHABURI—Chanthaburi is not like any other provincial town in Thailand. It has a variety of peculiar attractions that foreign visitors find fascinating.

The sapphire mines—excavated in the valleys in and around Chanthaburi since the 18th century: the most easily accessible mining area for visitors today is at Khao Ploy Waen, along the Ta Mai Road.

Here, among the trees of an old rubber plantation, the prospectors dig holes about three or four feet wide, down, down, down through the soft loam soil to a depth of about twenty-five feet. At this level they hope to find a fault, or layer of gems, and they may dig small tunnels horizontally. The gems are usually in layers about twelve inches thick. It is messy, unenviable work. The miners take turns down the narrow shaft; each one gets in and out by pressing hands, back, and feet against the earthen walls to make a bridge and wriggling his way down or up. At the bottom ventilation is poor and there is little oxygen. The miner takes a candle with him to serve as a warning signal (the flame goes out when there is too little oxygen). There, in the cold, dank pit, the miner grovels and, with the aid of a small pick, fills a rattan basket with soil. On a signal, the basket is hauled up by rope with the aid of a long branch, pivoted and counterbalanced. The soil is tipped into a sieve, washed, and sedulously examined. Chancing upon what appears a small piece of dull coloured glass, the experienced hands will place it aside. Usually, it will be practically worthless but it could equal a fortune.

The soil around the top of the mine shafts is soft and

liable to crumble. Look carefully where you tread—a step backwards without thinking might be fatal!

Talad Rong See (marketplace for gems)—at the intersection of Hua Hin and Ta Mai roads: Talad Rong See, literally "rice-mill market," is the place where gem dealers gather from around 11:00 A.M. until dusk. It is fascinating to watch the dealers, miners, and shopkeepers bargaining energetically. Foreign visitors who have a good knowledge of gems may also buy from here at well below Bangkok prices.

CUTTING AND POLISHING GEMS—A shopkeeper or local guide could lead you to one of the numerous workshops, usually tucked behind a house or shop in a wooden shack. The gems are stuck onto a small holder with gum made from heated, powdered clay. The worker then applies the gem at different angles to his grinding and polishing wheel, which looks rather like a potter's wheel but is made of steel. The gem is dipped into water to cool it, and, from time to time, a diamond-edged bar is used to make the steel grinding wheel absolutely smooth. It takes about five years to acquire enough skill to cut and polish the best stones well, a job that would qualify for the top wage of about 500 *baht* ($25) a week.

Besides sapphires, one will probably see red and blue "rubies." These are not found locally but are bought raw from Australia.

THE JEWELLERY SHOPS—dozens of tempting shops in the main streets: never buy before comparing prices and stones in several shops. Prices should be lower than in Bangkok.

THE CHURCH OF THE IMMACULATE CONCEPTION—in a

Vietnamese quarter on the east bank of the river: this church is the largest in Thailand. Completely non-Oriental in appearance, it looks incongruous among the little wooden houses. How did this great Gothic cathedral come to be built here? Its history goes back to 1711, when 130 Vietnamese Christians, led by a French minister, arrived at Chanthaburi after a fifteen-day voyage from Annam.* On this spot they built a small wooden church that has been destroyed and rebuilt four times during conflicts with Burma and Cambodia. The present building was erected in 1903. The community, doubtless tired of rebuilding the church after every war, removed two very high spires during the Second World War as a precaution against bomb damage. The spires were never restored, so the towers have a stunted appearance today. Adjacent to the church is the Fatima Convent School.

The Vietnamese community has grown to a population of around 6,000. Thais call them "Yuan." Ethnically, they are Annamites and they speak a dialect of Vietnamese. Many of them have adopted Christian names such as Maria or Paulo, and almost all of them are Christians. There are estimated to be only 200,000 or so Christians in Thailand, approximately 0.5 per cent of the population.

The "Yuan" or Vietnamese/Thai are accepted by the Thai people, and they have Thai citizenship. Most of them are engaged in the business of producing and selling woven items made from reeds or rattan, such as handbags, purses, beach bags, and mats in a wide variety of colours and patterns. They can be seen on sale in the main street shops.

CHANTHABURI'S OTHER POINTS OF INTEREST—The Mon-

* The Kingdom of Annam existed until 1948. It is now part of Vietnam and Laos.

Khmers occupied this area until they were pushed out in the 14th century by the northern Thais. They left no great structures as at Angkor or Phimai, but some archeologists may be interested in the ruins of a Shiivite Temple east of Chanthaburi town down a side road about 5 miles away along the road to Trat. The ruins are badly worn, and little is left of the carved stonework that is found scattered in the grounds of Wat Tong Toer. Some of the larger blocks have been used in the foundation of the *wiharn.*

Another historical site is Khai Nern Wong, a quiet wooded hill 5 kilometres (3 miles) south of Chanthaburi. King Taksin retreated to Khai Nern Wong in the 18th century, after Ayutthaya was overrun by Burmese invaders. Taksin raised a new army and built warships. Then, within one year, he returned to Ayutthaya and succeeded in ousting the Burmese. Soon afterwards, he decided to move Siam's capital from Ayutthaya to Thon Buri, now Bangkok's twin city. King Taksin is a much venerated hero. On Khai Nern Wong hill is a shrine dedicated to him. Also on this hill and at Laem Sing there are fragments of a fortress built for defence in the 19th century by King Rama III. Scattered around it, among the undergrowth, are the barrels of huge cannons that the local residents believe are protected by spirits that will harm anyone who disturbs them. Laem Sing is on the coast just southwest of Chanthaburi and has a quiet sandy beach. From here one can find a fisherman willing to take visitors to Ko Chang Island, another tropical paradise island where, it is said, there is a plantation owner who sometimes thinks, sometimes sleeps, and sometimes just counts the coconuts that fall.

Queen Rambhai Barni has a palace in Chanthaburi. She was queeen to the last absolute monarch to rule Thailand, King Rama VII, who abdicated just after the revolution in 1932. He died in England, and later his queen came back to Thailand to live, staying at least part of the time in Chanthaburi.

Ornithologist, Ichthyologist, Entomologist, or Herpetologist?

The islands and shores along the east coast will be of interest to you, for there are wide varieties of sea birds, tropical fish, game fish (such as the marlin), and a host of sea creatures, butterflies, other insects, and reptiles to be found. The uninhabited islands are particularly fascinating, though their thorny vegetation may be difficult to penentrate.

Of special interest are the large communities of giant turtles whose tracks trace their meandering across the sands. In December, at night, there is a great invasion of these creatures coming ashore to lay eggs in the sand.

18

THE NORTHEAST

Few foreign visitors have ventured into this region but, with the building of the Friendship Highway in 1956, and with other excellent roads, the Northeast (Khorat Plateau) is no longer inaccessible. In fact, it is feasible to drive from Bangkok to Nong Khai, a distance of about 662 kilometres (411 miles), in one day. The places of special interest are closer to Bangkok than that and make a refreshing break from the humidity, noise, and bustle of the capital.

The approach to the plateau is exhilarating as one pulls away from the modern world and drives through vast primeval forests, lush and tropical, inhabited only by unfamiliar birds and other wild life. The views are magnificent and the distances great, but a good car eats away the highway soon to draw near to the dramatic escarpment of the plateau, where the road winds and climbs steeply. Higher, the bush is interspersed with clumps of bamboo that grow fifteen feet high or more yet bend resiliently in the wind. The vegetation becomes more sparse until, atop the rolling plateau, there are only patches of tough grass and occasional stunted pines. It is a harsh, inhospitable region. Flooded, malarial, and swampy in the monsoon season, dusty and parched for the rest of the year (with the exception of the wide lowland marshes), this area may not sound inviting. But the wild tropical rainforests and distant views are grand, and the cooler mountain air is fresh and invigorating. The southern steep escarpments of the Dang Rak range overlook expansive tracts of the Khmer plain. Eastwards, the plateau slopes gently towards the Mekong River, the frontier between Thailand and Laos. The arid plateau descends into a region of paludal marshland where, nearer the Mekong, there are several great lakes. The Mekong is unforgettable. It meanders north and east of the plateau, stretching from 2,000 to 4,000 feet wide. Its shimmering waters are dotted with islands and sometimes broken by rapids.

Phimai for sightseeing, Khao Yai for relaxation, and Surin (in November) for the spectacular elephant roundup are three good reasons for venturing into this region. For archeologists, the prospects are boundless. There is evidence that lost kingdoms, other ruined cities like Phimai, and treasure hoards dating back 5,000 years or more lie untouched beneath the dusty surface of the Northeast.

Khao Yai National Park

ACCESS—Situated 205 kilometres (122 miles) from Bangkok, Khao Yai can be reached only by road. The drive takes about 3½ hours along well-paved highways.

PREPARING FOR KHAO YAI—A pair of binoculars and a telephoto lens are almost essential items for viewing the birds and butterflies. Of course, strong walking shoes and warm clothes are necessary. Campers must bring their own mosquito nets. Anti-malaria pills are advisable too.

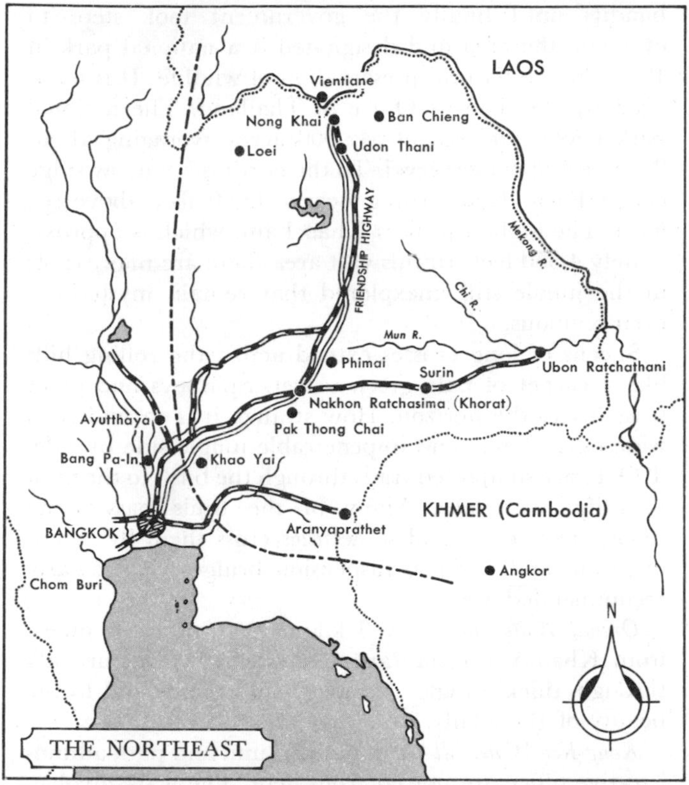

Exploring the jungles and highlands—This area used to be known as Khao Yai Forest. Khao Yai means "big mountain." There were few trails through the thick growth where only occasional hunters trekked. Then, about half a century ago, a few dozen families drifted into the area, made clearings, and started cultivation on a shifting system. This played havoc with the stream flow and affected the water supply in surrounding areas. Khao Yai Forest also became a notorious retreat for bandits until finally the government took steps to evacuate the area and designated it a national park in 1959, for the natural preservation of wildlife. It is managed by the Tourist Office of Thailand. The national park covers an area of 542,000 acres averaging about 2,500 feet above sea level. To the north is a narrow ridge called Khao Keow rising nearly 4,000 feet above sea level. The highest peak is Khao Lam, which is approximately 4,350 feet. In this vast area there are many spots in the jungle still unexplored that remain mysterious, even ominous.

Sheens of long grasses extend across the rolling hills like a carpet of pale green velvet. Spinneys and giant trees break the horizon. How strange it is to find such wide open spaces and impenetrable jungle side by side. T.O.T. has signposted trails through the bush to the most beautiful waterfalls. Many of the trails pass along mountain streams and sometimes cross them by means of rattan and bamboo suspension bridges. Particularly recommended are:

Orchid Waterfall—only 3 kilometres (almost 2 miles) from Khao Yai restaurant but a hearty two-hour walk through thick jungle. Various wild orchids add to the beauty of these falls;

Kong Keo Waterfall—camping ground and park administrative office are not far from here. The walk involves crossing a couple of suspension bridges;

Haew Suwat Waterfall—dropping seventy-five feet with thunderous force. The sunlight produces rainbow effects;

Haew Sai Waterfall—a further half-hour's hike along a narrow path by the stream.

A walk through real jungle is exciting. It is comparatively dark under the tall trees where narrow shafts of sunlight break through the umbrella-like dome of entangled branches and creepers. The gigantic trees are entwined with sturdy vines that sometimes fall across the trails, forcing the hiker to clamber, ungainly, over or under them. Off the popular tracks the going will be very strenuous. Adventurous, energetic hikers are advised to employ one of the local T.O.T. guides before venturing from the signposted trails, as it is very easy to become lost in the jungle.

PASTIMES AT KHAO YAI—Besides hiking, other popular activities at Khao Yai are bathing, golf, and watching the wildlife. There are natural bathing facilities at the pools by the waterfalls, where the Thais love to take cooling dips. Most foreigners find the water too cold. A less primary pastime is golf. Here is a fine, eighteen-hole golf course in a silvan setting. The greens fee is nominal. Another facility is the Wildlife Watch Tower, for which advance arrangements must be made through T.O.T.

MIDNIGHT SAFARI—At 11:00 P.M. a Landrover moves off on the narrow roads through the jungle. A searchlight is mounted on the roof of the vehicle and, in the pitch dark, the man on the roof aims its beam into the bush. With luck it will cross the path of some creature. Startled, the animal freezes and stares into the beam of light, eyes gleaming. When one's own eyes adjust to the sharp light, perhaps with the aid of binoculars, the creature can be recognized and observed, often for several minutes. Most animals seem not unduly disturbed by the intruders.

Among the Khao Yai inhabitants are various types of deer, bears, boars, oxen, porcupines, snakes, mongooses, and a wide variety of birds—small, large, colourful, and rare. T.O.T. also suggests that elephants and tigers are still roaming in the area, but this is more likely conjecture than fact.

ACCOMMODATION AT KHAO YAI—There is a choice of accommodation as follows:

Bungalows—Twenty-six two-bedroomed bungalows with sitting room, terrace, shower, and refrigerator. Wooden buildings with mosquito screens. About 200 *baht* ($11) a night is charged. Gas stoves may be rented for an additional 10 *baht* (50 cents).

Motels—Ten single-bedroomed accommodations with shower, sitting room, and refrigerator. About 165 *baht* a night.

Tourist Houses—Four buildings for low-budget travellers with dormitory-style arrangements.

Camping—The site is near the Kong Keo Waterfall. Sleeping bags, cooking utensils, and mosquito nets are not provided.

There is an attractive restaurant built separately that serves Thai, Chinese, and European-style food. Bottles of Polaris drinking water may be bought here.

Booking can be made at the office of T.O.T., Mansion 2, Rajdamnern Ave., Bangkok. If possible, it is better to avoid thc weekends, as this is a popular resort. Any time of the year is suitable for a visit.

Pak Thong Chai Silk Village

ACCESS—About 27 kilometres (just 17 miles) south of Khorat, by a well-paved road.

Every household seems to be engaged in some stage of the production of silk material. Raw silk is dyed in tubs, dried in backyards. Housewives spin the thread while amusing their children, and the sound of hand-looms, "clack, bonk, tahi" (or is it "pak-thong, chai"?), can be heard in almost every street. This is one of Thailand's important silk centres supplying the silk shops in Bangkok. Several shops along the main street sell silk lengths —all less expensively than in the capital.

Khorat or Nakhon Rajsima

Nakhon Ratchasima or Nakhon Rajsima is the official name used on maps and by the post office. The town is more generally known as Khorat, and this name is more popular today.

ACCESS—About 256 kilometres (160 miles) from Bangkok. The drive takes about four hours, or one can go by train which takes five hours, forty minutes, arriving at Khorat at 1:10 A.M.—not a very convenient hour. Hotels will, however, send a representative to the station to meet clients if asked. There is also a bus service operated by The Transport Co., Ltd., Bangkok, from its northern route terminal at Phaholyothin Road at 5:00 A.M., arriving in Khorat about 9:30 A.M. daily.

KHORAT HOTEL AND TRANSPORTATION CENTRE—Because of its position, Khorat has naturally developed as a base for visitors to the Northeast, and an abundance of new hotels, some of which are air-conditioned, has been built here in recent years. Here are plenty of good restaurants, too, serving Thai, Chinese, and European dishes. It is the obvious stopover place for travellers passing through the Northeast. All transportation services (except air services) radiate from here.

SIGHTSEEING IN KHORAT—Driving through Khorat one may notice remains of the old city walls. These were built when King Narai founded Khorat as a frontier town in the 17th century. One of the gateways, called Chumphon Gate, is well preserved. The bronze statue in front of this old city gateway is of a famous Thai woman named Tao Suranari, in honour of her courageous fight against invaders from Laos in 1826.

Those interested in sculpture and archeology may

seek out the Mahavirawongse Museum, a branch of the National Museum, situated in the grounds of Wat Sutatchinda, which faces the provincial government office a few hundred yards south of the Tao Suranari statue.

Khorat is also a commercial centre for the silk produced in the province, and a good selection of materials can be purchased here.

Phimai—Thailand's Angkor

ACCESS—About 312 kilometres (195 miles) from Bangkok using the Friendship Highway: allow about five hours for the drive. From Khorat (see preceding text) it is only 56 kilometres (35 miles) by an excellent road, making Khorat the obvious place to stay, since there is no good hotel in Phimai. A round trip to Phimai can be arranged easily through most hotels, or one may simply charter a taxi for about 100 *baht* ($5). There is also a local bus service for those with strong nerves. Some tourists stay overnight at Khao Yai National Park, which is 187 kilometres (117 miles) south of Phimai, just off the Friendship Highway.

It is not practical to think of flying to Khon Kaen, the nearest airport, which is more than 100 miles away to the north.

PHIMAI, AFTER 1,000 YEARS—Phimai is one of the oldest cities of Thailand, representing the splendour of the Khmer Empire that spread across the southern portion of the Khorat Plateau. It is the most impressive of dozens and dozens of archeological sites that are scattered around the plateau, many of which have not yet been properly excavated.

There are no records to show exactly when Phimai was founded but the French archeologist Parmentier found similarities here to Angkor Wat in Cambodia. He finally concluded that parts of the sanctuary were constructed in the reign of King Surijavaman (A.D. 1002–49), which makes Phimai older than Angkor. The type of architecture is called "Prasad Hin," literally "Rock Castle." It is peculiar to northeast Thailand and refers to the sanctuaries constructed either for Buddhist temples or for Hindu shrines. They had tall spires on tiered bases and were intricately carved with figures and inscriptions. At Phimai, no one can fail to be impressed by the beauty of the sculpture and bas-reliefs, which could be compared with the works of ancient Greeks or to the Hindu art found in India. The tedious excavation and reconstruction of the Phimai Sanctuary began in the 1950's. Now, it is the most magnificent example of Khmer architecture in existence apart from Angkor, which is, for the time being, impossible to visit.

SIGHTSEEING AT PHIMAI

The town as it was originally laid out was enclosed within four great stone walls that formed a perfect rectangle 1,031 by 565 metres (1,134 by 621 yards). The east wall has been mostly demolished by the Mun River, but remains of the other three can still be seen. Each wall had a gateway. Driving from Khorat one will pass through a breach in the north wall (this is not the original gateway).

The focal point of the ancient city was, and still is, the main sanctuary, which is also within four red sandstone walls forming a rectangle 280 by 250 metres (308 by 275 yards), each with a gateway. Visitors enter through the southern gate, which is believed to have been the main entrance, for an admission fee of 2 *baht* (10 cents).

Naga gate—Two stone lions guard the entrance. Stone serpents form the railings of the Naga Bridge.

Outer courtyard—This contains a reservoir at each corner, and there were also four Buddhist temples, each containing a Buddha image. Now, only two of the images remain.

Main sanctuary—Four galleries surround the central compound, in which are three *prang* or pagodas. Each gallery has a gateway. Looking back, one can see that the gateways are in direct lines to the outer gate. The three *prang* have been painstakingly re-constructed. Original stone slabs and lintels have been remounted on their former positions and pinned or cemented. Sometimes new stone blocks were specially hewn and carved to replace missing sections. The main *prang* in the centre is built of laterite and sandstone and is covered with exquisite carvings of Buddhist saints, Hindu gods and goddesses, scenes from the Indian epic Ramayana, and ancient inscriptions dated between A.D. 1036 and 1046. It stands about seventy feet high. To the left is a smaller, laterite *prang* that was named Prang Brahmadat after a statue of King Brahmadat was found inside. To the right of the main *prang* is Prang Hin Daeng (Red Stone Tower). Just behind this *prang* are the ruins of a small Hindu shrine that once housed *lingam* sculptures (phallic symbols of Siva). It is believed that worshippers would pour water, taken from the sacred reservoirs in the outer courtyard, over the *lingam*. The *lingam* sculptures are temporarily kept at Wat Derm nearby.

The entire sanctuary is fascinating, as it has not been completely reconstructed. One should allow one to two hours to wander around the stone ruins and slabs lying among the bush and palm trees in the compound. Many of the stone blocks are beautifully carved and seem to have been left lying as they have been for centuries.

PHIMAI OPEN-AIR MUSEUM—A few minutes' walk northeast from the main sanctuary is a small lawn, by a stream, on which treasured pieces of Khmer art are neatly arranged, some under cover. The works of art are not only from Phimai. All the items are labelled in English.

SAI NGARM (beautiful banyan tree)—About a kilometre east of the main sanctuary is an ideal picnic spot, situated near a reservoir and lovely parkland. One grove of banyan trees with interwoven branches forms a giant sunshade for visitors. Seats are provided, and soft drinks are sold from stalls.

Surin Elephant Round-Up

ACCESS—424 kilometres (265 miles) from Bangkok. A train journey of about ten hours is the only practical way to reach Surin. Reservations must be made through T.O.T. in Bangkok or through the office of the State Railways. The all-inclusive round trip costs around 1,250 *baht,* or $62.50 per person, including meals.

TIMETABLE—The elephant round-up, in mid-November (the exact date changes from year to year), is organized jointly by the Surin Provincial Office, T.O.T., and the State Railways, and the itinerary is usually as follows:

Day 1—8:00 P.M.	Depart from Bangkok by specially chartered night train
Day 2—6:00 A.M.	Arrive at Surin and transfer by bus to a local school for breakfast
7:30 A.M.	Bus transfer to round-up site
8:00 A.M.–12:00 noon	Round-up demonstrations
12:00 noon–3:00 P.M.	Lunch and leisure time
3:00 P.M.	Special train leaves for Bangkok, arriving around midnight. Dinner is served on the train.

Catching a wild elephant—The people of Surin, together with a hundred or more elephants, enact the entire procedure of an elephant hunt. Elephants used to be hunted at night from December until March but now Surin may be the only place in the world where one can see a hunt demonstrated. After the pre-hunting rituals to ensure protection from accidents, dozens of the lumbering beasts charge with frightening impetus but under the control of their skillful, diminutive mahouts. The "wild" elephants are caught with a lasso and grounded by teams of men. The hunt is followed by a round-up and playful demonstrations such as a tug of war between one elephant and lines of men. Finally, there is a grand parade of the elephants in traditional battledress with their mahouts dressed as ancient warriors.

The siamese elephant era—Elephants played an important role in the history and life of the Siamese. Not only symbols of power and prestige, they were also military assets in several wars against the Malays, Burmese, and Cambodians, thus keeping Siam from domination. The respected elephant was chosen to appear on Siam's first national flag and it is depicted on the country's first coins.

Until the 19th century hundreds of thousands of elephants, both wild and domesticated, could be found in Siam, but the 20th century seems to be marking the end of their glorious era. In 1951 the government enacted a new law to stop the hunting, killing, and export of elephants. Now only a few thousand exist in Thailand, mostly working in the forests in the north.

Loei

Access—About 682 kilometres (approximately 426 miles) by road from Bangkok.

MOUNTAINS, TIGERS, AND WILD ORCHIDS—For adventurous nature lovers who find Khao Yai too developed, Loei (or Loey) Province will be rewarding. The Phukadung District, just south of Loei, has been designated a national park, and bungalows may be rented.

The area is very mountainous, with unique scenery not to be seen elsewhere in Thailand. Thick jungle clings to the mountainsides, and great plateaus are found further up, scattered with pine trees, wild shrubs, and flowers such as rhododendrons and wild orchids. Orchids, especially, grow abundantly here. To explore and enjoy the area one must employ local guides to lead the way through the jungle. At the top of the mountains, climbers are rewarded with spectacular vistas of other mountains, also smothered with lush vegetation. Recent visitors to the Pu Luang Mountain found elephant trails and fresh tiger spoors. In later years the area may become more popular for visitors but, at present, it remains an untroubled, mostly unexplored wildlife sanctuary.

Archeological Sites in the Northeast

Remains of the Khmer Empire—temples, shrines, and ancient cities, some excavated, some just discovered, and many more untouched under centuries of dust and dirt —are scattered across Khorat Plateau.

Sculptures 1,000 years old and structures older than Phimai have been unearthed near Sungnoen, about 21 miles southwest of Khorat. A few miles north of Khorat is the 11th-century Wat Phanom Wan, still being excavated by the Fine Arts Department.

Visitors with a special interest in archeology are advised to contact the Fine Arts Department at the National Museum, Bangkok, as most sites are not easily accessible. Many are found in the southern part of the Khorat Plateau, but archeologists may make finds

Ban Chieng pottery.

further north, as one young visitor to Ban Chieng did in 1966. He spotted fragments of pottery by the side of the dusty road in this small, remote village. Puzzled, he brought some back to Bangkok, where experts at the National Museum examined them and confirmed that they were old—in fact, about 5,000 years old! Expeditions to Ban Chieng recovered beautiful examples of the bronze-age pottery with lovely swirling patterns, including one pot used by a villager in his pig sty.

Prehistoric relics have been excavated in other regions of Thailand but in the Northeast there are still, undoubtedly, hidden treasure hoards.

And to Vientiane, Laos

Access—678 kilometres (424 miles) by road: one may fly direct by Thai Airways. Alternatively, fly or drive or take the train to Nong Khai on the Mekong River. A taxi or pedicab will bring you to the river, where you can take a ferry boat across the water and a taxi to Vientiane (about three miles). Entry visas are required for all visitors except Thai nationals, and exit visas are also necessary. These are obtained from the Immigration Police in Laos but can be arranged at the main hotels within twenty-four hours.

19

CHIENGMAI AND THE NORTH

Chiengmai is among the most delightful and charming cities in Asia. The local people always smile, and the girls are graceful and soft spoken. The girls are also stunningly beautiful and well known for their attractive features. The shops compete to employ the prettiest, who are considered certain lures for customers. Chiengmai must be one of the few places in the world where a young man can smile at a pretty girl and be sure he will receive a warm smile in return, even when she is with her father. Their smiling is infectious, welcoming visitors as friends rather than tourists.

The people of Chiengmai seem to have no feeling of inferiority or fear towards strangers (which is at the root of aggressiveness). They regard themselves as culturally superior to the more prosperous modern Thais of Bangkok and the South. Naturally they are proud of their heritage and are obviously pleased when they have a chance to show an enthusiastic visitor around, telling him their tales and legends.

Luckily, their local arts and crafts have found recognition and new markets with the recent influx of tourists. On the outskirts of Chiengmai several villages each specialise in one of the traditional handicrafts, making silverware, umbrellas, temple bells, and so on, providing fascinating glimpses of the ancient methods and processes still employed.

The old walled city, which dates from the 13th century, has narrow streets where children play, quiet monasteries where monks glide in and out of princely buildings, and quaint homes with pretty gardens. It has managed to retain a village-like atmosphere although Chiengmai has grown to be Thailand's second largest city, with a population approaching 100,000. It lies on a plain, 1,000 feet or so above sea level, and is surrounded by distant green hills and purple, misty mountains.

It is not surprising that the King chose these hills for his summer palace. Visitors are allowed to wander through his palace grounds, which have gorgeous displays of roses. (Chiengmai is known as "Rose of the North.") From near Pu Ping Palace or Doi Suthep superb views across Chiengmai and the plains can be enjoyed. These hills have more to offer, however, including at least fourteen different tribes who for centuries have passed freely among the hills of Thailand, Burma, Laos, and Vietnam. Now they are having a hard time as the governments are trying to persuade them to settle, or at least to stop wandering back and forth across the borders at whim. The governments wish they would stop cultivating opium, too, and pressures will no doubt, in time, bring about their integration. For the time being, hardy tourists can still seek them out and observe their odd customs and strange mode of living, totally cut off from the rest of the world.

Allow at least three days to settle into the gentle ambiance of the Chiengmai area. Shorter stays will be regretted.

Some of the other small towns and sites in the North

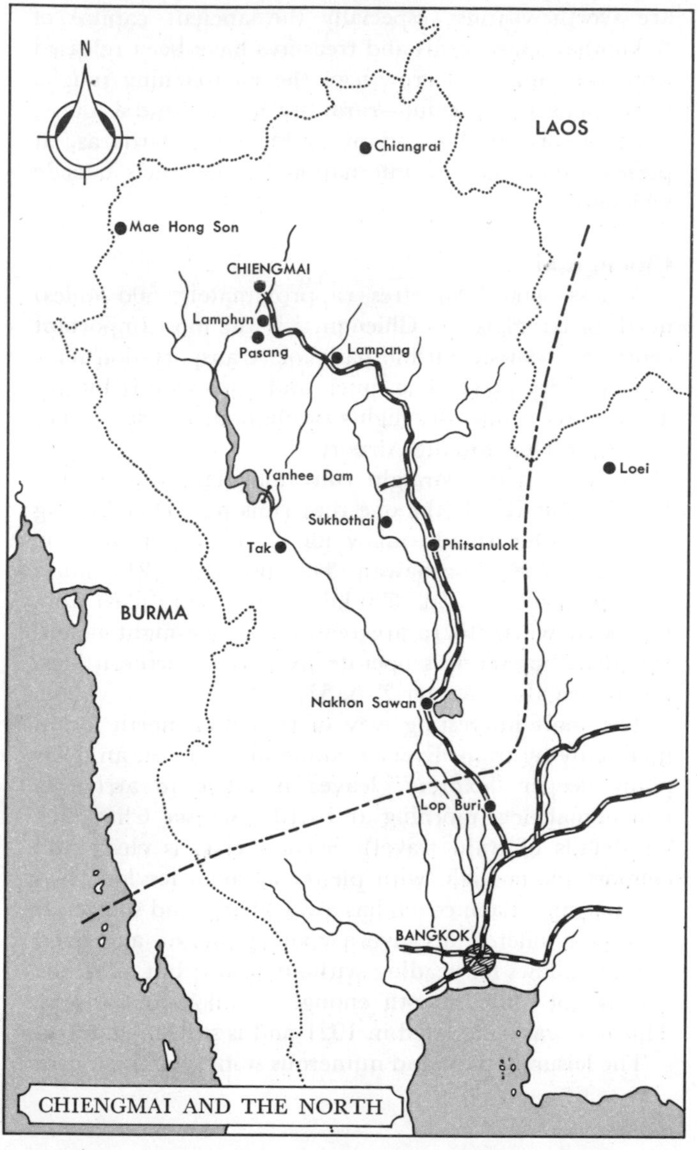

CHIENGMAI AND THE NORTH

are worth visiting, especially the ancient capital of Sukhothai whose ruins and treasures have been released from the vines and growth of the encroaching jungle. Conditions are peaceful—rural but harsh—and a tourist must be prepared to adapt to local standards as, at present, there are no international-style hotels outside Chiengmai.

Chiengmai

ACCESS—800 kilometres (approximately 500 miles) north of Bangkok. As Chiengmai is the most important centre for tourists outside Bangkok, transportation services are very good. The quick and easy way is by air. Thai Airways operates flights throughout the day, every day, from Don Muang Airport.

By road, it is a straight run along Highway 1—the Paholyothin Road (the one that runs past Don Muang Airport). One should allow for an overnight stop on the way, at Nakhon Sawan, 342 kilometres (214 miles) from Bangkok, or Tak, 520 kilometres (325 miles) from Bangkok, where there are reasonable one-night hotels. Frequent bus services operate from the Northern Terminal (see also Chapter 7, p. 57).

The most interesting way of travelling north is undoubtedly by train. Every evening at 5:05 P.M. an overnight sleeper "express" leaves Bangkok to arrive in Chiengmai next morning at 10:10 A.M. (see Chapter 7 for details of train travel). Second class is clean and comfortable enough, with plenty of room for long legs and luggage. Each coach has a washbasin and shower as well as a toilet. Fans give a cooling breeze, and good lighting allows for reading without strain; but, alas, the ride is not quite smooth enough to allow for writing. This line was completed in 1921 and is still single track.

The leisurely pace and numerous stops give the tourist

plenty of opportunities to observe and photograph the scenery and, after nightfall, to make friends with fellow passengers. On leaving Bangkok one can catch a glimpse of a smart new station—the King's own station; then the train passes through a depressing slum area beside the dark, stagnant waters of a disused *klong*. After that, the scenery is beautiful. Although utterly flat, the landscape changes with unending fascination as the sun sets in a blaze of colour. The plains are covered with thousands of acres of lotus plants (they bloom pink and white in October), and with rice paddy fields all interspersed with *klong* that stretch into the distance as far as the eye can see; country houses high on stilts, occasional *wat*, palm trees, tall *taln* trees, water buffalo, and so on. Of course, in the rainy season the plains are flooded, which can sometimes disrupt this train service. At each stop local food and drink are offered by hawkers in their traditional costumes and food and soft drinks are served on the train too. After nightfall, the berths are folded down. (The upper berths in second class have no windows.)

In the morning the air feels cool and fresh. The track winds and climbs more sharply, and the steam engine strains more noisily.* Here is nothing but jungle, tall trees, creepers, and vines; then more hills and distant plains. This is the North, a world apart from Bangkok. A journey there by train is a memorable experience and a beautiful prelude to Chiengmai.

PUBLIC TRANSPORT IN CHIENGMAI—The tourist is advised to use taxis, which are cheap and numerous, or the 1-*baht* taxis or samlor. There are five principal bus

* New diesel locomotives were imported for use on this line, but, after all, it was found that the old steam engines were more suitable for the track.

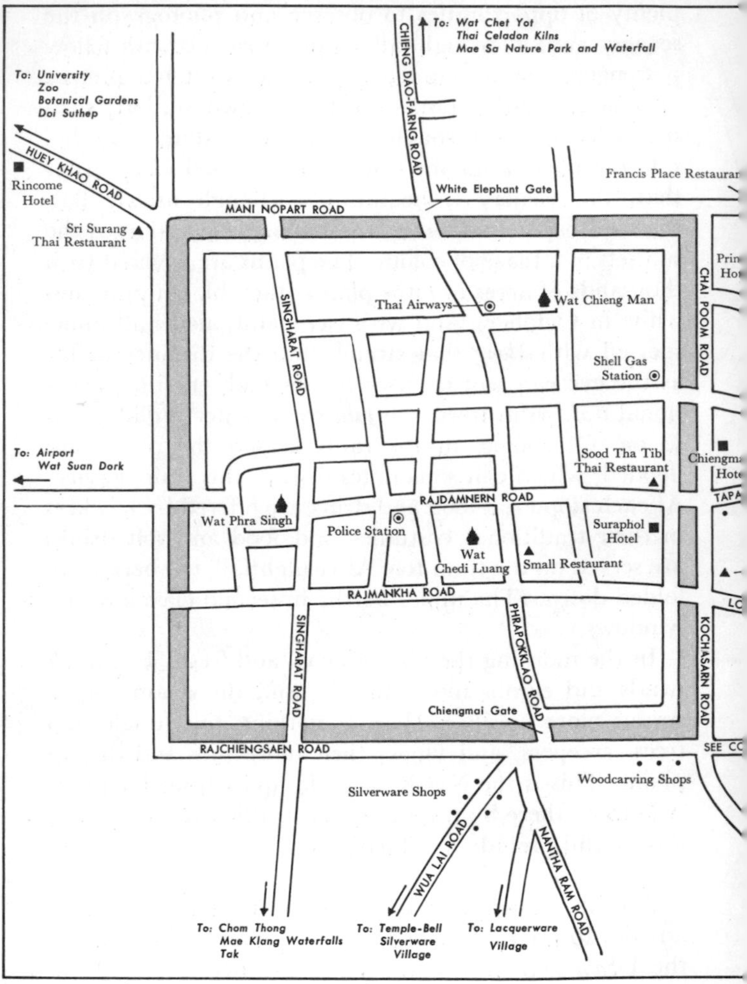
To: Wat Chet Yot
Thai Celadon Kilns
Mae Sa Nature Park and Waterfall
CHIENG DAO-FARNG ROAD
To: University
Zoo
Botanical Gardens
Doi Suthep
HUEY KHAO ROAD
Rincome Hotel
White Elephant Gate
Francis Place Restaurant
MANI NOPART ROAD
Sri Surang Thai Restaurant
SINGHARAT ROAD
Thai Airways
Wat Chieng Man
CHAI POOM ROAD
Shell Gas Station
To: Airport
Wat Suan Dork
Sood Tha Tib Thai Restaurant
RAJDAMNERN ROAD
Wat Phra Singh
Police Station
Wat Chedi Luang
Suraphol Hotel
Small Restaurant
RAJMANKHA ROAD
PHRAPOKKLAO ROAD
KOCHASARN ROAD
Chiengmai Gate
RAJCHIENGSAEN ROAD
Silverware Shops
Woodcarving Shops
WUA LAI ROAD
NANTHA RAM ROAD
To: Chom Thong
Mae Klang Waterfalls
Tak
To: Temple-Bell
Silverware
Village
To: Lacquerware
Village

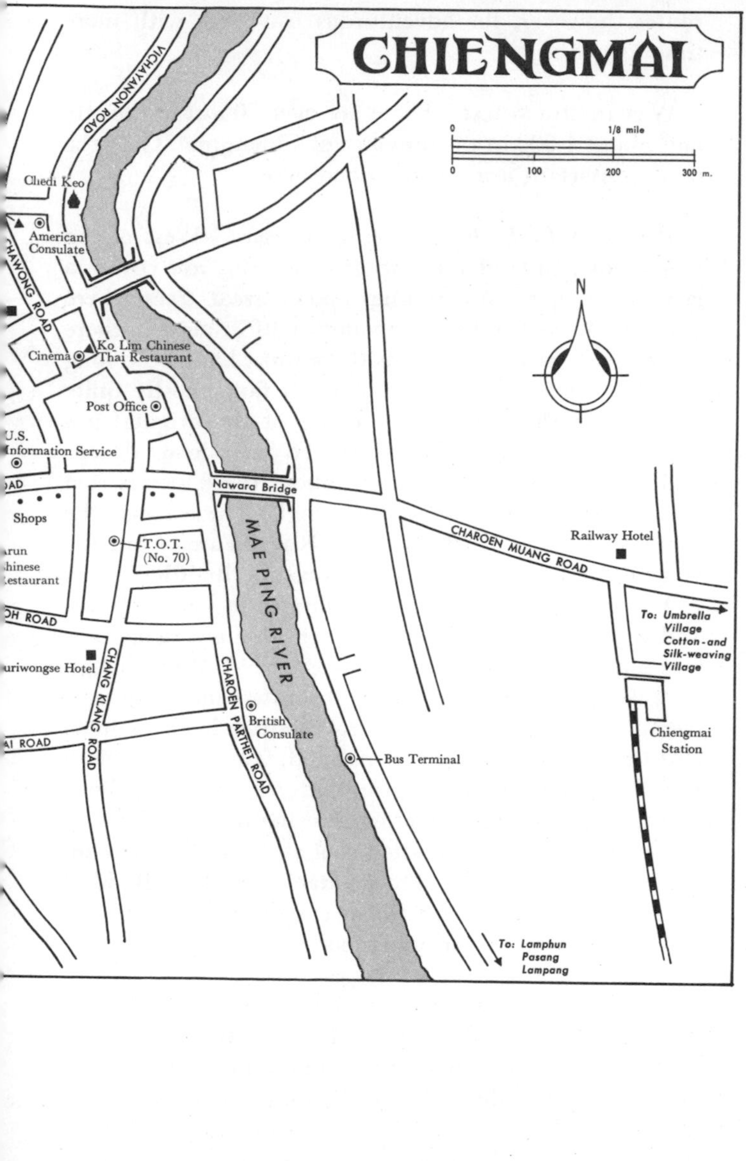
CHIENGMAI
0
1/8 mile
0
100
200
300 m.
N
VICHAYANON ROAD
Chedi Keo
American Consulate
CHAWONG ROAD
Ko Lim Chinese Thai Restaurant
Cinema
Post Office
U.S. Information Service
Nawara Bridge
Shops
T.O.T. (No. 70)
MAE PING RIVER
CHAROEN MUANG ROAD
Railway Hotel
To: Umbrella Village Cotton-and Silk-weaving Village
CHANG KLANG ROAD
CHAROEN PARTHET ROAD
British Consulate
Bus Terminal
Chiengmai Station
To: Lamphun Pasang Lampang

routes, however, for adventurous travellers with more time to spare.

WAT IN CHIENGMAI—There are over 70 *wat* in the city and about 1,000 in the province of Chiengmai. Only the more important *wat* are described here.

Wat Suan Dork (Flower Garden Temple)—West of old Chiengmai, just off the airport road, this *wat* covers a large area in a rural setting among great trees where cows graze even in the compound. Unfortunately, there is no flower garden today, as there must have been long ago. The present construction is, in fact, mostly quite new, although it occupies the site of the original *wat* that dated from the 14th century. To one side are dozens and dozens of small white *chedi,* about three metres (ten feet) to six metres (twenty feet) high. These house the ashes of many of the Chiengmai Royal Family but the largest one, just to the south, houses a Buddhist relic.

The *wiharn* is enormous—the largest in Chiengmai—and was built in 1932. Unlike other Thai *wat* structures, it is not very colourful, having a grey tiled roof, though the pillars and eaves are highly decorated and hung with trembling wind bells. Inside, bats twitter in the rafters, and the ceiling is brilliantly painted. The altar displays Buddha images of various sizes with a large sitting Buddha facing and a tall standing Buddha image behind.

The *bot* has an orange-tiled roof and is famous among Thais for housing the Phra Chao Kao Tue Buddha image, a very large bronze image cast in the 16th century.

The monks live nearby in wooden quarters.

Wat Phra Singh—Located on the west side of Singharat Road, within the old city walls. The main entrance, guarded by two enormous dragon-like "lions," is directly opposite the end of Rajdamnern Road.

One enters a spacious compound dotted with strikingly handsome buildings—in particular, the large *wiharn,* a magnificent structure built in 1518. A closer look reveals brilliantly carved and decorated panels at the front, glittering with coloured mirror chips and gilding. Behind this *wiharn* is a *chedi*, built by King Pa-Yu of Lanna Thai, the seventh King of the Mengrai dynasty, to house the ashes of King Khum Pu, his father. He then ordered a *wat* to be built on this site. In 1389 a revered Buddha image named Phra Singh, believed to have originated in Ceylon, was brought from Chiangrai and housed in a specially built crypt. However, this image had a confusing and muddled history. Before arriving at this *wat* it had passed through the hands of several kings, princes, and governors. Thus, the people of Bangkok maintain that this image was removed from Chiengmai in 1548 and is the one now in the National Museum. Chiengmai people say that the original image was returned to them by the King of Siam in 1767. To confuse historians more, the people of the South firmly believe that the original Phra Singh image is the one housed at Wat Mahatadt in Nakhon Si Thammarzt. All three images are identical. Such is the history of Thailand. One can see Chiengmai's "original" in the *wiharn ;* it is a fine work of art.

Also worth a closer look is the charming library building, near the front gate, built about 400 years ago. This *wat* is today an important centre for higher studies in Buddhism, and its school commands great respect.

Wat Chedi Luang—Located on the west side of Phrapokklao Road, within the old city walls, it is easily recognized from a distance by a tall, white-trunked gum tree that grows in the compound, towering above the surrounding buildings.

This *wat* is neatly kept, as befits a "royal" *wat* that,

for a time, housed the one and only Emerald Buddha. The interesting feature is the laterite and brick pagoda. Originally constructed in 1391 by King Saenmuangma (King Lukkhanaburagame—the eighth King of the Mengrai dynasty), it had a height of only twenty-four metres (seventy-nine feet) and was used as an animistic shrine. The present form of the *chedi* was made by King Tilokaraga (the tenth King of the Mengrai dynasty) who enlarged the structure to a height of eighty-six metres (282 feet) in 1454. This King established the site as a Royal Buddhist *wat* and housed the Emerald Buddha in a specially built *wiharn* where it remained from 1468 to 1552. The upper part of the *chedi* was toppled by a storm and earthquake in 1545, during the reign of Queen Mahadevi Jirapratha (the sixteenth monarch of the Mengrai dynasty). Some historians, however, believe that the damage was actually caused by King Taksin's guns in 1755.

The crumbling *chedi* contains two Buddha images; the other smaller *chedi* house various Buddhist relics. The existing *wiharn* is in fine condition and has particularly photogenic decorative *naga* (or serpents) at the entrance.

The Lak Muang (or Sao Intra Kin)—Just to the left of the gateway, within the compound of Wat Chedi Luang, is a little sanctuary constructed for the "spirit of the city"—the spirit that protects and guides the city. The original Lak Muang building stood on another site, and this one was built quite recently, in 1940. Celebrations and ceremonies are held annually.

Wat Chieng Man—Located in the northeastern section of the old city. This is the oldest temple in Chiengmai, built by King Mengrai in 1296 as Chiengmai's first royal *wat*. It has been restored several times and has a distinct

Burmese influence. The *wiharn* has a verandah across the front that is richly decorated with carvings of angels and flowers and with the three-headed Hindu elephant, Erawan. The doorways are decorated with coloured mirror pieces and inside, the walls are covered with murals. Painted red and gold pillars and ceiling beams and a stately Buddha in front of a canopy are spoiled by the inappropriate fluorescent strip lighting.

This *wat* is famous for several unusual images of Buddha. The most extraordinary is the Phra Kaew Kao or Crystal Buddha made in Lavo (Lop Buri) in the 2nd century and brought to rest in Chiengmai after journeys to Lamphun and Vientiane. It is believed to have the power to bring rain and therefore it is taken around the city in procession every year, if there is a drought, on the first of April. This image is kept in the abbot's residence and only a replica is displayed. Another interesting statue is the Phra Sethang Manee, an image made from white stone on a solid gold base. Brought here by King Mengrai from Haripoonchai (Lamphun) in 1281, it is believed to have originated in Ceylon.

Behind the *wiharn* is a large, gold-spired square *chedi* supported by fourteen life-sized elephants. Do not miss an inspection of the whitewashed earthen wall that surrounds the *wat*. It sags precariously but somehow blends well with the glittering, colourful buildings and luxuriant foliage. Sometimes travellers can stay overnight here with the monks, who are friendly and will easily strike up a conversation with foreign visitors in broken English.

Wat Bhodharam Maha Wiharn or Wat Chet Yot—This *wat*, situated down a left turn about a kilometre north of Chiengmai, off the Chieng Dao-Farng Road, is not easy to find without a guide.

It has the usual whitewashed wall surrounding the compound, set amidst banana-leaf-roofed houses in a quiet rural district. Its popular name, Wat Chet Yod, comes from the seven-spired *chedi* (Jed Yod=seven spires) in which are buried the ashes of King Tilokaraga. This king chose this site for a *wat* in 1455 and planted a *bhodi* tree, said to be taken from a *bhodi* tree in Ceylon. In 1477 he called the Eighth World Buddhist Council Meeting which was held at this very spot. Thus, when he died in 1487, it was natural that he should be cremated here.

The *wat* has been left in a poor, ruined state, partially overgrown by jungle, ever since the Burmese invasion in 1556. However these ruins give an impression of a noble past and an almost haunting peace.

WHITE ELEPHANT GATE—Along Farng Road, on the northern outskirts of Old Chiengmai. This pair of white elephant statues, placed in stalls facing north and west, commemorates the loyalty of two brave followers who saved the life of their king during a battle* on war elephants that took place when the King of Ayutthaya attacked Chiengmai. The statues were placed here by King Saen Muang Ma in the late 14th century but have since been restored.

MAE SA NATURE PARK AND WATERFALL—A 20-kilometre (12-mile) drive from Chiengmai, going north along the Farng Road and turning left at Mae Rim. There is a sign in English.

The drive is boring but patience is well rewarded by the beauty of this seemingly remote, forested park. The rush of water can be heard from the car park. A rocky

* A painting of the battle scene is in the "Varobhas Piman Pavilion" in Bang Pa-In.

path with stone steps winds alongside the cascades where torrents of water swirl and crash through the rocks, creating a heavenly white mist in the woodland. Walk 20 metres to the first viewing point, 100 metres to the first cascades, 320 metres to the second, 410 metres to the third, and 500 metres to the fourth. It is cool, refreshing, and beautiful all the way. Here are noticeably many varieties of butterflies and birds. Sensible walking shoes are essential.

BOTANICAL GARDENS (ARBORETUM)—Located alongside Huey Khao Road, next to the University on the way to Doi Suthep. Gardeners interested in roses should come here. There are interesting shrubs and trees too.

CHIENGMAI ZOO—A little beyond the Botanical Gardens (above), along Huey Khao Road. This was originally a private zoo belonging to an American named Harold Young. It seems it became so large that he finally invited the local government to take it over, although Mr. Young is still there. The zoo is carefully arranged on the hillside to allow the animals to enjoy a natural environment. The animals, birds, and snakes are almost all native to Thailand, especially northern Thailand.

CHEDI KEO—This white *chedi* is now used as a traffic circle near the American Consulate, along the Vichayanon Road. It contains the ashes of the Haw tribesmen (from western China) who made an unsuccessful attempt to invade Chiengmai around 1300.

QUEEN VICTORIA STATUE—A large statue of a middle-aged Queen Victoria stands outside the British Consulate by the junction of Charoen Phrathet Road and See Con Chai Road, near the Mae Ping River. The local people worship her as a fertility goddess. When she was temporarily boxed-up for protection during the Second World War, two holes had to be drilled near her eyes so that she could still look down upon her devotees, laden with offerings of flowers, food, and so on. The consulate was closed by the British government for two years as an economy measure, but, it seems, standing outside a closed consulate was too much for the venerable Queen Victoria to bear. It was reopened in 1971.

ELEPHANTS AT WORK—Local tours to see elephants at work involve a drive of about forty miles into the forests, where small teams of elephants push, drag, and pile up a few old logs. It looks contrived. Frankly, the drive is not worthwhile unless one has not seen elephants before and the tour is combined with other sightseeing spots.

CONFERENCE FACILITIES—Chiengmai University can accommodate 300 delegates in its auditorium. Also, the Buddha Satharn Meeting Hall and the Medical Science University are suitable convention sites. For full details, write to T.O.T. Convention Division, Bangkok.

Village Industries Around Chiengmai

The best way to visit all the interesting ones is to take a tour because only a short time is needed at each village and they are inconveniently scattered. At every village, the families work together as a group. Needless to say, buying articles direct from the place where they are produced can mean a considerable saving. As Chiengmai has expanded, many of these so-called "villages" are now really a part of the city.

SILVERWARE VILLAGE—located along Chom Tong Road, and Wua Lai Road south of Chiengmai Gate.

Hammering the silver.

Along here are rows of tiny wooden shops, packed with silver bowls, bracelets, belts, rings, and little trinkets. You hear the tap, tap, tapping of the silversmiths' hammers as they patiently form the extremely elaborate designs. Prospective shoppers are always welcome to go into the backroom workshops and watch the process.

The silver used is made by smelting old Burmese and Indian rupees (by courtesy of Queen Victoria) which are bought by the bagful in bartering with the hill-tribe people. Some of the coins, which have often been hidden in the mountains for many years, are quite rare and it is possible for numismatists to have an exciting time. Some shops have showcases displaying many of the coins. Queen Victoria's coins, which contain about eighty-five per cent silver, are smelted, then cooled and hammered into thin sheets. Next, the sheets are heated to make them pliable enough to wrap and hammer around wooden moulds that are intricately carved in relief.

Thus the designs, showing a strong Burmese influence, are stamped onto the silver objects. Popular designs include animals of the zodiac.

Prices are calculated according to the amount of work and weight but, confusing to the foreigner, the unit of weight is called the "baht"—the same as the unit of currency. The "baht" is about fifteen grammes; prices range from 15 to 20 *baht* (75 cents to $1) per "baht," according to the intricacy of the design. Of particular interest is the "betel set" which consists of four small boxes and a flat dish. The boxes are made to contain each ingredient for mixing into betel for chewing. The ingredients are: red lime; tobacco; areca nut; a salve to prevent the lips from staining; a *seri* leaf.

Little earrings and brooches are very delicate and the best value. Primitive hill-tribe silverware is also available.

LACQUERWARE VILLAGE—located just a little way beyond the silverware village at Ban Khoen, Chang Moi Road.

Again, there are rows of shops and workshops where one may watch the ancient process. Fine strips of bamboo are plaited for the base, which is then coated with about fifteen layers of lacquer gum, made from the ash of rice stalks and *lac,** or pounded, ground-up clay and *lac*. Each coating must be dried; it is then smoothed with rough leaves before the next layer is applied. The designs are painted on after the final coat has dried, and sometimes gold leaf is etched into the work.

Products include bowls, *khan toke* (small round tables), boxes for betel nut sets, cigarette boxes, hors d'oeuvres

* *Lac* is produced by a parasite that bores into the bark of the *lac* tree *(Melanorrhoea usitata)* and deposits a sap or excreta in the form of dark red blobs on the bark. This hard, pasty substance is then collected and made into liquid *lac*.

trays, and so on. Most designs employ red on black, or gold and silver on black, depicting flowers and dancers and similar patterns as found on the doors of *wat*.

A Japanese named Oyama has set up shop in Chiengmai (with a branch in Bangkok), producing Thai lacquerware by an improved method, with the addition of certain chemicals to make it more durable. Instead of woven bamboo he uses teakwood bases. His designs are more subdued.

TEMPLE-BELL VILLAGE—located just north of the silverware village. These are the bells that resound in the wind around a *wat*. The clapper has a hanging metal "leaf" to catch the breeze. First they make a model out of beeswax and then encase it in clay that is heated to melt away the beeswax. The clay mould is then ready for use, and the molten metal is poured in. Don't buy one without hearing the tone. Bronze images of Buddha are also made here.

COTTON- AND SILK-WEAVING VILLAGE—at the village of Sankampaeng 14 kilometres (about 8 miles) east of Chiengmai. A lovely drive along an avenue lined with *cham-churi* or monkey-pod trees (also called rain trees), *lamyai* (longans), small villages of teak-wood huts with leaf roofs, and a *klong* where people fish.

Sankampaeng has a long history, evident from the old *Wat Sai Mun* in Burmese style and from the discovery of ancient glazed pottery. Hand looms are worked by young girls in sheds behind the shops, just as in Lamphun and Pasang. Designs tend to be striped, using deep colours. Swiss and German dyes are generally used these days so colours are fast. Items are cheap if one bargains well.

UMBRELLA VILLAGE—at Bor Sarng, 9 kilometres

(about 5½ miles) from Chiengmai on the road to San-kampaeng, above.

About 300 families spend all their time producing paper umbrellas here. They make the paper from tree bark in different thicknesses, construct the frame from bamboo, and paint the umbrellas by hand with gay flower patterns. Finally, tassels are hung from each spoke of the frame, and they are sold for around 10 *baht* (50 cents) each. The people here have been devoted to this craft for several generations. The children do not appear to be receiving any formal education.

POTTERY VILLAGE AND THAI CELADON—Situated along Doi Chieng Dao Road, beyond the White Elephant Gate to the north. Frankly, the village is not very interesting, as the villagers are making only simple pots for household use. The potter families are said to have come here about four generations ago from the southern Shan states. More worthwhile is a visit to the Thai celadon kilns 6 kilometres (about 3½ miles) along the Chieng Dao-Farng Road.

Thai celadon is a high-fired, vitrified stoneware with a finely-crackled, pale green glaze created by using only natural wood ash in white-heat kilns. No synthetic materials or dyes are used. This is a "re-incarnation" of the celadon produced in northern China more than 2,000 years ago, and of the "Sawank'alok" or "Sank'alok" stoneware produced by Chinese potters in Sukhothai during the 14th century. The workshop and kilns here, at 62 Chieng Dao-Farng Road, were established in 1959. Open to visitors from 8:00 A.M. to 12 noon and from 1:00 P.M. to 5:00 P.M. every day except the first and sixteenth of each month (the days after payday, when nobody turns up for work and the kilns are closed).

Woodcarving district—Located near Chiengmai Gate, along the south side of Rajchiengsaen Road.

Carved elephants, furniture (it can be shipped), Scandinavian-style bowls, wall plaques, and so on are produced on the premises and sold at very reasonable prices—the labour is cheap. Teak wood is now rarely used. Instead, another more rosy-coloured hardwood called *mai-daeng* is substituted. Few tourists ever know the difference.

Laddaland—Well signposted at a right turning off Huay Khao Road, on the way to Doi Suthep. Entrance fee 100 *baht* ($5).

This is a specially built "Disneyland" of Chiengmai spreading over about fifty acres. It contains such attractions as "genuine" hill-tribe huts, antique Thai houses, landscaped flower gardens, a craft shop, restaurant, amphitheatre where northern dances are performed, stalls selling soft drinks, postcards, and so on. One can tour Laddaland by horse-drawn cart and ride on an elephant. The author prefers to see the original sites of Chiengmai. Like TIMland in Bangkok, this kind of commercial development is fine for tourists who like to be passively entertained.

Doi Suthep

One of the best sightseeing trips in Thailand is to the mountain that rises 5,500 feet to the northwest of Chiengmai, taking in Wat Phra That—an exquisitely beautiful shrine at 3,500 feet—the Royal Palace at 4,300 feet, and a Meo hill-tribe village a little farther on. The mountain is thickly forested and affords breathtaking views across the broad plain with the city of Chiengmai in the centre. It is a most exhilarating journey.

Kruba srivichai—this is the name of a monk whose statue stands at the foot of Doi Suthep.

Until 1934 there was only a steep, narrow track to Wat Phra That, and at least five hours were needed for the climb, preventing weaker pilgrims from visiting the *wat*. The monk Kruba Srivichai, a greatly respected old man, suddenly announced that he would build a road to the summit of Suthep Mountain and that it would be completed in 172 days! Of course that was utterly impossible. How could anyone, let alone an elderly man with no money and no machinery or tools, imagine cutting a road through the rock on this mountain in less than six months? But, while people dismissed the project as impossible, Kruba Srivichai started work on 9 November, 1934, digging at the foot of the mountain. His extraordinary faith attracted twenty followers, and with simple farming tools they made a start. At the end of that day there was a long, long way to go, and accomplishment must have seemed hopeless, but Kruba would not allow his followers to be disheartened. His indomitable spirit and confidence kept them working with cheerful enthusiasm. As the news of this strange story spread, a remarkable thing happened: people came. They came from Chiengmai and the surrounding villages, they came from as far away as Phitsanulok. Between 3,000 and 4,000 people arrived each day to help Kruba. Those who could not work served food and drink. Kruba eventually had to ration the work to less than 15 feet of road per villages so everyone could contribute. Just as he predicted, the road was completed in 172 days, entirely by volunteers using only bare hands and simple farm tools. It is 11 kilometres (6½ miles) long and has recently been widened to allow buses to pass.

Now, watch the Thais as they pass Kruba's statue. When they make a *wai*, you will know why.

WAT PHRA THAT—is perched on the hilltop named Doi Suthep. Visitors must walk up 300 steps, flanked on both sides by an elongated, wavy, snake-like body of a seven-headed *naga* and beds of frangipanis and cassias. The climber is rewarded at the top by a gorgeous and richly adorned *wat*. (Also, cold drinks can be bought here.) The *wat* has six doorways, but visitors usually pass through one of the west entrances, next to the *bot*. Near the left entrance is a shrine dedicated to the white elephant that found this site (see below). Going in, one enters a marble-paved square surrounded by a white-walled gallery. In the centre is the *chedi*, twenty-two metres (seventy-two feet) high, sheathed in copper plate overlaid with gold and surrounded by red and gold railings with golden lace umbrellas at each corner. The roofs of the buildings are tiled yellow ochre and brown, avoiding the gaudiness of some of the Bangkok temples. The whole *wat* covers quite a small area. At the west side is the *bot* (one of four chapels), in which a really handsome golden Buddha image of considerable size benevolently smiles, looking down from his pedestal at the stream of pilgrims who bring flowers and incense. In front of the image are dozens of little altar tables, stacked and piled high with gilded objects. Behind the image, the wall is covered with diamond-shaped pieces of coloured mirror, like luminous mosaic, and the ceiling is decorated with gold and blue flower designs.

Saffron-robed monks come by the bus-load to prostrate themselves and chant before the revered relic buried beneath the *chedi*.

In the courtyard there is a *bo* tree, shading statues of monks in meditation. Also, one should see the huge bronze temple bell. When the sky is blue and the air is clear, the view will be unforgettable. The Thais are justified in their saying "Visiting Chiengmai without going to Doi Suthep is no better than not visiting Chiengmai at all."

History of Wat Phra That, Doi Suthep—*Doi* means "hilltop" and *suthep* is derived from the name of a hermit named Sudeva who lived on this mountain. In fact, Doi Suthep is just a hilltop on the mountain, and there are other hills nearby such as Doi Ngam and Doi Chang Norn. The story of the founding of the *wat* is strange, if not comical, and the reader may decide whether to believe it or not.

There was in Sukhothai a monk named Sumana who had been educated in Ceylon. He had a dream that led him to the ruins of the ancient city of Pang Cha where, buried beneath a bush shaped like a stool, he found a relic of Buddha. The relic was the size of a pea, in a round container shaped like a pomegranate fruit, which in turn was in a coral urn . . . inside a gold urn . . . in a silver urn . . . in a brass urn . . . under a stone slab beneath a layer of bricks!

King Kuna in A.D. 1367 built Wat Phra Yun in Lamphun to house the relic, and Sumana stayed there. A few years later, the relic was brought to Chiengmai for the people to revere. When the box was opened, the relic, to everyone's amazement, had split into two, and furthermore, one part was the original size. The larger (original) part was enshrined at Wat Suan Dork as King Kuna had planned. The smaller part was placed on the back of an anointed white elephant to seek another suitable site. The elephant went into the mountains, followed by the King and his retinue, and, after much wandering, arrived at Doi Suthep. Here, it trumpeted three times, walked around in three counter-clockwise circles, and knelt down. The King at once knew that this was the chosen site, and the relic was promptly removed from the elephant's back, the hilltop was leveled, and the construction of Wat Phra That began. Successive kings have kept the *wat* well maintained, adding chapels and various embellishments.

Pu Ping Rajaniwat (Royal Palace)

Situated 5 kilometres (3 miles) beyond Doi Suthep along the forested, winding mountain road: the gardens are open to the public only on Saturdays, Sundays, and on national holidays, providing the Royal Family is not in residence. Lawns, shrubs, flower beds, and thousands of well-tended rose bushes are beautifully laid out in undulating patterns around the palace building and lake. This is used as a country villa by the Royal Family. It is 4,300 feet above sea level and so escapes the fierce heat and humidity during the Thai hot season.

Just a half mile away from Pu Ping Palace is a Meo hill-tribe village, known as Doi Bui. When the palace is open to the public, the Meo find it lucrative to come and pose before the queues of tourists at the entrance, collecting a fee for every camera click.

The Hill Tribes of Northern Thailand

In the lonely, desolate valleys and green mountains north of Chiengmai are strange tribes who have rarely had any contact with the Thais or other peoples, let alone white tourists. Mostly nomadic, some are quite sophisticated like the Meo, and some are very primitive like the Phi Thong Luang (Spirit of the Yellow Leaves), who were thought to have become extinct until re-discovered a few years ago by an expedition into the forested mountains. The number of distinct groups and sub-ethnic groups is uncertain. Even more uncertain are the wildly varying estimates of the numbers in each tribe. As far as is known, none of the tribes are hostile,

Hill-tribe dress.

so tourists have nothing to fear. On the other hand, many of the tribes believe that strangers bring evil spirits, which may account for their shyness and elusiveness.

One can imagine how stories of strange peoples can easily become exaggerated in this part of the world. The isolated, forested hills and frequent rain mists set the scene for mystery and imagination. Most if not all of the tribes originated in southern China and moved into the Indo-Chinese peninsula.

THE MEO OR MEOW—Official estimates say 45,000 to 50,000 are living in Thailand and they are also found in China, Burma, Vietnam, and Laos. The majority of Meo live on mountains along the border of Nan Province. Any tourist who visits Doi Suthep and Pu Ping Palace will have a chance to see some of them. One of their villages is easily accessible, about a mile down a track just beyond Pu Ping Palace on Doi Suthep. It is advisable to take a guide as there are several tracks. During or just after heavy rains, one should preferably walk or, rather, "climb," down the steep approach.

The Meo wear enormous turbans, heavy silver rings around their necks, silver bracelets, earrings, and decorative silver belts. The Meo take great care and trouble over their red and black costumes, far more than on their homes that are simple, thatched-roofed, wooden huts. Many are experts at embroidery who beautifully sew and decorate some costumes with captivatingly strange, primitive designs. Although they are quite proud of their dress they may appear to prefer not to be photographed. The author found that their shyness disappeared when they were offered a few *baht* for picture-taking.

The Meo are referred to in Chinese chronicles almost 4,000 years ago. About 800 B.C. the Chinese forced the Meo from the provinces of Kweichow and Hunnan, where they originated, into extreme southern China, from where they scattered into the provinces of Yunnan and Kwangsi. Later they evacuated into Tongking, Laos, Burma, and Thailand. They cultivate rice, maize, chillies, and opium, and keep domestic animals. Many are addicted to opium. The Meo believe in spirits and have a spirit doctor, though modern medical techniques are creeping in.

THE KAREN OR WHITE KAREN—These tribespeople are estimated to number 75,000 in Thailand, mostly living in the valleys along Mae Hongsawn, in the province of Chiengmai, the Mae Chan region of Chiangrai Province, and around Amphur Hod and Amphur Ban-Hoe in Lamphun Province. Little is known of their origin except that they belong to Tibetan-Burmese stock and, over the years, have drifted into Thailand from Burma and into sub-ethnic groups such as the Skaw, P'wo, B'ghwe, and Taungthu. They may have been in these northern hills even before the Thais came. Living in thatched-roofed or leaf-roofed bamboo homes, in villages of twenty to thirty houses, they believe in animistic spirits as well as professing to be Buddhist and Christian.

AKHA OR EKAW—Estimates vary from 9,000 to 28,000 for these people, as they avoid going into towns or other villages and retire from strangers, fearing evil spirits. Although they are very shy and elusive, they are not hostile. Their villages can be found only at Amphur Mae Sai and Mai Chan in Chiangrai Province. They are also of Tibeto-Burmese stock, belonging to the "LoLo" group. They probably emigrated from the Kweichow–Yunnan area of China about 4,000 years ago, first going to the Shan states in Burma and finally, to the Chiangrai hills in northern Thailand in this century. One group is said to have drifted into Thailand since the Second World War.

These are strange people indeed, living about 3,500 feet up the sides and tops of mountains. Their dress is distinctly more vivid than that of any other hill tribe and includes a head-dress decorated with silver coins, buttons, beads, tufts of fur, and embroidery. The men wear pigtails. They are said to eat more or less anything that moves or grows. Because of their belief that water contains spirits they never wash or bathe in their life. To clean themselves, they simply wipe and dust off the dirt from their bodies when dry.

The Akha cultivate rice, maize, cotton, chillies, and

opium and keep pigs and other domestic animals. The guide may describe the strange custom by which one tribesman deflowers all the virgins at a special ceremony but this is more likely legend than fact.

YAO—Believed to number 12,000 to 15,000 in Thailand, the Yao are said to have originated from the Szechuan, Hunnan, Kiangsi, and Kweichow regions of China, migrating southwards to Tongking, Laos, and the Chiangtung State of Burma, and to the Nan Province of northern Thailand. They now live in relatively large groups in the northern and eastern regions of Chiangrai Province and are not so nomadic as the other tribes. Large numbers are reportedly still in China.

The Yao are a house-proud and home-loving people. Two of their favourite pastimes are storytelling and drinking green tea. They grow rice, maize, and opium, and keep domestic animals.

LAHU—Some 10,000 Lahu are estimated to be living around Chiangrai, Chiengmai, Mae Hong Son, Lampang, and Tak, but they are nomadic. The Lahu are also of Tibeto-Burmese stock, originating from southwest Yunnan. They believe in spirits and have their own witch doctors. Cultivating rice, maize, a little opium, and still hunting for food, they are said to be very poor and kind.

LISU OR LISA—Numbering about 20,000, they are people of "LoLo" extraction, belonging to Tibeto-Burmese stock. They are Buddhists who used to grow opium but now cultivate rice, maize, and tea, and keep domestic animals.

Originally, the Lisu inhabited the regions around the upper reaches of the Salween River, later moving southwards into the Yunnan Province of China, into the state of Kachin, and the Shan states of Burma. Within this century, they have migrated into Thailand and now live on the sides of mountains in the provinces of Chiangrai, Chiengmai, Mae Hong Son, and Tak.

WHAT DOES THE FUTURE HOLD FOR THESE TRIBES?—Hill tribes bring problems when their simple way of life clashes with "progress." They clear forested land to grow their crops, exhaust the soil, and then move on. They grow opium, which is illegal. They are also seen as a political danger since they seem to have no regard for any government and naturally wander across borders.

Mainly because of the threat of Communist infiltration, the Thai government has made increasing efforts in recent years to try to assimilate these tribes into Thai life. This is a tremendously difficult task since many of the villages are so remote and often cannot be reached by road. Currently, Chiengmai radio broadcasts thirty minutes of tribal songs and speeches in Meo language and other tribal dialects every morning at 7:00 A.M. Surely, within a decade or two, it will be impossible to see these hill tribes as they exist today.

TRIBAL RESEARCH CENTRE—This anthropological study centre and small museum at the University of Chiengmai was founded in 1965 and is, in fact, attached to the Department of Public Welfare. Visitors are welcome.

HILL TRIBE HANDCRAFT CENTRE—Along Huey Kaew Road, the Centre sells native clothing and handicraft items made by the hill-tribe people.

Mae Klang Waterfalls

Well signposted in English, 9 kilometres (5 miles)

along a turning at Chom Tong, just past a temple on the right, coming from Chiengmai.

The falls are 91.4 metres (about 300 feet) high, set in thickly forested country. This is the King's favourite beauty spot, best seen during the rainy season, when the waters are high and the forests are perfectly green. Several viewing platforms have been built for sightseers. Local people sell drinks, fruit, and orchids.

A Walking Tour in Old Chiengmai ($2\frac{1}{2}$ kilometres or $1\frac{1}{2}$ miles)

This walk should best be made in the early morning when there is little traffic and the monks are pacing the streets to collect offerings of food.

Start from the Chiengmai Hotel that faces the old moat and tall trees on the opposite side of the road. Turn right, walking alongside this moat, and take the first turning left, across the moat, taking you into the old part of Chiengmai. Continue past the Shell gasoline station on the right and a small *wat* on the left to the first crossroads. There is a mailbox on the left hand corner, and behind a white fence is a most beautiful old Thai-style white house with a lovely lawn and garden. On the opposite corner is an attractive little spirit house facing an open-fronted Thai restaurant. Turn right here.

Now, one enters a quiet district where old wooden houses are set back from the road among coconut palms interspersed with modern concrete buildings. After a couple of minutes' walk there is a vividly coloured small *wat* on the right side. On the opposite side of the road is another whitewashed enclosure—Wat Chieng Man—with a gateway guarded by two orange-colored "lions" (see p. 304).

On coming out, turn right and right, following the road by the sagging old temple wall of Wat Chiang Man.

Along this narrow road on the left are little wooden houses. It is peaceful here with only the company of singing birds in the early morning. At the end of this road is a modern white concrete building on the right-hand corner—the Thai Airways Office. Turn left and immediately right across this main road to enter a similar narrow road.

Along here are a few of Chiengmai's most beautiful modern houses, with spacious lawns in front, edged with coconut palms and logan trees. Take the first turn to the left, passing through a quiet residential area. The houses look modern and comfortable. The upper parts are made of wood and the lower halves of concrete. The gardens have bamboo fences, spirit houses, lovely tropical plants and shrubs and sometimes chickens and even a pony. Walk straight on beyond the first crossroads (where a very grand ancient Thai-style wall surrounds some government buildings to the left), to the next crossroads which has traffic lights. Turn right here.

This is a busier road, still passing through a fine residential area. One will walk among saffron-robed monks, smiling women carrying baskets on bamboo shoulder poles, and an occasional pedicab that may stop and offer a ride. On the left is a pretty scene—green- and red-glazed tile roofs of a temple decorated with gold, gleaming and shining in the sun, set behind tall palm trees. At the crossroads, go straight across, past a row of shops on the left side. At the next crossroads there is a small restaurant in a wooden building on the right-hand corner. On the opposite corner is Wat Phra Singh (see p. 302). Cross over to the gateway where, as usual, two huge dragon-like lions stand guard.

After seeing this *wat,* come out of the main gateway and take the main road directly opposite. This road has a pavement on both sides. Along here one will pass two small *wat,* well maintained and attractively situated behind tall trees. Saffron robes hang over the balconies of the monks' quarters, rippling in the wind, and monks glide silently through the grounds. A little further on is a new grey-and-white building—a police station. Just ahead, to the right in the distance through the trees, one can see the ruins of the giant *prang* of Wat Chedi Luang. That is the next destination. To reach it, go straight on at the crossroads past yet another *wat* (rather modern) on the left, past two garages (one on each side of the street), and then take the narrow track to the right. This leads directly into the grounds of Wat Chedi Luang (see p. 303).

After viewing this *wat,* leave by the main gate—there is a tall white gum tree in the right-hand corner by the gate—and turn right. Across this busy road is a small restaurant where one can choose an iced, bottled drink from the refrigerator. Continuing along this street, one will pass a ruined red-bricked *chedi,* overgrown with shrubs and grass; a small *wat* with highly decorated eaves set among shaggy trees; and a shop on the right selling a curious assortment of water jars, colourful spirit houses, and water closets. Glimpses of daily home-life can be seen on the left, where there are old wooden houses with tiled roofs. The stroller will also pass another, poor-looking wat; a row of untidy cheap shops; and a garage where the 1-*baht* taxis are made by converting Japanese Daihatsu agricultural trucks. Then, opposite a Caltex garage, is yet another *wat.* Continue through a market area where shops occupy the ground floors of homes, and finally come to Chiengmai Gate, which has three tall gum trees next to it and a huge old red-brick wall by the moat outside. This corner is extremely busy, with buses, trucks, shops, stalls, and people walking about in every direction.

From here one could hire a pedicab for a few *baht* to go to the Silver Village, situated not far to the right down a road called Nantha Ram Road and then along Wua Lai Road to the left.

Alternatively, turn left at Chiengmai Gate and walk parallel to the old moat. Very soon, you will come across several woodcarving shops on the right side. Stop at two or three to compare prices before making a purchase. To return to the Chiengmai Hotel, follow the moat around to the left, walking for about seven minutes.

Entertainments in Chiengmai

Chiengmai has a few nightclubs and several cinemas that often show Western films, but in the author's opinion, the only way to spend an evening is to enjoy a *khan toke* dinner with dancing show. This form of entertaining is unique to northern Thailand and should definitely not be missed.

The meal is served on small, low, circular tables (or *toke*), usually lacquered red or black. These vary in size from around two to three feet in diameter, with larger ones for very special occasions. Every family in northern Thailand has one. One *toke* is for up to four guests, who sit on the floor to be served by hostesses who also sit

Khan toke dinner.

next to the guests, chatting and smiling, fetching more dishes, and anticipating every need. They, of course, wear traditional costume—ankle-length skirts called *bha sin,* with close-fitting, long-sleeved blouses called *sua khan krabok,* covered by a wrap or shawl called *sabai chiang.* The colours are magnificent, set off by a flower or two in the hair, usually orchids. Male guests are given a plain, shirt-type native costume to wear, usually dark blue or maroon. It is called a *sua maw hom* and is tied around the waist with a belt called a *bha ka ma.* Incidentally, these can be bought as souvenirs and make very comfortable sleeping attire.

The meal and show vary according to the establishment, but two that are good are at the Francis Place Restaurant Complex, 417/1 Vichayanon Road, near the American Consulate, and at the Rincome Hotel Banqueting Room. Reservations are always advisable. The cost for the set meal is about 120 *baht* ($6).

FRANCIS PLACE—has a fairly small *khan toke* room with a tiny stage. It caters to Thais as well as to foreigners. A typical meal here would include the following dishes: *gang kae*—a curry with vegetables, peculiar to the North; *nam*—a spicy, pickled sausage flavoured with lime, peanuts, or soybeans; *khao neo*—glutinous rice, served in a covered bamboo woven basket; *nam-prik*—the local sour fish sauce; several dishes of raw, fresh vegetables; fresh fruits such as *lamyai,* bananas, mangoes, and custard apple.

The show is excellent. About eight different northern and hill-tribe dances are performed. The hostesses are very attentive and explicit.

RINCOME HOTEL—has a large, paneled dining-room with red straw matting on the floor. It serves readily recognisable foods to cater to a primarily foreign clientele. A typical meal here would be: curried pork with tomato; fresh vegetables, such as cucumber, peas, lettuce, and spring onions; chicken and prawn spring roll; crispy noodles; fried, crispy pork skin; glutinous or plain boiled rice; fresh fruit such as pineapple, oranges, and papaya; *mieng gum*, a local chewing gum.

The food is beautifully served on celadon dishes and carved teak wood *toke* but the girls tend to act as waitresses rather than hostesses. The show is spectacular.

Restaurants and Local Dishes

Apart from *khan toke* described above, Chiengmai has some delightful Thai and Chinese restaurants such as the *Arun* or "Ah-room" (Chinese), set in a lovely garden at 55 Kochasarn Road; the *Sood Tha Tib* (Thai), open all night, opposite the Suraphol Hotel; and the *Ko Lim* (Chinese/Thai) near the Sri Nakhonping Cinema. The author's favourite is the *Sri Surang* Thai restaurant, situated on elevated ground along Huey Khao Road.

Two dishes to try are *kao soi,* a curry-with-noodles dish popular among Chiengmai people, and *mee krop*—thin crispy noodles fried with shrimp and pieces of pork, spicy and sweet.

A surprising variety of fresh fruit and vegetables is readily available in Chiengmai. Local farmers grow many varieties from the West that one would not normally associate with a tropical country, such as strawberries, sweetcorn, asparagus, and broccoli, as well as a range of exotic, unfamiliar produce. Chiengmai is particularly famous for *lamyai* (longans) which are harvested in late July/August. This fruit is so highly prized that it has inspired an annual "beauty contest festival" to celebrate the gathering of the fruit (see also "Food and Restaurants," Chapter 9, p. 74).

Lamphun

South of Chiengmai, 26 kilometres (16 miles) away, Lamphun makes a most pleasant excursion along a smooth, winding road lined with *yang* trees, tall and broad-leafed, and passing numerous little hamlets set among lush and colourful vegetation. The road also passes through Sarapee, once the site of Kum Kam, a town built by King Mengrai before he built Chiengmai. Finally, an avenue of cassias with yellow senna leaves leads into the town.

Lamphun was supposed to have been founded in the mid-7th century A.D. by a legendary hermit named Sudeva, after whom Doi Sutep is also named (see p. 316). This man, so the story goes, came to possess a holy relic. To house it suitably, he wanted to build a new town. With his friend, he commissioned a moat and a wall nearly three miles in circumference within which the town of Haripoonchai grew.

Sudeva then invited Princess Chama Tevi to be the Queen of Haripoonchai. She was the daughter of the Mon King of Lop Buri, who was so delighted that he donated a precious image of Buddha. It is believed she then built Wat Mahawan, now completely ruined, just outside the old city gateway in A.D. 657.

Haripoonchai existed for over 600 years as an independent kingdom until, in 1281, King Mengrai took over the city and incorporated it into his own kingdom—the Kingdom of Lanna-Thai. The town was razed to the ground, and only the brick *chedi* and remains of *wat* were left. King Mengrai then built a new town just northeast, where he stayed for three years while building Kum Kam (now Sarapee Village). He lived at flood-prone Kum Kam until 1291, when he moved to the site of Chiengmai, which is on high ground.

Lamphun was re-established during the 14th century

by a monk from Sukhothai named Sumana, who found the buried relic at Pang Cha. Ordained in Ceylon, he was sent to Lamphun by King Kuna, and he stayed at Wat Phra Yun (the Temple of the Standing Buddha), built to house the relic. In the 16th century, Lamphun fell to the Burmese (who also took Chiengmai), and it was not until 1775 that it was won back by King Taksin and Chao Kawila of Lampang. Since that date Lamphun has been a part of Thailand.

WAT PHRATADT HARIPOONCHAI—Situated between the Chiengmai-Lamphun main road and the Mae Kuang River, the *wat* has a front entrance guarded by two pink *rajasingh* (lions) next to a white gateway facing the river (where monks can often be seen washing their saffron robes). The rear entrance is generally used, as it faces the main road.

This wat covers an area of about ten acres. It was the site of a royal palace until A.D. 897, when the Mon King, Atityaraj, decided to convert it into a *wat* to enshrine a sacred relic of Buddha.

Entering from the main road, one passes school classrooms on the left and immediately encounters the great golden *chedi,* 51 metres (167 feet) high, topped by a tall eleven-tiered *chatri,* an umbrella of gold lace signifying royalty. The upper part of this *chedi* is in the Thai style, while the lower part is Burmese. The *chedi,* surrounded by inner and outer rectangular iron fences, is painted black and gold, and decorated with ornamental iron lamps. Tall gold-lace "umbrellas" stand at each corner; the pillars are decorated with shimmering pieces of mirror and yellow china in squares. No women are allowed within the inner fence. The temple bells tremble in the breeze, and bats squeak and squeal, hanging under the golden umbrellas. A pavement of very old flagstones has been laid around this monument, and little shrines have been added recently at each side. This *chedi* is as old as the *wat* itself, but it has suffered from invasions and has been re-constructed several times. In 1281, when King Mengrai conquered Lamphun, he covered the laterite and brick structure with copper and gold and raised its height to 30 metres (99 feet). In the mid-15th century King Tiloka increased the height further to 46 metres (151 feet), added an eleven-tiered umbrella in Ceylonese style, and recovered the whole structure with copper and gold. During the Burmese occupation, it was again repaired and enlarged.

To the east of this golden *chedi* is a large bell tower with an enormous gong, said to be the largest gong in Thailand and dating from A.D. 678. Formerly sounded every three hours, the gong is now used only during Buddhist festivals and special ceremonies.

There are four *wiharn* but these, like all the other buildings, are comparatively recent. The main *wiharn* was rebuilt in 1925 and shimmers with glass mosaics, gold leaf, shiny black pillars, and an orange-and-dark-green glazed tile roof. It has beautiful murals around it depicting the life of Buddha.

To the left of this *wiharn* is the *ho trai* or library, standing on tall red pillars to keep the contents dry, and safely guarded by crouching Chinese dogs. (Do not sit on the kneeling elephant statue nearby.) Villagers wander in through the main gate to draw water from the temple well.

Another square golden *chedi* about thirty feet high and covered with brass stands to the northeast. The *bot* is rather small and insignificant. There is a small museum in the compound, affiliated with the National Museum, Bangkok. If you can find a caretaker with a key, take a look inside to see items found on this site, such as Buddha images, votive tablets, and ancient coins. Wat Haripoonchai has a large, active school for monks, novices, and children. It is one of the most magnificent *wat* in Thailand—regal, carefully tended, suspended in time, and, as yet, undisturbed by bus loads of sightseers.

WAT CHAMA TEVI—Also known as Wat Kukut, this *wat* has a large square *chedi* in the Khmer style, with fifteen Buddha images on each side housing the ashes of Queen Chama Tevi. It was built by her son, King Mahandayok.

WAT PHRA YUN—Temple of the Standing Buddha—Located approximately 2 kilometres (about $1\frac{1}{5}$ miles) from Lamphun town on the east side of the Mae Kuang River, Wat Phra Yun is difficult to find without a guide. This is where the monk Sumana stayed; indeed, it is said to have been built in 1369 to house his holy relic. After the Burmese invasion in the 16th century, this *wat* was left to decay until 1900, when it was rebuilt.

SHOPPING—As in Pasang, cotton and silk are woven on hand looms behind the row of open-fronted shops along the main street. Attractive materials for tablecloths, hats, shirts, mats, and so on are inexpensive.

FOOD AND RESTAURANTS IN LAMPHUN—Only local-style restaurants exist here. An open-fronted one is situated right next to Wat Haripoonchai. Lamphun is renowned as the most fertile area in northern Thailand, and is famous for peanuts, tobacco, *lamyai* (longans), and, especially, garlic.

Pasang

About 10 kilometres (6 miles) south of Lamphun (use bus or taxi), along a road that passes through unspoilt rural villages, lies this small town famous for beautiful girls and for its cotton-weaving industry. The girls are fair-skinned and vivacious, and are said to be unfair competition in Chiengmai beauty contests. As in Chiengmai, the local stores vie to employ the most beautiful girls as shop assistants, in order to attract customers.

The main street is lined with open-fronted shops selling all kinds of hand-woven cotton goods, such as tablecloths, shirts, dresses, bedspreads, and even carpets made by weaving in loops. More than 2,000 hand looms are said to be in use in Pasang. One type of loom here requires two operators to weave a cloth twice the normal width. Also on sale are locally produced buttons made in unusual designs from wood and bamboo, painted necklaces, bracelets, and similar folksy trinkets.

Lampang

About 56 kilometres (33 miles) southeast beyond Lamphun, in all about 82 kilometres (49 miles) from Chiengmai, Lampang is easily accessible by train or road. Either way it is a pleasant trip, winding through jungle-covered hills.

Lampang city borders the river Kuang, though this is actually a narrow stream except during the monsoons. The city's rural quiet belies its twelve centuries of turbulent history. This ancient kingdom fought numerous wars and for a long period existed as a part of the Haripoonchai Kingdom (Lamphun) until, finally, it fell to the Burmese in the 16th century. Nowadays, it is the Burmese-style art and architecture that attract tourists. No one will be disappointed, for Lamphun's *wat* are huge, with ornate carvings, and are intricately decorated inside with multicoloured mirror pieces. Furthermore, one can tour Lampang not only by pedicab but also by pony-drawn carriage. The lack of cars and noise is notable.

WAT PHRATAD LAMPANG LUANG—located 11 kilometres (about 7 miles) south of the city is the largest *wat*, made mostly of wood rather than the usual stone or stucco, and exquisitely carved. Parts of the building are said to be 800 years old. Some of the woodcarvings are housed in a small museum in the compound.

WAT SRI RONG MUANG AND WAT CHEDI SAO (Temple of the Twenty Pagodas)—are the two other principal *wat*. In the latter, reputed to be over 1,000 years old, are unusual and most beautiful banana shrubs. The branches have to be propped up to support the great bunches that grow luxuriantly. These bananas are small and seedy, however, and not so enjoyable to eat.

Tak

Situated 525 kilometres (about 315 miles) from Bangkok or 290 kilometres (174 miles) from Chiengmai on Highway 1 (formerly Highway 5) that stretches from Bangkok to Chiangrai, this is a small, dusty town where bus routes converge. It is close to the range of hills that separates Burma from Thailand (said to be infested with bandits). Local taxi drivers and samlor are always to be found when the buses arrive. If one has to stay overnight, there are several Chinese-owned hotels of the usual provincial standard. The Tak Hotel (about 50 *baht*) or the Thaveesak Hotel (about 40 *baht*) are reasonable.

MEMORIAL SHRINE OF KING TAKSIN—this consists of a most beautiful and well-cared-for statue of King Taksin, seated, in an open-sided building by the main highway. King Taksin regained Thailand from the Burmese in 1767, assisted by his commander General Chakri (see Wat Arun in Bangkok chapter, p. 163, for details).

BHUMIPOL (OR YANHEE) DAM—the dam is situated about 65 kilometres (40 miles) northwest of Tak. One must either take a shared taxi or charter a taxi for about 60 *baht* ($3).

The dam is enormous, said to be the eighth largest in the world and the highest dam of its kind in Asia, representing the largest public investment project in Thailand. Villages had to be moved in Lamphun Province because of the flood of the reservoir. The first phase of this multi-purpose project, designed to have a total capacity of 560,000 KW in order to supply electricity to thirty-seven provinces, was completed in 1964.

Beautifully situated in the hills near the dam and reservoir are a rest house and golf course. Prior reservations are recommended for overnight stays.

Sukhothai—"The Dawn of Happiness"

There are three Sukhothais—Sukhothai Province; Old Sukhothai (the ancient capital); and New Sukhothai, a town founded in 1786 just 12 kilometres (8 miles) from the ancient capital.

ACCESS—Approximately 450 kilometres (270 miles) north of Bangkok and 330 kilometres (200 miles) south of Chiengmai. The distance is longer by road. The most convenient route is via Phitsanulok, which can be reached either by plane or train direct from Bangkok or Chiengmai (see p. 341). From Phitsanulok one must go by road, a distance of 58 kilometres (36 miles) west to New Sukhothai and a further 12 kilometres (8 miles) to Old Sukhothai. Taxis can be hired or shared, or there are intermittent "1-*baht*" taxi-trucks as well as occasional open-sided provincial buses operating. Alternatively, one may travel by bus all the way from Bangkok or Chiengmai to Tak (see p. 334) which is 68 kilometres

(42 miles) to Old Sukhothai (and a further 12 kilometres or 8 miles east to New Sukhothai). As from Phitsanulok, one must take a taxi or bus.

SIGHTSEEING IN SUKHOTHAI—As yet this area is rarely visited by foreign tourists and so facilities are limited, to say the least. Hotels are such that it is strongly recommended to stay either in Phitsanulok or Tak and then, ideally, charter a taxi for the day for around 200 *baht* (U.S. $10).* Once in Old Sukhothai, visit the museum first and purchase its "Guide to the Old Town of Sukhothai" which contains a map. The sites are clearly marked with numbers that correspond to those on the map. It is still wise to keep your chartered taxi as the sites are scattered and continuous walking over rough ground would be tiring, especially in the hot season (March–May) when the area is uncomfortably warm and dusty.

THE STORY OF SUKHOTHAI—The ancient city was founded around 1257 by the Thais, who had been migrating into the Indo-Chinese peninsula, steadily gaining in strength and numbers. By the 13th century, they had formed several separate states, Sukhothai being one of them. However, Sukhothai is regarded as the first capital of Thailand. In other words, it was the capital of the first state that unified the Thai people, where Thai art and culture were born. This achievement is largely attributed to the first King, Phor Khun Sri

* Note, however, that accommodations at a comfortable modern guest house in Old Sukhothai are available under the auspices of the Thai Fine Arts Department, for visitors who wish to study the ruins of the ancient capital. Reservations should be requested well in advance from the Department of Fine Arts of Thailand, Na Phra Lam Road, Bangkok.

Indrathit, more popularly known as Phra Ruang. Not only is he known to have conquered the Khmers and established his own kingdom, but also he is said to have possessed wonderful, mythical talents, which, to some extent, must shroud the real truth of his character. Today, the Thai expression "to have the tongue of Phra Ruang" means that a person's words can make what he says come true.

Romantic legends were replaced by documented, historical accounts when King Ramkamhaeng (Lord Rama the Brave, second son of Phra Ruang) reigned, 1277–1317. The creation of the first Thai alphabet is attributed to him. His inscribed stele (now in the National Museum, Bangkok) gives us an insight into 13th-century life in Sukhothai. Records show that he was indeed a great warrior, expanding his kingdom to include areas that now belong to neighbouring countries. He visited China twice and returned with artisans, including potters, to teach the Thais new crafts. One result is the coveted Sukhothai and Sawank'alok stoneware. The methods of production are now imitated by the Thai celadon kilns, in Chiengmai. Another account tells how this great king hung a bell in front of his palace gate, so that any of his subjects could ring for him whenever a dispute required mediation. King Ramkamhaeng would come out, listen carefully to each person's grievances, and then decide the right sequel. This King also encouraged the teaching of Buddhism and the classic arts. The era is referred to as the Thais' "Golden Age."

Sukhothai prospered and six kings ruled, but decline began during the reign of the last two as states tried to overpower one another. Eventually, in 1365, Sukhothai became a vassal state of Ayutthaya, and finally, in 1378, it fell when the people abandoned the city during the war between Ayutthaya and the Burmese. The jungle took over, and until the 1950's the site was almost totally obliterated by dense undergrowth. The ruins of this great city are still being uncovered; the finds include many Buddha images, pottery, and other objects that have become treasures of the National Museum in Bangkok or the New Ramkamhaeng Museum in Old Sukhothai. Chinese and Burmese records have also helped to build up a picture of life in Old Sukhothai.

The old city was surrounded by three walls separated by moats, the north and south walls measuring 1,360 metres (4,420 feet), and the east and west walls measuring 1,840 metres (6,813 feet). Each wall had a gateway. Within the walls, the ruins of twenty-one *wat,* four ponds, and the royal palace have been found. Outside the city, but in the vicinity, three Hindu temples, about a dozen *wat,* twelve kilns, and an earthen dam have so far been discovered. The dam is believed to have had a capacity of about ten million cubic metres of water—a good supply—being about 300 metres (985 feet) long, 4 metres (13 feet) high and just 3 kilometres (nearly 2 miles) from the city. It was discovered in 1964. Many more *wat* are known to have existed but still lie hidden by the thick jungle.

WAT TRAPHANG THONG LANG—is a cube-like ruined *mondop* of red brick situated just before the entrance to the old city on the left, coming from New Sukhothai. The *wat* is at the end of a farm track just past a few wooden houses. Almost opposite the entrance of the track is a wooden shop called "Old Objects of Sukhothai Art" where odd bits of pottery are for sale.

Twenty laterite pillars remain in the front, and the brick plinth is almost intact. Fine examples of Sukhothai art can be seen in statues on the walls and inside the niches on each side. The rear side is badly worn. The relief work depicts the story of Buddha returning to earth after having ascended to heaven to preach to his mother, who is supposed to have died before he preached on earth.

NEW RAMKAMHAENG MUSEUM—open: 9:00 A.M.–12:00 noon and 1:00–4:00 P.M. daily except Mondays, Tuesdays, and national holidays. Two-*baht* admission fee is charged on Saturdays and Sundays only. Entering the town from New Sukhothai, one passes through an arch bearing the name "Sukhothai" in ancient script. The museum is on the left.

It contains bronze and stone Buddha images, votive tablets, ceramics, and various objets d'art excavated in the area.

WAT MAHATHAT—Monastery of the Great Relic—the most impressive monument in Sukhothai. Walk along a dusty path from the west gate of the museum, through a well-kept lawn dotted with beautiful, shady trees. Before entering the *wat* compound one can see a huge, straight-backed Buddha image seated between two ruddy brown pillars, a white band across his chest. This is one of many images here. Red and black *chedi* point skywards, with grass and plants protruding from the cracks. There is a pond nearby filled with lotus. Cows graze freely and strange butterflies flutter across one's path. With only the sound of birds and rattling cowbells, this huge *wat,* silhouetted against the still blue sky in its jungle setting, appears mysterious and ominous.

Entering, one is soon surrounded by crumbling laterite *chedi,* pillars, and a great many Buddha images including standing Buddhas to the right. One image, frequently visited by local people, is spattered with squares of gold leaf. A mat, burning incense, and an oil lamp are signs of a recent visit. Carefree children play among the numerous tapering pillars. The main *chedi* has a well-preserved base decorated with a frieze of pink-coloured walking Buddhas. There are said to be 189 separate structures of Thai and Ceylonese styles.

WAT SRI SAWAI—To the west or behind Wat Mahathat is a small stretch of water and a moat. Turn left along the narrow dirt track here, passing some wooden monks' huts where saffron robes hang over the balconies. Wat Sri Sawai is straight ahead. In the distance are green wooded hills.

Wat Sri Sawai means either Monastery of the Glorious Mango Tree or Monastery of the Glorious Siva. It appears to have been a Sivaite temple originally, later to become a Buddhist *wat*. It consists of three Khmer-style *prang* with laterite outer walls. Ruins of two *wiharn* are in front. Beautiful stucco work with dancing figures, *garuda*, and so on are believed to date from the 15th century.

WAT CHETUPON—meaning Monastery of the Grove of Prince Jeta, can be reached by a five-minute bumpy drive through bush and scrub south of the museum, just beyond the old South Gate.

A huge grey and red stone, standing, "walking" Buddha image, though headless, gives a fluid impression of movement. The original *wat* is almost totally destroyed.

Nearby is a newly built *wat* with bright red eaves and one building with a thatched roof. Pillars of ruined buildings can be seen, like petrified tree-trunks, above the surrounding undergrowth and scrub.

OTHER SITES OF INTEREST ARE—*Wat Phra Phai Luang,*

Monastery of the Great Wind—the central *prang* resembles that of Phimai; *Wat Sri Chum,* famous for possessing the earliest known specimens of Thai pictorial art. This building has extremely thick walls and a passage containing a dangerously aged stairway. A huge Buddha, measuring some 11 metres (36 feet) across, from knee to knee, is housed inside. Pilgrims leave incense burning, and the image's long fingers have been plastered with gold-leaf. Notice *the Thuriang kilns;* remains of about fifty have been discovered and the ground is still littered with shards; *Wat Sapan Hin,* involving a climb of 50 metres (164 feet) to a beautiful Standing Buddha; *Wat Sra Sri,* Monastery of the Glorious Pond, just off the main road. Perhaps the most photogenic ruin consists of a massive, elegant, seated Buddha image surrounded by broken laterite brown pillars and a Ceylonese-style *chedi.* The hardy traveller and archeologist will enjoy seeking other sites.

New Sukhothai

In 1786, King Rama II ordered New Sukhothai to be built. Largely reconstructed following a great fire in 1968, the town has a small rural market, a few hotels (suitable for only the hardiest of travellers), and one *wat,* Wat Rajadhani, Monastery of the City of the King. This temple is of simple design and was built only a century ago. The abbot is known to be responsible for many of the great finds and treasures now kept in the museums.

Phitsanulok

By road, 590 kilometres (about 370 miles) from Bangkok: by train, Phitsanulok is a stop on the Bangkok–Chiengmai route. The 5:05 P.M. Northern Express from Bangkok arrives at Phitsanulok just after midnight.

Slower but more pleasant for enjoying the scenery is a daytime train departing at 7:00 A.M. from Bangkok, arriving at around 5:00 P.M. in Phitsanulok. By air, it takes about one hour from Bangkok. Many Chiengmai-bound planes touch down here.

Phitsanulok is a spacious town with wide streets, divided by the murky river Yom. It was almost completely rebuilt following a great fire a few years ago. In front of the railway station is an old steam engine. Next to it is a large hotel aptly called Phitsanulok Hotel. It is reasonably comfortable and good value at around 50 *baht* a night.

THE FLOATING HOUSES—Walking straight ahead from the station past the hotel (the local market place and shopping street are to the right), for five to seven minutes past banks, shops, and offices, one will come to a road next to the river Yom. Cross over and turn right, strolling in the shade of beautiful *bauhinia* trees as far as the bridge.

Along this part of the river on both sides are floating houses—primitive-looking rafts made of wood except for their corrugated iron roofs. Long gangplanks lead across the muddy river banks. It is not really a pretty sight and rather unhealthy looking.

WAT PHRA SRI RATANA MAHATHAT—On the same side of the river, one will see the orange, green-bordered, glazed-tile roofs of this *wat* and a tall *prang*. A beautiful tile path leads from the gateway, guarded by two small lion-like statues that have been covered with tiny squares of gold leaf stuck on by devout pilgrims. The *wat* is perfectly maintained. Lawns and large trees with circular marble walls built in steps around their trunks make a pleasant picture. In the porch of the *wiharn* a musician plays a *ranad ek* (Thai xylophone). Pilgrims pass in and out constantly, carrying lotus flowers and incense to lay before the image of Buddha.

Before entering, look closely at the heavy black wooden doors, magnificently decorated with inlaid mother-of-pearl in designs of *naga*. They glisten pale pink, green, and white in the tropical sunlight. Just inside the entrance a gallery surrounds the hall. This is lined by dozens and dozens of golden Buddha images; most are seated but a few are standing, Sukhothai style. Many are roughly life-size. Each image has a slightly different expression but all have a look of peace and contentment.

Further inside, one comes into the main hall of the *wiharn*. It is quite dark, not very large, and dominated by the Phra Buddha Chinaraj, a serene figure, seated on a throne-like platform. This figure was cast in A.D. 1300 and is regarded as one of the most beautiful images in Thailand. A replica is in the *bot* of the Marble Temple (Wat Benchamabopitr) in Bangkok. The pilgrims kneel down and bow to one side in front of the image, touching their foreheads to the cold tiled floor.

Above, the beams and roof are painted bright red, the pillars black, and all are decorated with intricate patterns in gold. There are also some fine murals depicting the life of Buddha.

The adjacent *prang*, which is about 100 feet high, contains a holy relic and signifies that this is a royal *wat*, as does the name Mahathat. It is said to have been founded by King Boromtrailokanat (his title is more usually shortened to King Trailok) who reigned from 1448–88 during the Ayutthaya period, succeeding his father at the age of only seventeen. This King was famous for reorganizing and centralizing the government and strengthening the state. (Sukhothai lost its independence to King Boromaraja I of Ayutthaya in 1378).

THE MEMORIAL SHRINE OF KING NARESUAN—Coming from Wat Phra Sri Ratana Mahathat, take a samlor for 5 *baht* or so, go over the bridge, turn right, and drive along the road by the river until you reach Pitsanulok School on the left-hand side—five minutes' journey in all. The Memorial is situated in the grounds.

This spacious government school has a wide central avenue lined with trees and shrubs, leading from the gateway straight to the memorial between two rows of well-kept wooden classroom buildings. The presence of foreign tourists may distract the children and disrupt the classes, but never mind. The statue is bronze, life-size, and grandly housed in an open-fronted structure with marble steps. The King looks more like a boy soldier with a funny hair style. His knees are spattered with squares of gold leaf stuck on by people who come to pay their respects. They burn incense too.

This King is known as Naresuan the Great, for it was he who liberated the Thais from the Burmese in 1584 after fifteen years of subjugation. It is a remarkable story outlined in the footnote on page 228. He was once appointed Viceroy of Pitsanulok, and it was in this town that he trained men for his army.

20

SOUTHERN PENINSULA

Southwest from Bangkok, the country of Thailand stretches to the border of Malaysia, along a narrow strip of mountainous land, green and lush. The land here is well developed and rich with coconut, fruit, and rubber plantations. Its affluence is a sharp contrast to the poverty of northern Thailand. Many of the towns have good hotels and comfortable facilities for foreign visitors.

The main attraction to this part of Thailand is the kind of peace that comes from the untroubled, wealthy, rural communities settled between the mountains and the sea—peace, away from the busy traffic and crowds of Bangkok. The area shown on the map contains a population of only four million or so. Motoring is highly recommended as the main roads are in good condition and there is hardly any traffic.

Prospective visitors should know that the seasons on the east side occur at different times from those on the west side. On the east, the rainy season is from October until late January or early February, while on the west side it is from late May until September. In other words, one can always find suitable weather for sunbathing and swimming on one side or the other. Also, there is an abundance of fruit the year round. Of course, seafood is always available too—fresh and delicious.

Besides beaches and sun there are numerous old cities with interesting long histories and many fine buildings. Another important attraction in this region is cost. All prices are nonsensically low when compared to Bangkok or beach resorts in the southeast such as Pattaya.

The far south is popular for Malaysians, who easily cross the border by the International Express. (Details in the chapter on Transport). Similarly, one should also consider going into Malaysia for a visit to Penang—the exotic island, free port, and tourist resort that seems one day destined to become another Hawaii.

Phet Buri (Petchaburi)

About 170 kilometres (just over 100 miles) south from Bangkok or about 40 miles from Hua Hin, Phet Buri can be reached by car, along good roads; by train; or by bus from Thon Buri.

One has to be a really enthusiastic sightseer who enjoys getting off the beaten track to go to Phet Buri. Among the most interesting sights is Tham Khao Luand, an enormous cave with an open shaft in the roof. It contains dozens of Buddhist images and is open weekends only, when hordes of Thai pilgrims come to pay homage, offer flowers, burn incense, and paste little squares of gold leaf onto the images. The largest Buddha image, a seated figure spattered with gold, is about twenty feet high.

Khao Wang (Palace Hill) nearby is the site of King Mongkut's summer palace. This also is open only at weekends for a small fee. Visitors can see some of King Mongkut's furniture and wander around the old structures including some temple buildings and the King's observatory, all atop this hill. A tiring climb.

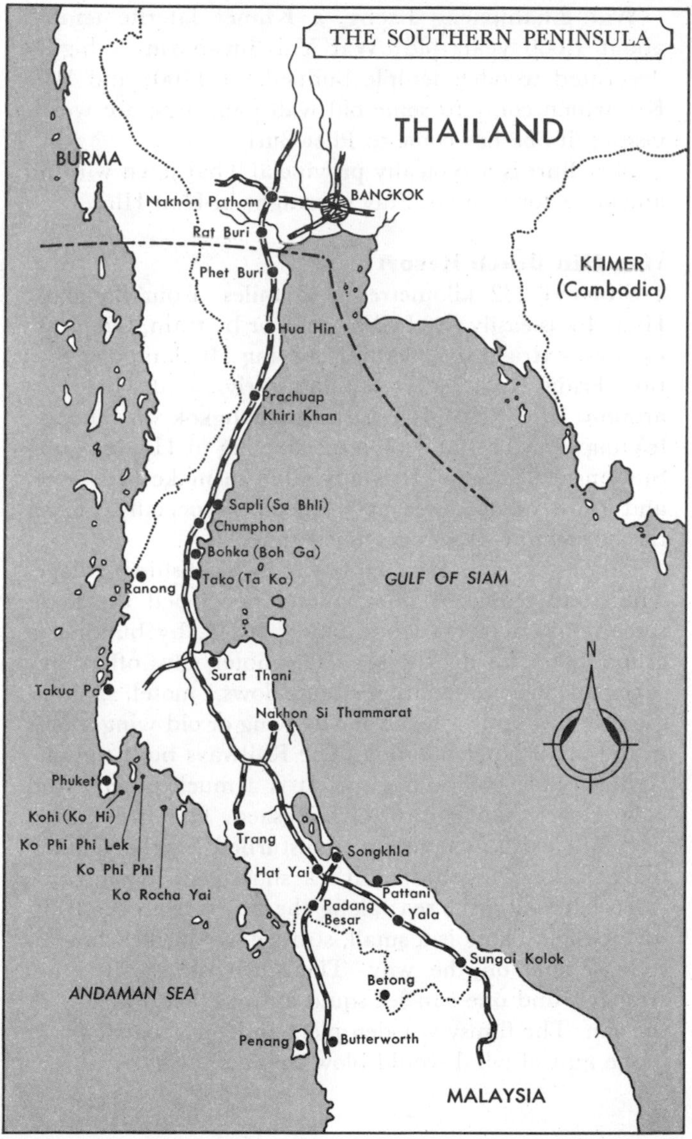
THE SOUTHERN PENINSULA
THAILAND
BURMA
Nakhon Pathom
BANGKOK
Rat Buri
KHMER
(Cambodia)
Phet Buri
Hua Hin
Prachuap
Khiri Khan
Sapli (Sa Bhli)
Chumphon
Bohka (Boh Ga)
Ranong
Tako (Ta Ko)
GULF OF SIAM
N
Surat Thani
Takua Pa
Nakhon Si Thammarat
Phuket
Kohi (Ko Hi)
Ko Phi Phi Lek
Ko Phi Phi
Ko Rocha Yai
Trang
Songkhla
Hat Yai
Pattani
Padang
Besar
Yala
Sungai Kolok
Betong
ANDAMAN SEA
Penang
Butterworth
MALAYSIA

Wat Khampaeng Laeng, a Khmer laterite temple about 1,000 years old; Wat Yai Suvanarm, a highly decorated wooden temple built about 1700; and Wat Ko, which contains some old wall paintings, are worth visiting if one has come to Phet Buri.

Phet Buri is a typically provincial Thai town with no amenities for tourists. Stay overnight in Hua Hin.

Hua Hin Beach Resort

Situated 232 kilometres (145 miles) from Bangkok, Hua Hin is easily reached by road or by train. On weekends an extra train operates, leaving Hualampong Station Fridays at 5:30 P.M., and arriving at Hua Hin around 10:00 P.M. It returns to Bangkok on Sunday, leaving Hua Hin at 4:00 P.M., arriving at Hualampong Station at 8:35 P.M. It is advisable to make firm hotel and train reservations at weekends, especially during the hot season—February until June.

Fifty years ago Hua Hin was just a fishing village. The State Railways of Thailand developed the area, since it has a lovely white sandy beach, by building a grand hotel facing the sea. The hotel now offers five types of accommodation—bungalows, motel, golfers' guest house, and a choice of new-wing or old-wing rooms in the main hotel building. The Railways built the fine eighteen-hole golf course too. It is a much quieter and older resort than Pattaya or Bangsaen. The little fishing port still exists, seemingly undisturbed by the holiday makers along the beach; it's a short walk northwards (turn left facing the sea) along the beach from the Railway Hotel. There is a small, strange, colourful Chinese-style temple on the way. The smell of fish becomes stronger, and one can see squid and cuttlefish drying in the sun. The flimsy wooden piers and tiny boats look as if one gust of wind would blow them all away.

Besides golf, Hua Hin offers other sports—tennis, fishing, boating, horse riding, and skin-diving. The latter is not recommended, as the waters are usually too cloudy. Also, to wile away the time, one might like to take a samlor for about 10 *baht* and go to the Royal Summer Palace of Klai Kangwen a mile or two away. It is still used by the King and Queen during the hot season. The palace has beautiful gardens and grounds with a wide variety of trees providing plenty of shade. Visitors are not allowed to enter the palace building, which is disappointing and unimpressive from the exterior. The grounds are closed when Their Majesties are in residence.

ACCOMMODATION AT HUA HIN—The Railway Hotel is comfortable, spacious, and gracefully old fashioned. A double costs around 170–200 *baht* a night. The gardens are littered with some odd pieces of topiary that are amusing to children. Alternative accommodation is limited, but the new Subhamitra Hotel offers clean, simple rooms at 80–140 *baht* for one night with air conditioning. It is not far from the sea front, near the market in the main street. Tel. Hua Hin 94.

Prachuap Khiri Khan

Easily reached by road or train 322 kilometres (201 miles) from Bangkok; if arriving by train, look for the little country-style station with a main street nearby resembling a street from a Wild West movie.

The town's most attractive buildings are the municipal and provincial government offices. Near these government buildings, a short samlor ride from the station, are a few wooden bungalows along one of the finest beaches in Thailand. The bungalows can be rented for about 50 *baht* a night. They may be comfortable for people who like camping but are sub-standard for most foreign tourists. There is no hot water, no porterage service, no cooking facilities, the walls are caked with dust, and they are infested with ants. If it were only cleaned it would be a wonderful place to stay. Until that happens, the King Hotel in town (not far away) offers cleaner accommodation and is the best alternative. One room costs about 40 *baht* a night. There is also a hotel on the beach by the bungalows offering rooms at around 20 *baht* a night. This hotel and the bungalows are owned by the government, and reservations should be made through T.O.T.

Prachuap Khiri Khan is one of those unforgettable beauty spots. Here is a vast, semicircular-shaped bay sheltered by a chain of rugged islands on the south. The beach is very narrow but there is plenty of space. One can walk for miles along the soft, pale-lemon-coloured sands, shaded by a few palms and pine trees. The peace is striking. It is ideal for swimming and, if one is lucky enough to meet some of the friendly fishermen, one may make a trip with them offshore.

Local food is excellent Chinese-Thai style, but do not expect to see a menu in English. Apart from enjoying the uncrowded beach and the seafood, one should make the effort to climb the hill that rises behind the provincial offices. It has steps, guarded by *naga,* all the way to the top (about 500 feet) where there is a small *wat* with trembling temple bells hanging from the eaves. The view across the bay and pine-studded hills is magnificent. There is a small community of monkeys that live around the bottom of this hill. They are not very tame and should be left alone.

Prachuap Khiri Khan is an ideal spot to spend a day swimming, fishing, or picnicking, but stay overnight at Hua Hin, 90 kilometres (56 miles) north, or at Chumphon, 177 kilometres (110 miles) south.

Prachuap Khiri Khan to Chumphon

By road or rail this route offers vivid tropical scenery, passing through banana plantations and dozens of villages nestled among tall coconut palms. The terrain is generally hilly, giving occasional distant views, making the journey time pass quickly.

Chumphon

This is a clean town with some handsome modern buildings. There is nothing for a tourist to see here, but it makes a convenient stopover place for a night's rest when travelling down or up the peninsula. Two clean hotels operate almost side by side in direct competition, with rooms available at around 40 *baht* a night. They are the Suriwongse Hotel and the Chumphon Hotel, both very near the railway station. The shopping centre nearby is fairly well stocked, and there is a market with an interesting variety of local fruits and vegetables. There is even a smart new cinema a hundred yards or so from the hotels. It seems that the local people here are largely Chinese.

Chumphon to Ranong

The railway goes directly south from Chumphon, so Ranong can be reached only by road through the hills, teak forests, and some of the best jungle scenery in Thailand. The terrain is rough but the road is well-paved. It has many severe bends that reduce the average motoring speed to around fifty kilometres per hour. The jungle and undergrowth are completely wild, with extremely tall trees overhung with creepers. Some parts have been cleared to make space for paddy fields or small banana plantations. In this region elephants are still used for work in the forests. Early in the morning they can be seen chained near the frail wooden huts. Later in the day, one is certain to pass a few on the road with their mahouts perched above their heads.

There are magnificent views across the hills to the river that forms part of the border between Thailand and Burma. The green hills of Burma are clearly visible across the water. As the mouth of this river widens one nears Ranong. The southern tip of mainland Burma—Victoria Point—is almost opposite. Small outlying islands make the scene very picturesque.

Ranong

An uninteresting provincial town 619 kilometres (287 miles) from Bangkok, Ranong has become more prosperous than most others through tin mining and rice marketing. It has two hotels with just adequate facilities for an overnight stay—the Sin Ranong Hotel and the Asia Hotel, almost opposite each other in the main street. Rates are about 30 *baht* a night. However, only two kilometres from the town centre (5 *baht* by taxi), is the smart new Thara Hotel, tel: 813341, situated at the foot of thickly wooded hills, a quiet and peaceful spot. Its hot water comes from a nearby natural hotspring. The rates range from 60 to 220 *baht* a room.

Ranong to Takua Pa

A curvy road through wild forest and jungle, passing occasional rubber plantations, tin mines, and elephants, makes this an attractive and dramatically scenic drive.

Takua Pa

A small, seemingly remote town that must have seen remarkable activity long ago, Takua Pa is on the ancient trade route where goods from India and the West were transported overland across the Isthmus of Kra to be re-shipped from Surat Thani to the far eastern countries.

Greek and Roman remains have recently been found in the area, indicating that further archeological excavation could be exciting. Part of the original portage route is followed by the modern, well-paved road that crosses the peninsula to Surat Thani. Takua Pa is a useful route centre if one is travelling by bus. There are regular services to Hat Yai, Phuket, Chumphon, or to Surat Thani.

Takua Pa to Phuket

Continuing south by road (there is no alternative), one passes by a large, open tin mine on the right and then enters perhaps the most beautiful part of Thailand. It is quite hilly, and the road winds gently up and down, through spectacular jungle with trees of amazing height. Half-revealed, through the tropical bush, are fine views of inviting coves and wide bays along the coast. The warm blue waters belong to the Andaman Sea. This area is remote and lonely but, if one is keen on diving and has brought equipment, the waters will be irresistible—deep and well-stocked with fish of the Indian Ocean. After passing a couple of rubber plantations one reaches a small town named Khok Kloi. Here the routes diverge, eastwards to Hat Yai and southwards to Phuket Island, which has been connected to the mainland by one long bridge.

Phuket

Phuket, pronounced more like Bhuket, is approximately 888 kilometres (555 miles) from Bangkok. It can be reached either by road or by air. Thai Airways operates a daily service. The quickest alternative route is to take a train as far as Surat Thani and then use a local, provincial bus.

The only travel agent operating regular tours to Phuket is Tour Royale, 392/27–28 Siam Square, Soi 5,

Bangkok, tel: 56888 (opposite the Siam Intercontinental Hotel). The tour lasts five days and uses an air-conditioned bus all the way via Prachuap Khiri Khan, Chumphon, and Ranong, to Phuket and back to Bangkok. It costs 1,100 *baht* including all meals, accommodation, and a visit to some of the little islands near Phuket.

Few places in the world can match this island's natural beauty. When facilities are improved it may well become the "Caribbean of the Orient." For the time being, however, Phuket Island lies basking peacefully in the sun, fanned by its swaying palms and bathed by the wash of the Andaman Sea. The clear, warm waters are blessed with coral and dotted with tiny, alluring islands. There is enough here to fulfill anyone's dream of a tropical island in the sun.

For a few years more Phuket may be allowed to sleep undisturbed, for this island province is not yet ready to cater to the needs of foreign tourists. There are no first-class hotels or restaurants and no hotels facing or even near a beach; as of now, it is not an ideal place to stay with children.

PHUKET TOWN—Phuket Island is about twelve miles wide and thirty miles long. Phuket town is situated in the southern part of the island and should be used as a base since the more comfortable hotels are here. From Phuket Airport, in the northwest, one must take a taxi. There are only a few taxis and bargaining will be hard for the 30- to 40-minute drive to Phuket town. The Tavorn Hotel is the best, offering a range of rooms at 50–150 *baht* a night, including some air-conditioned rooms. This hotel has an excellent restaurant serving Thai, Chinese, or Western-style dishes at low prices. The town has many Thai-Chinese local restaurants, but very few have menus in English. Seafood dishes are the obvious choice—Phuket is famous for its shellfish. Other local specialities include turtle eggs, available in November, December, and January; *satay*—the Malaysian dish; *gang hunglay*—curry with pork; and *gang luam*—a yellow curry dish with fish bladders. The local people also produce cashew nuts and eat cooked crickets.

Apart from hotels and restaurants, Phuket town really has nothing more to interest a tourist except for a few shops that sell seashells and locally produced pearls. There are three cinemas (one is very modern), three dismal nightclubs, and a dance-hall entertainment called Ram Wong which may be peculiar only to Phuket. An enterprising Chinese founded and manages this theatre, which is near the clock tower at an intersection just southeast of the town. He brings hostesses, aged from twelve to twenty, from the poor villages in the north of Thailand to work and live here. The girls dance in miniskirts on a low platform in the middle of the hall for five hours every night, from 8:00 P.M. to 1:00 A.M. No wonder they look so bored. Young men sit at tables around the platform, sipping Coca-Cola. For half a *baht* they may go on the platform and have one dance with a girl, and for a fee of 10 *baht* one of the hostesses will sit at the table for thirty minutes. The girls are paid 400 *baht* a month, plus full board and lodging. It is said that their purity is carefully guarded. It is also said that when they reach the age of twenty, they are sold as maids for around 1,500 *baht* each. Clearly, Phuket's attractions lie beyond the town.

BEACHES AND SIGHTSEEING SPOTS IN THE PHUKET AREA —the most popular beach, and the nearest to Phuket town, is at PaTorng Bay, about 12 kilometres ($7\frac{1}{2}$ miles) west of town. One route passes through the village of Ban PaTorng. Take the road into the Kathu Valley, now a mass of tin mines, then turn left to pass through the small hamlets of palm-leaf-roofed huts. Further on, the road runs along the coast near the beach. There are excellent picnic spots around here, beneath the palms. The beach, spacious, clean, and usually deserted, is bordered by a line of strange, "primeval" trees locally called *laam jaik,* that bear a useless, inedible green fruit resembling a pineapple. The road, now a track, returns eastwards past more native houses. Children will grin with delight at foreigners, while chickens squawk and small, long-snouted black pigs scamper away into the bush as a vehicle clatters by. The first village is a community of Moslem people. Further on, one finds Moslems and Chinese living side by side. By taxi this outing will cost around 60 *baht*.

In the same general direction is Kaw Rang, or Rang Hill, which is about 10 *baht* round trip by taxi from Phuket town. This hill is high enough for an extensive view across the hilly island, overlooking the Kathu Valley, the terra-cotta roofs of Phuket town to the east, and across yellow bays and turquoise sea to the chains of tiny, dark-green islands that stretch into the distance. This hill has been turned into a public park and has a well-paved road winding to the top. The summit is beautifully landscaped with gardens of trees, shrubs, and cacti, the trees carefully labelled with their Thai and Latin names. There are park-type benches for young lovers who come to watch the sunset and enjoy the fresh, cool air. The higher hill nearby is Kaw To Saa or Toh Seh Hill, which has a communication station at the top.

PUNG BEACH, OR BAHNG TAW BAY—is another beauty spot. The area is hilly but easily accessible by a good paved road (30 *baht* by taxi or 3 *baht* per person by shared long-distance taxi-truck from the marketplace).

Edged by tall pines and luxuriant palms, the sand is warm and soft, but the water is rather murky and the heavy waves make this a place for strong swimmers only. It is fine for a picnic. There are several small restaurant stalls along the beach that serve tasty hot dishes, Thai-style. Fishing boats gather at the north end of this bay.

PHUKET NINE-HOLE GOLF COURSE—faces the bay, attractively set across small hills landscaped with palms and purple flowers. Among the local hazards are the buffalo that sometimes wander on this course. No balls are for sale here. The club's address is P.O. Box, 42, Phuket, Thailand.

SURIN BEACH (pronounced Soo-Rin)—is just south of the golf course at Bahng Taw Bay and can be reached by walking over the high promontory in about seven to ten minutes. As one reaches the top of this promontory there is a magnificent view to the south. The rocky cove is Surin Beach, and beyond is a larger bay that is also calm and sandy. It is called Governor's Bay. A few miles further is Komla Bay. All are superb beaches for swimming. The beaches on this side of Phuket Island have whiter sand, and the sea is usually calm except during the monsoon season, from May–June until October, when the beaches on the other side of the island are more appealing. They are more muddy than sandy but are preferred by Thais.

LAAM KO OR PINEAPPLE BEACH AND RAWAI BEACH—seem to be the best for safe swimming. The former is about 9 miles south of Phuket town on the way to Rawai Beach. The bays are well-sheltered, the water crystal clear and shallow and quite safe for children. Small villages (though sleepy) provide a little interest and life for the bays. Here one can laze for hours, watching the fishing boats pass to and fro and the villagers saunter to meet the fishermen as they moor their craft beneath the coconut palms leaning across the sands. And if one feels the urge to explore the islands across the sea, a few simple gestures and a friendly smile will be enough to hire one of the fishing boats. Try the villagers' favourite baked fish and live like a native for a day. A taxi to Rawai Beach costs around 30 *baht* one way.

A worthwhile side trip to a remote beauty spot is about two miles further south from Rawai Beach. Attempt this only in a fourwheel-drive Landrover (as the author did) or walk. From the top of the southernmost promontory you get an awe-inspiring view over four desolate bays and islands, the best coastal scenery in the Far East. At the moment the steep hills here prevent easy access to the fine beaches below, but Japan's Mitsui Company has plans to construct a new hotel in one of the placid bays that would then be served by hydrofoils.

Phuket has another excellent beach near the airport, appropriately known as the Airport Beach, just a couple of miles beyond the airport.

THE SEA GYPSIES—Besides Thais, Chinese, and Moslems (of Malay origin) on Phuket, there is an odd tribe which has maintained its own identity, language, and habits for so long that no one knows where they originated. Known as the sea gypsies because they frequently move their villages, they have at the time of writing a community directly east of Phuket town at a bay between Ban Laam Mai Phai and Ban Laam Phap Pha and a few others on the islands around Phuket. The former village can be reached by taxi (about 15 *baht*) along an abominable track across a rickety wooden bridge over *klong* Thachin and through thick jungle to the coast.

There are about 200 inhabitants here, living in huts with walls of interlaced bamboo set among a coconut grove. The children have matted hair but play happily on the sand. Their elders are dark, handsome, and brimming with health. They all have the same surname, Pra Mongit, and all of them earn their living fishing from gaily painted boats. Freshly caught fish hang on a stick like washing on a line as the menfolk approach visitors with exquisite specimens of seashells at wildly variable prices. The local government has taken initial steps to integrate these people by sending a schoolteacher to their village but integration will doubtless take several decades and, even then, the mystery of their origin may remain unsolved forever.

Directly southeast of Phuket town is Rong Rian Bang Nieo, an area of land being reclaimed to make a new park. This is where dredging for tin first occurred, bringing to Phuket the dawn of a new era. A Captain Edward Miles and his sons began the first tin dredge at this site in 1907, an historic fact marked by a monument erected in November, 1969. Resembling a bucket with a hole in it, the monument is pleasing, compared with many modern works. Local residents wander round and round it, peering at it from every angle.

PHUKET MARINE FISHERIES STATION—is situated about 8 kilometres (5 miles) directly south of Phuket town along a well-paved road, past rubber plantations and coconut groves, on the very tip of Ko Phuket Peninsula. It has interesting aquariums and a fine display of shells and sea creatures. One of particular interest is the dugong, a rare sea cow with pectoral fins. This creature has breasts like a human and is known to "sit" upon a rock while suckling its young. No doubt this, long ago, inspired stories of elusive mermaids.

A couple of miles further around the Ko Peninsula is the Phuket Marine Biological Centre. This was opened in 1970, following an agreement with Denmark to set up a marine research centre and oceanarium for training Thai students at university level. The Danish director is hoping to further conservation as well as study the lesser-known sea creatures.

Finally, just worthy of mention is Num Tok Ton Sy or Tonsai Waterfall, a lovely picnic spot in a jungle-like botanical park a couple of miles along the road going east out of Thalang. Nearby is the most notable temple on Phuket, Wat Prathong. Also, as one drives in and out of Phuket, or to Surin Beach, one will notice a charming statue of two sisters who have been honoured because of their efforts to defend Thalang (Phuket's old capital) during a Burmese invasion in 1785.

THE ISLANDS AROUND PHUKET—are in an area that bears some resemblance to the Inland Sea in Japan. Ko Yao Yai, or long island, is the largest. The Japanese Murata Pearl Company has established a joint venture with the Thai Marine Products Company to produce cultured pearls here, specializing in big pearls. The waters near the rafts (used to support baskets of oysters) are beautifully clear, and one can easily see small, colourful fishes. This island is almost uninhabited and has an extreme tide of about a kilometre. Other islands—Ko Phi Phi, Ko Phi Phi Lek, to the east, Ko Hi, Ko Racha Yai, and Ko Racha Noi to the south, to mention just a few—are occasionally inhabited by sea gypsies. The former two are noted as a source of swifts' nests used by the Chinese for their renowned birds' nest soup. They all have wild attractions that will appeal to nature lovers who are seeking a remote, unspoiled tropical island in the sun.

Phuket to Hat Yai

There is a daily morning flight on Thai Airways from Phuket to Songkhla, 31 kilometres (19 miles) from Hat Yai.

It is also possible to make this journey, about 480 kilometres (300 miles), in one day by bus or by car if the driving can be shared. The drive seems long, as there is little variety in the scenery. The roads pass through jungle, broken only by a few dusty hamlets and some peculiar clastic rock areas. The route, via Trang, is well-paved all the way, but the roads are often rather too narrow for the speeding buses.

TRANG—about two-thirds of the way from Phuket, would be the least uncomfortable place en route to break the journey. A number of long-distance bus routes converge here, and therefore a few hotels (of dubious standards) have emerged. From Trang the road goes over the hills in a series of not-too-tortuous curves to descend on the east side of the peninsula. Travelling south from Bangkok, one notices how the regions become steadily more prosperous. The peak of wealth is reached at Hat Yai, home of the rich plantation owners and the commercial centre of the south.

Hat Yai

Located 1,291 kilometres (806 miles) from Bangkok, Hat Yai can easily be reached by a daily overnight train from Bangkok in eighteen to nineteen hours; by car (a more direct highway is being built from Chumphon via Surat Thani to Songkhla so that soon one will not need to cross to the west coast in order to drive south); or by Thai Airways in less than three hours on the daily flight from Bangkok via Phuket to Songkhla or by direct flight to Songkhla (three times a week) in about two hours from Bangkok. Hat Yai is a half-hour drive from Songkhla.

Hat Yai in the old days was called The Mount, as it is elevated, and it became renowned as a town that was never flooded. No doubt this reputation contributed to its present prosperity. Nowadays it is one of the cleanest towns in Thailand, with a fine array of shops, restaurants, a few nightclubs, and several hotels that could be termed first class. Growing into an impressive centre for higher education too, the town proudly boasts modern buildings of distinctive architectural design. Hat Yai is a suitable place for a businessman to stay or for tourists who are based in Songkhla to visit for a special evening out. (A taxi from Songkhla to Hat Yai costs only 25 *baht* per car!)

LOCAL TRANSPORT AND SIGHTSEEING—Pedicabs are everywhere. They cost just a few *baht* for short trips or can be hired by the hour for 20–25 *baht*. However, the three- and four-wheeled, 1-*baht* taxis are the most popular and convenient form of local transport.

Although Hat Yai is a neat, attractive town, there is really little to interest a tourist. Architects will enjoy seeing the recently constructed Prince of Songkhla University, which has a pleasing design and is set in spacious grounds near an artificial lake. Golfers will want to visit the 3,400-yard golf course at Senanarong Military Camp, five kilometres from the town centre. It is open to non-members for a green fee of 10 *baht* a day. Tourists will find few souvenirs here as Hat Yai is a centre for rubber and tin, but there are some fine pieces of batik and Thai cloth in the local shops.

Hat Yai to Songkhla

The easiest way to Songkhla is to jump on a 1-*baht*

taxi anywhere in town and ask for "Songkhla taxi." The driver will go to a side street where cars are parked waiting for passengers to Songkhla. The fare is only 5 *baht* per person if one is prepared to wait indefinitely until there are five passengers. Alternatively, the whole car can be chartered for 25 *baht*. The ride takes about twenty to thirty minutes (depending on the condition of the car), and the driver will deliver each passenger to any destination in Songkhla as part of the deal. In Songkhla, follow the same procedure to travel to Hat Yai. There is a local rail service but it is more comfortable to go by road. The drive is pleasant, along a good, smooth road winding and undulating through rural countryside.

Songkhla (seaside resort)

Located 1,321 kilometres (825 miles) from Bangkok, Songkhla is 31 kilometres (19 miles) from Hat Yai. For information about travelling from Bangkok, see under "Hat Yai," p. 361, in preceding text. There is also a cheap coastal shipping service available. For details, see "Water Transport," beginning on page 62.

Songkhla is *sabii.** It is a place for rest and peace, totally uncommercialized apart from one charming hotel, the new Samila Hotel on the beach. The beach, after all, is Songkhla's principal attraction. It stretches in a graceful curve for miles, miles of soft, powdery, virgin sand, gently washed by white-crested waves that leave behind lovely ripple patterns. Sand bars form shallow, lukewarm backwaters, ideal for toddlers. The entire beach is edged with tall, swaying pine trees that provide plenty of shade: *sabii* indeed.

The town itself is more or less on the tip of the peninsula at the north end of this fine beach. On the other

* *Sabii* is Thai for "very pleasant."

side of the peninsula is Thale Saap Songkhla or Lake Songkhla, a very large stretch of pellucid water with a few islands waiting to be discovered by anyone with enough enterprise to contact a local fisherman. There is an intimate fishing harbour that makes the whole of Songkhla another of Thailand's "picture postcard" resorts. Not everyone is suited to this sort of place. One has to be lazy to enjoy the quiet and sleepy atmosphere that is almost overbearing. Who could guess that Songkhla has suffered a most inconstant and violent past?

It has been suggested that Songkhla was the site of Stone Age settlements. What is known more definitely is that Songkhla grew to importance in the Srivajaya period (8th–13th centuries) when it was called Singla or sometimes Singora, a name derived from the two islands offshore said to give the impression of lions.* It developed from a fishing village to a commercial centre of considerable standing as Indian, Persian, and Arab merchants came to trade here. Even today, Songkhla is the largest port of Thailand south of Bangkok.

In the Sukhothai period (13th–14th centuries) the name became Songkhla. The town suffered from repeated invasions and once came under the rule of Ayutthaya. Invasions came from Malayan pirates and from nearby states but the city always grew again. In 1769, King Taksin once more brought Songkhla under Siamese rule. There was no peace, however, until King Narai restored order in 1860, driving out the rebels forever. Remains of a fortress and city walls, built between invasions, can still be seen.

LOCAL TRANSPORT—Songkhla has trishaws (different from those anywhere else in Thailand). They are simply

* Now called the Cat and Rat Islands.

made from bicycles with wicker chairs attached like sidecars. The seats are strong and designed to carry two small people. Trimmings are in bamboo, and an umbrella of oiled paper protects passengers from the strong sunshine or rain. Short trips cost just a few *baht*. Apart from ordinary taxis, one can easily use the 1-*baht* taxis that ply the main roads from town.

Sightseeing around Songkhla

Except for the scenery there is nothing fantastic or spectacular. Of course, one can spend a few days just wandering here and there, enjoying the local colour, visiting the morning produce market or fish market in Songkhla. Also of interest are the following places:

MOUNT TANG KUAN—a hill about 650 metres (2,000 feet) high, situated a short trishaw ride from the Samila Hotel. It has stone steps to the top but some of these have disintegrated, which makes the climb steep and hard. The climb is really worth the effort, however, for the exhilarating view over Songkhla Lake, the harbour with its tiny fishing boats, and the green-hilled islands famous for fruit and nests for birds' nest soup. Also, a little to the south, there is a view of Cat and Rat Islands offshore among white-crested waves, and the sandy bay with the Samila Hotel. There is a small monastery atop this hill, with a *chedi* built by King Rama IV in the mid-19th century.

SUAN TUL—is a small public park and, at the same time, Thailand's largest coconut plantation. It was given by King Chulalongkorn to a former governor of Songkhla.

WAT CHAI MONGKHON—on Thale Luang Street, has

a small *chedi* housing a Buddha relic from Sri Lanka.

THE PATRSEE MUSEUM—in Majimawat Temple grounds, is more popularly known as Wat Klang, situated in Sraiburi Street (5 *baht* by trishaw from the Samila Hotel). This little local museum contains relics from the Stone Age, Buddha images, idols that seem to stem from Brahminism, and some fine pieces of china and Chinese porcelain. Visitors are asked to sign the visitors' book, for which a donation is expected. Allow time to find the abbot or someone to unlock the museum door.

KAONOI SUAN SERI RECREATION PARK—popularly known as Kao Noi, is a small (if not puny) park just near the Samila Hotel, through the trees from the beach. Children will delight at seeing the bushes trimmed into the shapes of animals of all kinds.

THONGYAI GOLF COURSE—nine holes, next to the Samila Hotel, is rather plain and uninteresting compared to others in Thailand.

MOW AND NO (CAT AND RAT) ISLANDS—are visible just offshore, and can be reached easily by hiring a fishing boat(pay about 20 to 25 *baht* an hour). No Island is the larger and has some particularly nice picnic spots and quiet bathing beaches.

KAO SENG OR GOWSENT—is a fishing village to the south, about 5 *baht* by trishaw from the Samila Hotel. On the beach is a huge rock known as Nai Rang's Head. It is the subject of an extraordinary legend that has several variations and embellishments. In outline, the story goes that a millionaire named Nai Rang arrived at Kao Seng with his vessel brimming with treasures that he intended to use to build a temple at Nakhon Si Thammarat, about 130 kilometres (80 miles) from here. Apparently he was so upset to find that this temple had already been constructed that, in despair, he buried his treasures and held his breath until he died! His spirit is believed to have remained in the rock, guarding his buried fortune.

BULL FIGHTS (bull versus bull) are still held on the last weekend of every month. While there is nothing to commend this "sport," it can be interesting for a visitor just to watch the crowds who gather around the market place. Vendors set up flimsy stalls under the palm trees, and old women, chewing betel nut, crouch along the wayside cooking obscure delicacies in sizzling pans of coconut oil. Perhaps, apart from the milling crowds, one might see the local residents betting over a game called *sabah* in which a dealer knocks down small stones with a larger one.

SONGKHLA'S BEACH—remains the prime attraction. At the south end facing the sea are a few local restaurants where Thai, Chinese, and vaguely Japanese-style dishes are available. Close by the Samila Hotel is a lovely statue of a mermaid next to a rocky section of the beach. Around here one can while away the time watching (or helping) the fishermen wading thigh deep in the sea and casting their weighted nets with a lifetime's dexterity. Finally, one should remember that the seasons here are not the same as on the Andaman Sea side of the peninsula. It is hot from April to August and the rainy season here lasts from September to March.

Hat Yai to Penang (Malaysia)

Having come so far south in Thailand, you should

seriously consider crossing the border to Malaysia and visiting Penang, especially if you are unlikely to return to this part of the world.

If driving, follow the road from Hat Yai to Khlong Ngae and Sadao. Alternatively, one can join the International Express from Bangkok and jog along southwards, as far as Singapore (see p. 51 for times and days of services). There is also talk of a bus service starting soon. For this, one would have to inquire locally. As the scenery is monotonous, the train offers more interest. Indian, Chinese, Thai, and Malay passengers in an array of colourful costumes fill the train. The Thais smile and chat freely with foreigners, while the Malays are more reserved. They travel as the British do in trains, sitting stiffly. At each step, young Thai girls and children come aboard selling ices, hot steaming noodles, something called *tzuk* (a rice gruel), *makan ketchi* (a small, spicy Indian-Malay dish), and cashew nuts, fruit, tea, and so on. The train has a kitchen car, and a waiter constantly carries dishes up and down the aisle, but the food is mediocre and the smells can be upsetting to squeamish foreigners.

The route passes through millions of avenues of rubber trees until well across the border into Malaysia, where the terrain becomes hilly, almost mountainous. The immigration and customs at the border (Padang Besar) are cursory. Railway stations in Malaysia have melodious names and are noticeably neater than in Thailand. They each have rows of flowering shrubs and bushes. If travelling at night, one will see nothing at all and will be annoyed by the flying insects attracted into the train by the lights from the carriages. It takes less than six hours from Hat Yai to Butterworth (the terminal for Penang). Remember that Malaysian time is thirty minutes ahead of Thai time.

Penang Island (Malaysia)

Situated about two miles offshore from the west coast of Malaysia, Penang is accessible by a very frequent ferryboat service operated from a pier next to Butterworth Station.

Penang is an idyllic holiday spot. It is warm and sunny all the year round. Temperatures hardly ever fall below seventy degrees, and mostly stay in the eighties. The humidity is comfortable, and regular rains keep the hills lush and green. When it rains, it is usually at night. Penang is known as "Malaysia in Miniature" because, like Malaysia, the island has a population consisting of Malays, Chinese, Indians, and a few Europeans and Arabs. With this variety of races comes an interesting variety of cultures and religions. Though the island is a mere fifteen miles by nine miles, there is plenty to see and do. Attractions include miles of sandy beaches, good hotels, good roads, and fine scenery. Penang is a free port too. For further information about Malaysia write to: Department of Tourism, P.O. Box. 328, Kuala Lumpur, Malaysia.

Nakhon Si Thammarat

Located 1,196 kilometres (748 miles) from Bangkok, this is just one more place in the Southern Peninsula that is worth a visit. It will be easier to reach by car when the new road from Chumphon to Songkhla is completed. At present, the most practical route is from Trang or Krabi via Huay Yod, which is about 108 kilometres (68 miles) from "Nakhon," as it is locally called. By train, one should disembark at Thung Song if coming from Bangkok or at RonPibun if coming from the south. From either of these stations, it is easy to find a taxi to go to Nakhon. The charge should be not more than 60 *baht* per car. The drive takes about one hour.

The town of Nakhon is a ribbon development along one main street—Rajdamnern Avenue—which runs north/south for several miles. It is surrounded by thickly forested hills that make one wonder how a town ever came to be here. In fact, Nakhon was once a seaport though it is now at least three miles from the coast. As a trading port, Nakhon grew to importance. It still claims to have more *wat* than any other city of similar size in Thailand, a fact that has earned it the name "City of Priests."

Earliest records show that it was a part of the Srivajaya Empire which brought the Brahmin influence (Brahmin temples here are still active). Later, at the turn of the 11th century, it became a part of the Khmer Empire; it fell under Sukhothai rule in the 13th century, and then under the rule of Ayutthaya a few hundred years later. After the fall of Ayutthaya, King Taksin re-established control over Nakhon in the 18th century. The only clues to past disturbances are the traces of an old city wall and moat that can be seen about halfway along Rajdamnern Avenue.

SIGHTSEEING IN NAKHON SI THAMMARAT—Archaeological remains are still being unearthed at a number of sites in and around the town. Unless one is interested in archeology, a few hours here will be sufficient. Unfortunately, many of the *wat* have deteriorated and are left neglected.

Wat Mahatadt—Situated on Rajdamnern Avenue, this *wat* is worth a visit to see the lovely stone carvings and distinctive architecture. It must be as old as Nakhon. In the 12th century it was remodeled by Ceylonese monks, though one section is in the Ayutthaya style. In the precincts is a museum containing interesting items relating to Nakhon's past. If it is closed, ask one of the monks to find the curator. Also at this *wat* you will find another "original" Phra Singh image of Buddha (see p. 302 under *Wat Phra Singh*).

Sao Chingcha (The Giant Swing)—This enormous swing is situated in the precincts of the largest Brahmin temple, also along Rajdamnern Avenue. Formerly it was used for a Brahminic annual festival. An identical swing is in Bangkok (see page 179 under *Wat Sutat* for a fuller explanation).

USEFUL ADDRESSES AND INFORMATION

Emergency Medical Treatment
The hotel manager will know where to find a doctor or dentist quickly.

Emergency Telephone Numbers
Ambulance—54121
Fire—199-816666
Police—199-811644

Airlines
Air Siam, Rajprasong Trade Centre, tel: 56081-5
Cathay Pacific, Narai Hotel, 222 Silom Road, tel: 35911-3
Thai Airways, 6 Larn Luang Road, tel: 811633
Thai International, C.M.M.C. Building, 1043 Phaholyothin Road and 412 Rama I Road, tel: 72040, 54181, 512738

Business and Commercial Services, Bangkok
Export Promotion Board, Mansion A, Rajdamnern Avenue, tel: 24660
Thai Chamber of Commerce, 150 Rajabopit Road, tel: 23351
Thai Product Display Centre, Mansion C, Rajdamnern Avenue, tel: 20615

Business Hours

Banks: 8:30 A.M. to 3:30 P.M. Closed on Saturdays

Offices: 8:30 A.M. to 12 noon, 1:00 P.M. to 4.30 P.M., Saturdays, 9:00 A.M. to 12 noon

Shops: 8:30 A.M. to 6:00 P.M.

Church Services

In Bangkok there are quite a number of Roman Catholic and Protestant churches with services in English and other Western languages. It is best to obtain details on the spot from the hotel receptionist, who should have an up-to-date list.

In Chiengmai, the Seven Fountains Chapel, Huey Khao Road near Chiengmai University, has Roman Catholic Mass in English, Sundays at 9:30 A.M. Interdenominational Protestant services in English are held at the Chiengmai Community Church, Chiengmai School of Nursing, Keo Nawarat Road, Sundays at 5:00 P.M.

Other churches are also available. Ask at your hotel desk for the latest schedules.

Clubs and Societies, Bangkok

American Club, 65 Wireless Road, tel: 57012

American University Alumni, 179 Rajdamri Road, tel: 57067

Asia Foundation, 283 Silom Road, tel: 31962

British Club, Suriwongse Road, tel: 30274

Lions Club of Bangkok (Wednesdays), Manohra Hotel, tel: 37070, ext. 565

Press Association of Thailand, North Rajsima Road, tel: 815666

Rotary Club of Bangkok (Thursdays), Erawan Hotel, tel: 59870

Rotary Club of Bangkok South (Fridays), Rama Hotel, Silom Road, tel: 31030

Rotary Club of Thon Buri (Wednesdays), Royal Hotel, tel: 29020

Siam Society, 131 Asoke Lane, tel: 914401

Y.M.C.A. Headquarters, 100 Vorachak Road, tel: 22921

Embassies

American Consulate, Chiengmai, Vichayanon Road, tel: 4466-9
American Embassy, Wireless Road, tel: 59800
British Embassy, 1031 Ploenchit Road, tel: 53291
U.S. Information Service Library, Patpong Road, tel: 34911-3
Information Service, South Sathorn Road, tel: 31060-6
U.S.I.S. Chiengmai, Tae Pae Road, tel: 6024

Highway Department

At the same intersection as the SEATO Headquarters (see below): this office publishes excellent maps, as mentioned on page 55.

Public Relations Office

Located at the Phramane Ground end of Rajdamnern Avenue on the opposite side from the Royal Hotel. Just walk upstairs and ask for a copy of *Vistas of Thailand,* published by the office and distributed free. It is a small paperback book with a collection of articles by Thai writers on various aspects of Thai culture, economy, foreign policy, and other more general subjects. It is also available from the Royal Thai Embassy, Washington, D.C.

Radio and T.V.

Programmes are almost all in Thai but there is a news broadcast and several hours of English-language programming on the radio. Some English-language television soundtracks are broadcast over FM radio simultaneously with the Thai television versions of the same programmes.

SEATO Headquarters

Situated on the corner of Rama VI Road and Sri Ayutthaya Road: SEATO was formed by a treaty signed in Manila on 8 September, 1954 by Australia, France, New Zealand, Pakistan, the Republic of the Philippines, Thailand, the U.K., and the U.S.A. for "collective defence and mutual aid in Southeast Asia."

Shops (Government Sponsored)

Narayana Phand (handicrafts), 275/2 Larn Luang Road, tel: 810496

Border Crafts of Thailand (hill-tribe products), Chiengmai, Huey Khao Road

Telephone

Operator, information—13

Overseas calls (via satellite)—0-32054, 0-34076

SOME OVERSEAS CALL CHANGES:

	First 3 minutes	Each additional minute
Australia	240 *baht*	80
Canada	252	84
Hong Kong	147	49
Japan	156	52
New Zealand	252	84
U.K.	255	85
U.S.A. (except Alaska)	252	84

These rates are, of course, subject to change. Ask at your hotel for current charges.

Tourist Information Offices

Tourist Organization of Thailand (T.O.T.—government-run) Head Office: Mansion 2, Rajdamnern Avenue, Bangkok, tel: 28611-7; Don Muang Airport Office, tel: 814363 or 72780; Chiengmai Office, 70 Chang Klan Road, tel: 35354

Tour Royale, Siam Square, opposite Siam Intercontinental Hotel, Bangkok (specializes in deluxe bus tours to places provincial and remote at reasonable, all-inclusive rates)

Voltage

The voltage is 220 volts, 50 cycles, but a few areas have different voltages. Several hotels in Bangkok have 110-volt circuits.

INDEX

airlines
  addresses, 373
  domestic services, 63
annual events, 20–23
antiques, 110
archeological sites, 259, 288, 293–4
Ayutthaya, 227–35
  Ayutthaya Museum, 233–4
  Chao Sam Praya Museum, 235
  elephant kraal, 233
  Royal Ancient Palace, 232
  Wat Logya Sutha (Temple of the Reclining Buddha), 232
  Wat Panan Cherng, 229–31
  Wat Phra Mahathat, 235
  Wat Phra Sri Sanphet, 231–2
  Wat Phu Kae Thong (Temple of the Golden Mount), 233
  Wat Rajaburana, 234–5
  Wat Yai Chai Mongkol, 228–9
  Wiharn Phra Mongkol Bopit, 231

Bang Pa-In (Royal Palace and Gardens), 235–7
Bangkok, 153–221
  Chinatown, 198–200
  Chulalongkorn University, 212–13
  day excursions from, 222–63
  Dusit Zoo, 213–14
  Emerald Buddha, 170–74
  floating market, 159–63
  Giant Swing, 181–2
  Golden Mount, 182–7
  Grand Palace, 167–70
  Jim Thompson's Thai house, 216–17

Bangkok *(cont'd.)*
Lacquer Pavilion, 215–16
Lumpini Park, 209
market(s)
Bangkok, 197
floating, 159–63
flower, 197
Pratunam, 197
Sam Yan, 198
"Thieves" (Nakhon Kasem), 199
weekend, 196
Monument of Democracy, 195
National Assembly Hall, 24
National Museum, 192–4
National Theatre, 195
public transport in, 154–6
rice barge tours, 246
Royal Bangkok Sports Club, 213
royal barges, 166–7
sightseeing tours, 156–8
snake farm, 209–211
statues
equestrian, King Chulalongkorn, 214–15
King Rama VI, 200–201
Suan Pakkad Palace (and Lacquer Pavilion), 215–16
Victory Monument, 195–6
walking tour, 217–21
Wang Na Palace, 194–5
Wat Arun (Temple of the Dawn), 163–6
Wat Benchamabopitr (Marble Temple), 187–8
Wat Bovornivet, 190–91
Wat Indra Wiharn, 178–9
Wat Mahathad, 177–8
Wat Phra Jetupon (Wat Po), 174–6
Wat Phra Keo (Emerald Buddha Temple), 170–74
Wat Po; *see* Wat Phra Jetupon
Wat Rajabopit, 177
Wat Rajapradit, 190
Wat Sraket, 182–7
Wat Sutat, 179–82
Wat Trimitr (Temple of the Golden Buddha), 189–90
Bangphra (golf course), 268–9
Bangsaen (beach resort), 267–8
banks, hours of opening, 374
bars, 98–9
beach resorts
Bangsaen, 267–8
Hua Hin, 348–9
Pattaya, 270–73
Rayong Province, 273–5
Songkhla, 362–7
beetle fighting, 105
Bhumipol (or Yanhee) Dam, 335
boxing, Thai, 100–101
bronzeware, 110
Buddhism, 135–8, 146–50
budget tips for travellers, 15
bus services, 57
business hours, 374

business services, 373

celadon, Thai, 111, 312
ceramics, 110–11
Chanthaburi
  Church of the Immaculate Conception, 277–8
  historical sites, 279–80
  jewellery shops, 267
  sapphire mines, 276–7
Chiengmai, 295–328
  access to, 298–9
  botanical gardens (arboretum), 307
  celadon works, 312
  Chedi Keo, 307
  conference facilities, 308
  cotton- and silk-weaving village, 311
  Doi Suthep, 313–17
  elephants at work, 308
  entertainments, 326–8
  hill tribes, 317–22
  lacquerware village, 310
  Laddaland, 313
  Lak Muang, 304
  Mae Klang waterfalls, 322–3
  Mae Sa nature park and waterfall, 306–307
  pottery village, 312
  public transport, 299
  Pu Ping Rajaniwat (Royal Palace), 317
  Queen Victoria statue, 307–308
  restaurants, 328
  silverware village, 308–310
  temple-bell village, 311
  umbrella village, 311–12
  walking tour in, 323–6
  Wat Bhodharam Maha Wiharn (Wat Chet Yot), 305–306
  Wat Chedi Luang, 303–304
  Wat Chieng Man, 304–305
  Wat Phra Singh, 302–303
  Wat Phra That (Doi Suthep), 315–17
  Wat Suan Dork (Flower Garden Temple), 302
  White Elephant Gate, 306
  woodcarving district, 313
  zoo, 307
Chinese New Year, 20
Chon Buri (Cholburi), 266–7
Chumphon, 351
church services, 374
cinema, 99
climate, 19–20
clothing, 31–4
clubs and societies, 374
coastal shipping services, 62
cock fighting, 104
convention/conference facilities, 44, 308
cotton, Thai, 111, 311, 333
crocodile farm, Paknam, 244–5
crocodile-skin products, 111
currency, 28, 35
customs, meeting a Thai, 64–6
customs regulations, 35–6

dance

classical, 91–4
folk, 95–6
modern, 96
where to see, 96–8
Dhonburi (Thon Buri), 160
dishes, Thai
local, 254, 326–8, 354–5
popular, 80–90; *see also* food
dolls, Thai, 111–12

education in villages, 132–3
elephant(s),
kraal, 233, 242
round-up (Surin), 23, 291
sacred (Dusit Zoo), 213
Siamese elephant era, 292
at TIMLAND, 262–3
at work, 308
emergency medical treatment, 373
emergency telephone numbers, 373
employment in Thailand, 26–7

farming, 128–9
festivals, 20–23
fish fighting, 104–105
fishing, 267, 270–71, 349
floating market, Bangkok, 159–63
food and drink, 68–80; *see also* dishes
fruits, 70–77

Giant Swing, 181–2, 371
gifts, 29–30
golf, 105–106, 268–9, 357, 362, 366
Grand Palace (Bangkok), 167–70

Hat Yai, 361–2
sightseeing, 362
hill tribes, 317–22
Akha (or Ekaw), 320–21
Handicraft Centre, 322
Karen (or White Karen), 319–20
Lahu, 321
Lisu (or Lisa), 321–2
Meo (or Meow), 318–19
Phi Thong Luang (Spirit of the Yellow Leaves), 317
Tribal Research Centre, 322
Yao, 321
hotel(s)
international style, 38–41
local (Thai) style, 41–4
reservations, 28
Hua Hin beach resort, 348–9
hydrofoil services, 62

ice cream, 69
insurance
medical, 27
motor, 29

jewellery, 112–14

Kanchanaburi (Kwai bridge), 256–8
Chung Kai or Hospital Cemetery, 258
Neolithic artifacts at, 253–9

Donrak Cemetery, 258
Khao Yai National Park, 282–6
midnight safari at, 285
preparing for, 282
sights at, 284
Khorat (Nakhon Rajsima), 287–8
Khorat Plateau, 281–2, 293
kite-fighting, 100
Kwai, bridge over river, 257–8

lacquerware, 115, 310–11
Lampang, 333–4
Wat Phratad Lampang Luang, 334
Wat Sri Rong Muang and Wat Chedi Sao (Temple of the Twenty Pagodas) 334
Lamphun, 329–32
Wat Chama Tevi, 332
Wat Phra Yun (Temple of the Standing Buddha), 332
Wat Phratadt Haripoonchai, 330–32
language, 45–47
Laos, 294
local government system, 132
Loei, 292–3
Lop Buri, 240–44
Constantine Phaulkon's residence, 244
elephant kraal, 242
Kala Shrine (San Phragan), 242–3
Lop Buri Museum (Narai Raja Niwes Palace), 243–4
Phra Prang Sam Yod, 244
Wat Indra, 243
Wat Nakhon Kosa, 243
Wat Phra Sri Ratana Mahadat, 243

Mae Klang waterfalls, 322–3
Malaysia, 367–9
medical requirements, 27
motoring
hiring a car, 54–5
importing your car, 28
insurance, 29
road conditions, 53–4
road maps, 55
road signs, 55–6
musical instruments, 115

Nakhon Nayok, 222–3
Nakhon Pathom, 246–55
food and restaurants, 254–5
November Fair, 251
Phra Pathom Chedi, 248–53
Sanam Chan Palace, 253–4
Wat Phra Gnam, 254
Wat Phra Meru, 254
Wat Phra Pathom, 248–53
Nakhon Rajsima (Khorat), 287–8
Nakhon Si Thammarat, 369–71
Sao Chingcha (Giant Swing), 371
Wat Mahatadt, 370–71
name cards, 29

national parks
Khao Yai, 282–6
Loei, 292–3
New Sukhothai, 341
nielloware, 115
nightlife, 98–9, 326–8, 355

Pak Thong Chai silk village, 286
Paknam
crocodile farm, 244–5
festival, 22
Pasang, 332–3
Pattaya beach resort, 270–73
Penang (Malaysia), 369
Phet Buri (Petchaburi), 346–8
Phimai (Thailand's Angkor), 288–91
Sai Ngarm (beautiful banyan tree), 291
sightseeing at, 289–91
Phitsanulok, 341–4
floating houses, 342
Wat Phra Sri Ratana Mahathat, 342–3
Phrapadeang village, 245–6
Phuket 353–60
beaches, 355–8
golf course, 357
Island, 354
islands around, 360
Marine Fisheries Station, 359–60
nightlife, 355
sea gypsies, 358–9
town, 354–5
Prachuap Khiri Khan, 349–50
princess ring, 113–14
Pukae, botanical gardens at, 240

radio (and T.V.), 375
railways, 48–53
Ranong, 352
Rat Buri (Ratchaburi), 259–61
caves of Khao Ngu, 260–61
Wat Mahathat, 260
Rayong, 273–5
restaurants, 78–80, 96–7
rice barge tours, 246, 256
rose garden
(Suan Sampran), 255–6

Sara Buri 237–40
Phra Buddha Bat, 238–40
Phra Buddha Bat festival, 20
Phra Buddha Chai, 240
Pukae Botanical Gardens, 240
Sattahip, 273
SEATO (headquarters), 375
sea gypsies, 358–9
shipping, coastal services, 62
shopping, 108–118
bargaining, 108–109
hours of opening, 109
markets, 108, 196–8
souvenir suggestions, 110–18
silk, Thai, 116, 216, 286
silverware, 116, 308–310
Siracha, 269–70

skin-diving, 106–107
skins and hides, 117
snake farm (Bangkok), 209–211
snakebite treatment, 211–12
Songkhla (seaside resort), 362–7
  beach, 367
  bull fights, 367
  Kao Seng (or Gowsent), 366–7
  Kaonoi Suan Seri Recreation Park, 366
  local transport, 364–5
  Mount Tang Kuam, 365
  Mow and No (Cat and Rat) Islands, 366
  Patrsee Museum, 366
  Suan Tul (public park), 365
  Thongyai Golf Course, 366
  Wat Chai Mongkhon, 365–6
sports
  national, 99–103
  rural, 103–105
  Western, 105–107
Sukhothai, 335–41
  New Ramkamhaeng Museum, 339
  New Sukhothai, 341
  story of, 336–8
  Wat Chetupon, 340
  Wat Mahathat, 339
  Wat Sri Sawai, 340
  Wat Traphang Tong Lang, 338–9
Surin elephant round-up, 291–2
swimming, 106
sword and pole fighting (Krabi-Krabong), 102–103

tailoring, 117
Tak, 334–5
  memorial shrine of King Taksin, 334
Takraw, 99–100
Takua Pa, 352–3
taxis, 58–61
telephone, 376
temperature, 20
Thai language, 45–7, 109
Theatre, National, 98
theatre restaurants, 96–7, 327–8
Thon Buri (Dhonburi), 160
TIMLand (Thailand in Miniature), 98, 261–3
tipping, 39
tourist information offices, 376
transport
  airport to city centre, 36
  public, 48–53, 57–61
  seaport to city centre, 36–7
  water, 62
T.V. (and radio), 375

vaccinations (medical requirements), 27
Vientiane (Laos), 294
village life, 121–34
visas, 24–6
voltage, 376

walking tours

Bangkok, 217–21
Old Chiengmai, 323–6
Wang Takrai country retreat, 224
wat, buildings within, 138–46
water, drinking, 69, 90
water skiing, 107
women, status of, 66–7
woodcarving, 117, 313

yacht, chartering, 63
yachting, 107

zoos
Bangkok (Dusit), 213–14
Chiengmai, 307